KOREAN YEARBOOK OF
INTERNATIONAL LAW

KOREAN YEARBOOK OF INTERNATIONAL LAW

Volume 7
2019

PARKYOUNGSA

THE KOREAN BRANCH OF THE INTERNATIONAL LAW ASSOCIATION

KOREAN YEARBOOK OF INTERNATIONAL LAW

Copyright ⓒ The Korean Branch of the International Law Association 2020
Published by PARKYOUNGSA

PARKYOUNG Publishing&Company
210-ho, 53, Gasan digital 2-ro, Geumcheon-gu, Seoul, 08588, Korea
Tel 82-2-733-6771
Fax 82-2-736-4818

First published 2020
Printed in Seoul, Korea
ISSN 2635-8484 87

For subscriptions to this Yearbook, please contact the sole distributor, PARKYOUNG Publishing&Company
210-ho, 53, Gasan digital 2-ro, Geumcheon-gu, Seoul, 08588, Korea
Tel 82-2-733-6771   Fax 82-2-736-4818   E-mail: pys@pybook.co.kr

THE KOREAN BRANCH OF THE INTERNATIONAL LAW ASSOCIATION

PRESIDENT

SUNG Jae-Ho

HONORARY PRESIDENT

LIMB Thok-Kyu

VICE-PRESIDENTS

LEE Chang-Wee

LEE Keun-Gwan

LEE Hwan-Gyu

YANG Hee-Cheol

SECRETARY-GENERAL & TREASURER

LEE Kil-Won

MEMBERS OF EXECUTIVE COUNCIL

DOH See-Hwan

LEE Chang-Youl

LEE Chang-Wee

LEE Gyooho

LEE Keun-Gwan

LEE Hwan-Gyu

LEE Kil-Won

LEE Seryon

PARK Young-Kil

SUNG Jae-Ho

YANG Hee-Cheol

YOO Joon-Koo

SUPPORTING MEMBERS

CONTENTS

EDITORIAL NOTE

It is my pleasure to present the Volume 7 of the *Korean Yearbook of International Law*, which addresses issues in international law with emphasis on topics of special interest for Korea.

The Articles Section covers 5 articles and offers a forum to discuss broad issues related to interpretation of treaties, international human rights law and international environmental law. First, Professor Jae-Ho Sung at Sungkyunkwan University traces back the historical circumstances surrounding the conclusion of the Protectorate Treaty between Korea and Japan in 1905 and thoroughly analyzes numerous relevant legal materials to support the view that the 1905 Treaty through coercion was both procedurally and substantially invalid under international law.

The second article by Dr. See-Hwan Doh at Northeast Asian History Foundation focuses on the recent Korean Supreme Court case brought by the Korean victims of wartime forced labor against Japanese corporations and Japan's subsequent measure against Korea to restrict export on certain materials essential for manufacturing semiconductors and displays. He addresses the importance of victim-centered approach and universal value of human rights in resolving the forced labor issues.

The third article by Professor Paolo Palchetti at University of Paris 1 analyzes the cases on wartime compensation claims decided by Italian and Korean courts. Professor Palchetti introduces the historical background of the two cases one involving Italy and Germany and the other between Korea and Japan to present similarities between the two cases, followed by discussion on three key issues on the interpretation of waiver clauses in post-war agreement, law of state immunity concerning compensation claims filed by the victims of international crimes and potential conflict between domestic constitutional principles and the rule of state immunity in international law.

The fourth article by Professor Kil-Won Lee at Chungnam National University examines the key features and limitations of the environmental impact assessment system under the Madrid Protocol and the London Convention. He identifies the environmental impact assessment as an general obligation under international law and highlights the factors to be considered when adopting environmental impact assessment procedures.

The last article in Articles Section by Dr. Seoji Choe presents updates on the progress made by Korea's Refugee Act by introducing some of the key standards in relevant court cases and issues related to the amendment to the Refugee Act.

The Special Report Section includes the topics that cover both the public and private international law issues as follows: the trade tension between the United States and Japan and its implication for Korea, opening of Korea's legal service based on Korea-EU FTA, comfort women lawsuits from a legal point of view from private international law, crowdfunding regulation in Korea from private international law perspective, secured transaction in Korea.

The Recent Development Section assembles a selection of recent issues including nuclear energy cooperation between Korea and the United States, entry of China and Russia into Korea's Air Defense Identification Zone, deportation of the fishermen from North Korea, pending cases at WTO involving Korea, a brief summary on Singapore Convention on Mediation and Resolutions made by the National Assembly during the second half of 2019.

The Contemporary Practice and Judicial Decisions Section

introduces selected court cases related to public international law and private international law rendered in 2019. The judicial decisions in public international law cover the Constitution Court case, which deals with the constitutionality of Korea's Act on National Human Rights Commission, Seoul High Court's decision involving revocation of refugee status, the Supreme Court's decision on the interpretation of a domicile under the Enforcement Decree of the Income Tax Act. The court cases in private international law are provided by Judge Jiyong Jang at Judicial Policy Research Institute. The judicial decisions in private international law cover the Supreme Court's decisions on standard of determining international jurisdiction, law applicable to torts, and insurable interest under the U.K Life Assurance Act.

We would like to express our appreciation to all the authors for making this volume possible. My special gratitude must go to Professor Seung-Hwan Choi, Editor-in-Chief of KYIL for his guidance and support for the editorial team. I also take this opportunity to welcome and thank our new staff editor, Dr. Taewon Kim whose role has been vital in ensuring the high standards of KYIL.

I truthfully hope that you will find the issues in this volume interest and welcome your contribution.

Lee Seryon
Executive Editor
Korean Yearbook of International Law

ARTICLES

Re-examination of Invalidity of the Protectorate Treaty between Korea and Japan Concluded in 1905

SUNG Jae-Ho
Professor
Sungkyunkwan University Law School, Seoul, Korea

Abstract

After the Russo-Japanese War, Japan pillaged Korea through a series of coercive treaties between 1905 and 1910. The second Japan-Korea Agreement which was called the Protectorate Treaty on November 17, 1905 took away the diplomatic sovereignty of the Daehan Empire. As such, Japan coerced Korea into concluding a series of treaties in order to legalize the colonization and aggression and claim the legal justification along with elaborate political and military preparations.

Emperor Gojong of the Daehan Empire discerned Japan's covert intentions and implemented various activities to protect the Empire's sovereignty in response. His handwritten letter to the United States through his presidential envoy Hulbert on November 22, 1905 clearly stated that the protectorate treaty was coerced by the guns and swords and he did never ratify the treaty. This was clearly evidenced in the paper of FrancisRey. He pointed out in his paper "La Situation International de la Corée" in 1906 that there were two defects that completely nullified the Treaty. According to the conclusion that can be made through the examination and analysis of writings regarding international law at that time, a treaty concluded by coercion to a representative of a state cannot come into force. Moreover, a claim that coercion to a state does not affect the validity of a treaty also cannot be considered the common view at that time. The function of ratification is, therefore, to make the treaty binding, and, if it is refused, the treaty falls to the ground in consequence. E. Hall, J. Lawrence, L. Oppenheim supported this assertion. In addition, Emperor Gojong tried to secure the international legal status of the Daehan Empire as an independent sovereign state through the Declaration of Neutrality during Wartime.

Claims of the Japanese scholars and arguments by the Korean scholars have been comparatively and thoroughly reviewed in terms of international law. Re-examination of circumstances and relevant legal materials in terms of theory of international law of those times make it certain that the Protectorate Treaty between Korea and Japan concluded in 1905 was invalid since Japan forced the ministers of the Daehan Empire to sign the Treaty. Furthermore, the Treaty was an unfinished draft treaty not ratified by Emperor Gojong who was the right holder to conclude a treaty under the law of the Daehan Empire.

Key Words

Protectorate Treaty of 1905 between Korean and Japan, Invalidity of Treaty, Coercion, Ratification

1. INTRODUCTION

Japan's pillage of the Daehan Empire (also known as the Korean Empire) planned legally and precisely based on the scenario turned out to be an incontestable fact through the literature. After the Russo-Japanese War, Japan pillaged Korea through a series of coercive treaties between 1905 and 1910.[1] Japan took away the right to use the territory through the Japan-Korea Treaty of 1904 on February 23, 1904, and concluded the First Japan-Korea Agreement on August 22, 1904, with Korea. Japan concluded the second Japan-Korea Agreement with Korea, which was called the Protectorate Treaty between Korea and Japan on November 17, 1905, and took away the diplomatic sovereignty of the Daehan Empire. The Protectorate

Treaty between Korea and Japan provided that the Japanese government supervised and directed the diplomacy of Korea via the Ministry of Foreign Affairs in Tokyo in Chapter 1 and the Korean government promised not to conclude any future international treaty or agreement without mediation by the Japanese government in Chapter 2. Japan took away the military power and the right for internal affairs through the third Japan-Korea Agreement which was called the Japan–Korea Treaty of 1907 on July 24, 1907, and completed the pillage of the Daehan Empire through the Japan-Korea Treaty of 1910 on August 22, 1910. As such, Japan coerced Korea into concluding a series of treaties intentionally in order to legalize the colonization and aggression and claim the legal justification along with elaborate political and military preparations.[2] No world powers at that time had officially called Japan's protectorate over Korea into question. However, Jurist Francis Rey of Paris criticized the coercive protectorate treaty which Japan concluded with Korea to be deplorable in 1906.[3]

In this process, Emperor Gojong of the Daehan Empire discerned Japan's hidden intentions and implemented various activities to protect the Empire's sovereignty in response. One of these was the diplomatic strategy to nullify the Protectorate Treaty between Korea and Japan by notifying the coerciveness. The following record left by H. Hulbert, who was Gojong's special diplomatic envoy, supports such a fact.

> "I testify the most important acts that will be surely recorded in history. The Gwangmu Emperor has never submitted to Japan. The Gwangmu Emperor has never obeyed willingly to Japan, damaging the national system. The Gwangmu Emperor may have bent over once but has never submitted to Japan to the end. In terror for his life, he asked for the cooperation of the United States but his petition did not work. Under the same circumstances, he appealed to the International Peace Conference but this also failed. He appealed

to the European powers as he faced this terror for his life but Japan forced him to abdicate the throne so that his appeal was never delivered. He was the king of isolation. All those in Joseon, remember the eternal loyalty displayed by the Emperor forever."[4]

For the Protectorate Treaty between Korea and Japan, which was one of the elaborate steps to pillage the national sovereignty by Japan, Emperor Gojong clarified that he did not ratify the Treaty and claimed its invalidity by disclosing the fact that the Treaty was concluded by coercion through various diplomatic channels. In addition, Emperor Gojong tried to secure the International Legal status of the Daehan Empire as an independent sovereign state through the Declaration of Neutrality during Wartime. Emperor Gojong established the Red Cross in October 1905 and joined the International Red Cross and Red Crescent Movement, disclosing that the Daehan Empire was an internationally independent state and emphasizing the image of a sovereign state that actively participated in humanitarian activities. Such specific and practical efforts were not noticed significantly due to negative views of Emperor Gojong,[5] but it is an undeniable fact his various diplomatic activities were to maintain the independence as a sovereign state. Therefore, this paper evaluates Emperor Gojong's activities to protect the Empire's sovereignty and examines in terms of international law the legal principles that support the invalidity of the Protectorate Treaty between Korea and Japan that was concluded without the Emperor's ratification.

2. EMPEROR GOJONG'S NEUTRALIZATION PLAN AND DIPLOMACY FOR SOVEREIGNTY

The Daehan Empire already established diplomatic relations with the United States, England, Germany, Italy, Russia, France, and Austria before concluding the Japan-Korea Treaty of 1904 with Japan. This means that the Daehan Empire expressed its sovereignty abroad independently as an established state and the Daehan Empire was approved by partner countries. Moreover, the relations between the Daehan Empire and those countries should be regulated according to international law and rules. In Henry Wheaton's writing 'Elements of International Law' translated as public international law in Chinese, external sovereignty inhered in the independence of a political society in the relations with another political society.[6] Therefore, Japan was obligated not to damage the dignity, independence, and territorial independence of the Daehan Empire approved by Japan and the United States. However, Japan intruded the sovereignty of the Daehan Empire by force and coercion and Emperor Gojong tried to tell the whole world about the unlawfulness through various international legal activities to protect sovereignty available as a sovereign state. Such representative activities are the Declaration of Neutrality during Wartime and diplomatic efforts through the dispatch of a special envoy.

2-1. Neutralization Plan

The Daehan Empire promoted neutralization through international law or via an international organization while conducting diplomacy with powers. This tactic was the diplomatic plan promoted since 1880 with heavy reliance.[7] In international law, neutrality is the status of a country that does not participate in a war viewed from the state of war.[8] The contents regarding neutrality also appear in a writing regarding international law at that time, and Wheaton explains neutrality according to the international law in his work published in 1866. Neutrality is acknowledged as the right which all sovereign states should observe with regard to a war with a different state. That is, the right of a sovereign state to maintain peace while other states go to war is an obvious attribute of sovereignty.[9] Since the right of neutrality is linked to a corresponding obligation, the obligation to maintain impartiality occurs between states at war.[10] A neutral state should not use weapons except for self-defense against an attack and should not volunteer itself into an international responsibility that could directly lead to a war.[11] A neutral state should avoid dispatching troops or weapons to belligerent states, prevent its territory to be used by belligerent states, and uphold its obligation to tolerate certain sanctions of a belligerent state applied to a neutral state supporting the other belligerent state. An action for a certain state to become a neutral state is carried out through an international treaty between a powerful state and the said state, and the independence and territorial integrity of the state that declares neutrality are secured collectively through such a treaty.[12] However, modern international law did not force a third state to assume a general obligation that the third state should maintain neutrality during war and did not prohibit a belligerent state from starting a war with a neutral state. In this regard, neutrality depended upon a neutral state's decision and the maintenance of its position of a neutral state depended upon a belligerent state's decision.[13] Therefore, such an issue was that of international politics, rather than a direct issue of international law.[14] According to Wheaton's or Oppenheim's explanation, the Declaration of Neutrality during Wartime issued by the Daehan Empire has merely a declarative meaning. However, it is necessary to examine whether or not the declaration of neutrality is considered a sovereign action of a sovereign state beyond the issue that the position of neutrality was or was not actually granted through the declaration of neutrality.

Emperor Gojong carried out the Emperor's coronation ceremony on October 5, 1897, based on the public international law and promulgated the Constitution of the Daehan Empire on August 17, 1899. The Daehan Empire demanded the recognition of its sovereignty within the structure of international law by participating in the public international law system and found the grounds from the neutrality provision included in public international law that enabled the promotion of the neutralization.[15] In addition, the Daehan Empire obtained the draft of the Geneva Conventions from the Swiss government in 1901 with intentions to have the Daehan Empire recognized as a neutral region using the Red Cross in the event of a war.[16] Joining the International Red Cross in October 1905 was also an intention to clarify the Empire's position as a sovereign state in the international society.

The Korean government forecasted a war between Japan and Russia (Russo-Japanese War) and examined the declaration of a neutral state in August 1903. When the situation had escalated at the end of the year, the Korean government urgently declared neutrality on January 21, 1904,[17] and England, France, Germany, Italy, Denmark, and China approved the Declaration of Neutrality by the Daehan Empire. Right before the Russo-Japanese War, Emperor Gojong asked the United States to support the Daehan Empire's neutralization. His petition, however, ended in failure as the US government understood the international situation as well as that of the Daehan Empire, and upheld its principle of nonintervention on issues regarding the Daehan Empire.[18] On February 6, 1904, Japan severed diplomatic relations with Russia, entered into a war with Russia, and violated the neutrality of the Daehan Empire by occupying the territories of Korea using the expeditionary forces that were temporarily dispatched in advance. After the expeditionary forces arrived in Seoul, the Japanese army occupied the territories all across the country on a large scale by way of the excuse of the military and conquering army reinforcements. In the state of military occupation, Japan concluded the Japan-Korea Treaty of 1904 on February 23, 1904, with Korea by coercion in order to ignore Korea's declaration of neutrality unilaterally and legalize the occupation of the Korean Peninsula. The Japan-Korea Treaty of 1904 stipulated that the Daehan Empire was an independent sovereign state while allowing the Japanese army to station in the Daehan Empire.[19] The Japan-Korea Treaty of 1904 had a provision to guarantee the safety, independence, and territorial integrity of the royal family but also had provisions in Articles 1, 4, 5, and 6 that rationalized the pillage of sovereignty from the Daehan Empire in terms of politics, military, and diplomacy. In particular, Article 4 describes as follows.

> "The Imperial Japanese government shall take necessary measures immediately in case the peace or territorial integrity of the royal family of the Daehan Empire is at risk due to an invasion by a third state or rebellion. And, the government of the Daehan Empire shall provide sufficient convenience to facilitate the measures of the Imperial Japanese government."

This meant that the government of the Daehan Empire was obligated to provide convenience to Japan during its war with Russia even though Japan had already ignored the declaration of neutrality by the government of the Daehan Empire and dispatched its military to Korea. There was severe opposition from ministers including Emperor Gojong against this Treaty, but the Treaty was concluded anomalously by coercion through Japan's show of force. Therefore, the Daehan Empire consequentially broke the declaration of neutrality, facing the plight of indirectly participating in the Russo-Japanese War and losing its position as a neutral state.[20] This was a preview of the Protectorate Treaty between Korea and Japan concluded in 1905 and the Japan-Korea Treaty of 1910.

In international law, neutrality is the status of a country that does not participate in a war viewed from the state of war.[21] The right of a sovereign state to maintain peace while other states go to war is an obvious attribute of sovereignty.[22] Since the right of neutrality is linked to a corresponding obligation, the obligation to maintain impartiality occurs between states at war.[23] A neutral state should avoid dispatching troops or weapons to belligerent states, prevent its territory to be used by belligerent states, and uphold its obligation to tolerate certain sanctions of a belligerent state applied to a neutral state supporting the other belligerent state. However, modern international law did not force a third state to assume a general obligation that the third state should maintain neutrality during war and did not prohibit a belligerent state from starting a war with a neutral state. In this regard, the neutrality depended upon a neutral state's decision and the maintenance of its position of a neutral state depended upon a belligerent state's decision.[24] Therefore, such an issue was that of international politics, rather than a direct issue of international law.[25] According to Wheaton's or Oppenheim's explanation, the Declaration of Neutrality during Wartime issued by the Daehan Empire has merely a declarative meaning. However, the declaration of neutrality is considered a sovereign action of a sovereign state beyond the issue that the position of neutrality was or was not actually granted through the declaration of neutrality.

2-2. Diplomatic Activity for the Protection of Sovereignty

When the pillage of sovereignty by Japan started in earnest, Emperor Gojong dispatched people to the countries that concluded the treaty of peace, commerce, and navigation with Korea, censured the invasion of Japan, and asked for help to protect sovereignty and maintain independence. Such dispatch of a special envoy by Emperor Gojong began after the beginning of the Russo-Japanese War in February 1904 and continued to the dispatch of a special envoy to the Hague in July 1907 for the invalidation of the Protectorate Treaty between Korea and Japan.[26] Emperor Gojong did not acknowledge the Protectorate Treaty between Korea and Japan from the beginning and continuously carried out diplomatic activities to reveal its unlawfulness and invalidity to world powers. Due to Japan's surveillance and control, the diplomatic activities of Emperor Gojong were mainly the petition for the preservation and maintenance of independence to world powers using the delivery of a personally handwritten letter and the dispatch of a special envoy.[27]

In December 1904, Emperor Gojong ordered Min-hee Cho, who was an envoy extraordinary and minister plenipotentiary to Japan, to deliver a secret letter to the US government. The letter contained the request for help to maintain the independence of and solve issues in Korea and the East as long as such help was not contradictory to the current relations of the treaty to the US Secretary of State.[28] In a secret telegram sent to the US representative department in Washington on July 24, 1905, Emperor Gojong claimed that he was unaware of the international treaties and other treaties regarding the rights and interests concluded between Japan and Korea since the Russo-Japanese War as the ministers of Korea were taking orders from Japan. In addition, Emperor Gojong also claimed that all telegrams that would subsequently be sent by the Korean government would be sent by coercion from Japan. As such, there would be no need to implement the petitions communicated in such telegrams.[29] As the Russo- Japanese War approached closer to the end in 1905, President Roosevelt held a Peace Conference in Portsmouth upon the agreement of both states and intervened in the process of negotiation. Kaneko Kentaro, who was Minister of Agriculture and Attorney General in the cabinet of Ito Hirobumi, influenced President Roosevelt using his tie with him.[30] When Emperor Gojong became aware of this fact, he judged that the decision on sovereignty would be decided at the Conference. In response, he secretly sent Syngman Rhee to the US in the summer of 1905 through the intercession by Yeong- hwan Min and Gyu-seol Han. However, President Roosevelt rejected the request of the Daehan Empire representative for participation in the Conference by reason of defect that he was not delegated the qualification of envoy extraordinary and minister plenipotentiary.[31] On September 9, 1905, President Roosevelt announced that he had no objection to

Japan's takeover of Korea's diplomatic sovereignty. Article 2 of the Treaty of Portsmouth provides that Japan had the right to control Korea, and the key point of this Article is that Korea was handed over to Japan. The Russo-Japanese War began with the attack of Port Arthur by Japan, and numerous battles took place in the territory of the Daehan Empire that had declared neutrality. The Treaty of Portsmouth was the agreement that asserted that Japan held the sovereignty of the Daehan Empire under the arbitration of the United States even though this was against the will of the Daehan Empire which was a sovereign state. This Treaty became the grounds for proving that the Protectorate Treaty between Korea and Japan in November 1905 was concluded regardless of the will of the Daehan Empire which was a sovereign state.

In October 1905, Emperor Gojong sent his personally handwritten letter to the President of the United States through his secret envoy Homer B. Hulbert.[32] In his letter, Emperor Gojong claimed that the act of Japan breaking the protection of the sovereignty promoted to Korea in the Japan-Korea Treaty of 1904 and attempting to make Korea a Japanese protectorate broke faith and such an act was not demonstrative of a civilized power. He requested help to prevent the protective rule of Japan, showing concern about Japan's ambition to be displayed against Korea in the future.[33] However, President Roosevelt wished to have American dominance over the Philippines recognized in return for the approval of Japanese dominance over Korea. Consequently, he delayed the reception of Emperor Gojong's personally handwritten letter and even refused an interview with Hulbert. According to President Roosevelt's later recalled thoughts, "It is certain that the fact that the independence of Korea should be maintained has been stipulated solemnly in the Treaty. However, considering there is a state that is willing to take action for the Korean people who cannot defend themselves without any interest by putting the nation on the line deviates from the point."[34] That is,

President Roosevelt believed that autonomy was not appropriate for Korea even though he recognized the United States-Korea Treaty.[35] In fact, Hulbert arrived in Washington on the day after the Protectorate Treaty between Korea and Japan, which meant the Daehan Empire's loss of sovereignty was concluded by coercion. With the United States in the lead, 11 countries that had diplomatic relations with the Daehan Empire pulled out their legation at that time. The United States, which was the first to establish diplomatic relations with Korea, was also the first to sever these ties with Korea.[36]

In order to support the negotiation between Dr. Hulbert and diplomatic minister Min, Emperor Gojong sent a telegram of the full text of annulment of the Japan-Korea Treaty of 1905 to Hulbert via China branch and delivered it to the US government. However, it was also disregarded by the US government.[37] Hubert's manuscript contained Emperor Gojong's request for cooperation in the protection of sovereignty. The manuscript was sent to President Roosevelt to request diplomatic cooperation from the United States according to Article 1 "If other powers deal unjustly or oppressively with either Government, the other will exert their good offices on being informed of the case to bring about an amicable arrangement, thus showing their amity" of the United States-Korea Treaty concluded by Joseon and the United States in 1882 when Japan pressed the Daehan Empire in order to conclude the Protectorate Treaty between Korea and Japan in November 1905. Hulbert's manuscript candidly expressed Emperor Gojong's sincere request to the United States to apply diplomatic and military pressure against Japan, citing the United States-Korea Treaty in 1882. However, the United States judged that the situation had already leaned in favor of Japan and refused the request, responding against the Treaty. When Dr. Hulbert tried to deliver this letter of request for cooperation to the US government, the US government refused its reception citing the reason that a new treaty (Protectorate Treaty between Korea and

Japan) was concluded between the Daehan Empire and Japan on November 18, 1905, and diplomatic sovereignty was transferred voluntarily to Japan. Therefore, the United States-Korea Treaty was no longer valid. The diplomatic activities of Emperor Gojong clearly indicate that the Protectorate Treaty between Korea and Japan that led to the pillage of diplomatic sovereignty was concluded regardless of the will of the Daehan Empire. Accordingly, the Emperor's diplomatic activities were significant as the legal and realistic grounds for claiming the invalidity of the Treaty under international law.

Emperor Gojong sent his personally handwritten letter again to each state through Hulbert in June 1906, and he presented three grounds indicating that the Protectorate Treaty between Korea and Japan was concluded by coercion. In his letter sent to the Emperor of Russia, Emperor Gojong claimed that it was not true that the minister of the Daehan Empire signed the Treaty voluntarily and it was done by coercion under threats. He stated that he never approved the government to sign the Treaty. Moreover, although the Japanese government claimed that it was a government conference, they actually locked up the minister by coercion and held the conference by themselves in contrary to the national law.[38] He also mentioned that such a conclusion of the Treaty violated public law of Korea and was thus invalid and the Daehan Empire intended to bring it to trial at the international trial court in the Hague in the future.[39] In this way, Emperor Gojong continued his efforts to restore sovereignty from Japan by presenting a specific proposal such as an international trial. Emperor Gojong stood firm on his will as demonstrated in the documents he sent, which included his personally handwritten letter sent in 1905 to the power of attorney given to his special envoy in 1907. That is, the Protectorate Treaty between Korea and Japan was not prepared upon the Emperor's agreement and it was not the treaty between states ratified by the Emperor. Emperor Gojong claimed that the Protectorate Treaty between Korea and Japan was illegal and invalid under international law and it was not even concluded. Emperor Gojong's personally handwritten letter dated June 22, 1906, is a historical record proving that the transfer of diplomatic sovereignty according to the Protectorate Treaty between Korea and Japan was an illegal action which was neither agreed upon nor ratified by the Emperor, and that Japan had invaded the Daehan Empire by force. A measure by Emperor Gojong of the Daehan Empire as a sovereign state to appoint Dr. Hulbert as his special envoy, entrust him with full powers, and delegate him to deliver his personally handwritten letter was a flawless action by formality according to the international law of that time.

Since no result was obtained despite such efforts, Emperor Gojong dispatched special envoys again, counting on the 2nd Hague Peace Conference held in June 1907. Yi Sang-seol, Eee Joon, and Yi Wi-jong were selected as the special envoys and they arrived in Hague on June 25, 1907. Hulbert also joined them and began the activities. Emperor Gojong's personally handwritten letter shows the following content.

> "This letter is sent by the Emperor of the Daehan Empire to the Hague Peace Conference held in Holland. The situation has changed significantly and our diplomatic sovereignty was robbed and our independence was damaged due to the severe invasion of power. We would be grateful if our allied states helped us to protect our independence and sovereignty."

The special envoys were not officially granted the qualification to attend the Hague Peace Conference, so they also could not achieve their goal at the Conference. Instead, as the incident of the special envoys sent to Hague became known, Japan forced Emperor Gojong to abdicate the throne on the grounds of such an incident, so Emperor Gojong's policy for special envoys was not successful. However, Francis Rey, a French scholar of international law, claimed that the Treaty concluded in 1905 was invalid through his paper "La Situation Internationale de la Coree" published in early 1906. His work cited the fact that coercion was used at the time of concluding the Treaty and the Emperor immediately displayed diplomatic protests in order to show that such Treaty was illegal and invalid.[40] With regard to the adoption of the Convention on the Law of Treaties, the report submitted by the United Nations International Law Commission to the UN General Assembly held in 1963 also stated the threat to the Emperor of Korea and the Minister for agreeing on the Protectorate Treaty between Korea and Japan as a standard example of the treaty concluded by coercion in 1905, citing the Draft Convention on the Law of Treaties prepared by Harvard University.[41]

3. INVALIDITY OF THE PROTECTORATE TREATY BETWEEN KOREA AND JAPAN CONCLUDED IN 1905 UNDER THE INTERNATIONAL LAW

The Vienna Convention on the Law of Treaties (VCLT) adopted in 1969 provides 8 grounds for invalidating a treaty. Those grounds include the violation of a provision of domestic law regarding the competence to conclude treaties (Article 46), violation of specific restrictions on authority to express the consent of a state (Article 47), error (Article 48), fraud (Article 49), corruption of a representative of a state (Article 50), coercion of a representative of a state (Article 51), coercion of a state by the threat or use of force (Article 52), and the case of conflicting with a peremptory norm of general international law (Article 53). The former's argument is the matter regarding Article 46 which mentions the violation of a provision of domestic law regarding the competence to conclude treaties and the latter's argument is the matter regarding Articles 51 and 52 of the

VCLT. It is necessary to examine the fact with regard to the nullity of the Protectorate Treaty between Korea and Japan concluded in 1905 that the treaty was not ratified by the Emperor of the Daehan Empire at that time.

With regard to the validity of the Japan-Korea Treaty of 1910, a Japanese scholar claims that the annexation of Korea was carried out within legal limits in accordance with external formalities.[42] This claim is based on the explanation that the views of the majority of scholars of international law at that time divided coercion into coercion of a representative of a state and coercion of a state and regarded the former as invalid but the latter as valid. Such difference originates from the premise that there is a difference between the Convention on the Law of Treaties according to modern international law and the international law in the 1910s. That is, the Convention on the Law of Treaties clarifies that both the coercion of a representative of a state and the coercion of a state are invalid. However, there is a claim in a writing in the 1910s that classified the two sides and regarded the coercion of a state as valid. If this was the case, it is necessary to examine what the legal basis is for classifying an act as the coercion of a representative of a state and the coercion of a state in the writings regarding international law at the time and whether or not such a classification is valid. It is also necessary to examine whether or not all writings regarding international law at that time adopted dichotomous classification and whether or not all scholars who adopted dichotomous classification regarded the coercion of a state as valid. For this, it is necessary to extract the grounds adopted by scholars in both Korea and Japan through precedent studies in both countries and macroscopically analyze the original text of Western scholars quoted by Japanese scholars. Unfortunately, the precedent studies of domestic scholars of international law seem to accept the dichotomous description of a British scholar, who claimed that coercion applied to a representative of a state at the time of concluding a treaty under international law in the 1910s becomes the grounds for the invalidity of the treaty but coercion applied to a state is not the grounds for the invalidity of the treaty.[43]

The mainstream at that time in the 1910s politically adopted absolutism and legally followed legal positivism. Therefore, it is necessary to investigate the understanding of the international law at that time through the existence of the positive law from the viewpoint of legal positivism. It is because legal positivism focuses more on what is the law through systematic research of state practice, unlike the previous natural law theory.[44] The legal positivists understood that only positive laws such as treaties between countries and customary international law were accepted as international law. However, as there was no international law of general nature such as the current Convention on the Law of Treaties at that time, it is necessary to examine the substance of international law from the customary international law. Even if an international practice is verified from state practice, it cannot be elevated to common international law if it cannot be generally recognized. This is especially the case in the event that an international practice results in and is displayed as a state practice or bias according to an imperialist state. Since it is difficult to source empirical data regarding the international society of those days, it is necessary to find clues from theories by scholars of the time in this study. There is also a difference in the grounds for theories claiming the validity of coercion to a state, and some scholars explain that it is valid only in limited cases that satisfy a certain condition. Western scholars' opinions are also not unified and there are many who claim that there is no reason to handle the coercion of a state at the time of concluding the treaty differently from the coercion of a representative of a state.

The Protectorate Treaty between Korea and Japan concluded in 1905 was clearly the result of unjustified coercion through the use of force and was also prohibited under the legal positivism at the time of the Treaty conclusion. Therefore, no legal system as the positive law (de lege lata) that can be cited as grounds for validating a treaty concluded by coercion through the use of force exists.[45] However, the consistent standpoint of the Japanese government on the theory of legislation (lex ferenda) as the legal system based on such a legal definition should be judged by the intertemporal law which was the law at that time. And, the Japanese government has maintained the standpoint that a retroactive law (ex post facto law) cannot be acknowledged.[46]

3-1. The Deficit in the Ratification

The literature on the international law at the time the Protectorate Treaty between Korea and Japan was concluded in 1905 by coercion indicates that ratification is the requirement for the binding force of the treaty.[47] Ratification is the term for the final confirmation given by the parties to an international treaty concluded by their representatives. Although a treaty is concluded as soon as mutual consent is manifest from acts of the duly authorized representatives, its binding force is as a rule suspended until ratification is given. The function of ratification is, therefore, to make the treaty binding, and, if it is refused, the treaty falls to the ground in consequence.[48] There is no doubt that a mutual agreement between the parties to a treaty is essential[49] for the conclusion of the treaty. Hall stated that to make the treaty binding, it should be ratified by the highest state institution with the right to conclude a treaty,[50] and Lawrence asserted that a treaty which is not ratified does not have binding force unless there is a special agreement.[51] Oppenheim also said, "Although it is now a universally recognized customary rule of International Law that treaties are regularly in need of ratification, even if the latter was not expressly stipulated, there are exceptions to the rule."[52] But this opinion does not accord with the facts. For the representatives are authorized and intend to conclude a treaty by their signatures. The contracting States have always taken the standpoint that a treaty is concluded as soon as their mutual consent is clearly apparent.[53] Hall also said that a treaty that was not ratified was invalid unless there was a special agreement on the exemption of ratification.[54] There is a custom that the king's ratification is a requirement in order to establish a treaty, which is then concluded and becomes effective by an ambassador plenipotentiary. According to Bynkershoek, this was established in the early 18th century and it should be understood that a commission of full powers grants general authority to negotiate and conclude a treaty under the directions of the king.[55] It is also specified in a Japanese scholar's writing of those days that ratification was the requirement for the conclusion of a treaty: 'A treaty is enacted by a signature and it is concluded effectively by ratification'[56] or 'A signature establishes a treaty conditionally subject to ratification and ratification is required for finalizing the binding force of a treaty.'[57]

As mentioned earlier, domestic scholars present two grounds for the invalidity of the Japan-Korea Treaty of 1910. The first ground is that this treaty was invalid due to a defect of expression of will since it was concluded due to coercion or compulsion of Japan. The second ground is that this treaty was invalid due to a defect in the conclusion process as it was not signed by the emperor of the Daehan Empire. As the Protectorate Treaty between Korea and Japan concluded in 1905 was not ratified by Emperor Gojong, it had an irreparable defect as a treaty for dealing with an important duty such as the transfer of diplomatic sovereignty. Professor Tae-jin Yi, who produced an important research result through the historical verification of Japan-Korea Treaty of 1910, claims the doctrine of invalidity beginning from the point that an important treaty such as an annexation treaty is valid only when it is concluded as a formal treaty.[58] There is also a significant defect in the conclusion of the Protectorate Treaty between Korea and Japan concluded in 1905 since it was not ratified by the Emperor. As examined earlier, Emperor Gojong consistently and repeatedly claimed the invalidity of the Treaty for the reason that such Treaty was not ratified. This indicates that Emperor Gojong was aware of the legal definition of ratification. Although the explicit fact that the treaty was not ratified by Emperor Gojong alone is sufficient to prove the invalidity of the Japan-Korea Treaty of 1905, a series of actions taken by Emperor Gojong, who was the right holder to conclude a treaty complementally against the Japan-Korea Treaty of 1905 at that time, were sufficient to be indirect evidence that prove the intention of Emperor Gojong not to ratify the Treaty. The facts that the Treaty of Peace, Amity, Commerce and Navigation between Korea and the US was ratified through the exchange of instruments of ratification with U.S. Minister Foote who was assigned to Korea or that the Japan-Korea Treaty of 1876 concluded with Japan specifies the ratification are grounds for such a claim. Furthermore, there is also a claim that ratification by the modern definition was fully implemented at the time of the Korea-Japan Annexation Treaty in July 1882.[59] It is also necessary to observe the fact that the No. 1 imperial order in 1894 required the Emperor's signature, or the written signature and the seal of the State on the instrument of ratification for a treaty according to Article 18. It is noticeable that the system related to the Emperor's ratification was clearly provided in the imperial order which was the domestic law of the Daehan Empire at that time. The Constitution of the Daehan Empire proclaimed on August 14, 1899, after the name of the country was changed to the Daehan Empire in 1897, that the Emperor has the legislative, judicial, and administrative powers and the right to strengthen propaganda activities, and the person who has the right to conclude a treaty is the Emperor. Article 9 of the Constitution of the Daehan Empire states as follows.

"The Emperor of the Daehan Empire dispatches a stationary envoy to each ally state and concludes a treaty regarding the right to strengthen propaganda activities and other treaties."

In this regard, Professor Sakamoto of Japan presents that the domestic law cannot be quoted as the grounds for the justification of non-observance of the treaty according to Article 27 of the Vienna Convention on the Law of Treaties in 1969.[60] However, it is not appropriate to quote the Convention on the Law of Treaties concluded in the 1960s for the Protectorate Treaty between Korea and Japan concluded in 1905. It would be more appropriate to examine many diplomatic arrangements concluded at that time.[61] This indication is a claim that it is not appropriate to examine the Japan-Korea Treaty of 1910 based on the international law in 1969 and only the conclusion examined in terms of intertemporal law is appropriate.

It is the fact that Emperor Gojong repeatedly refused to ratify the Treaty through diplomacy using a personally handwritten letter. In particular, Ito Hirobumi threatened and requested for the official ratification of the Treaty several times until the abdication of Emperor Gojong. Since Japan demanded the official ratification for the treaty which was already promulgated and enforced in effect, this meant that Japan acknowledged that there was a defect in the conclusion of the Treaty so that the Treaty could not come into force legally.[62] This fact sufficiently verifies that Korea had no intention to conclude the Japan-Korea Treaty of 1905. As examined earlier, the scholars of international law at the time of the conclusion of the Protectorate Treaty between Korea and Japan in 1905 agreed that the ratification of a treaty was a necessary instrument under international law. Since the Japan-Korea Treaty of 1905 contained the signature and the seal of Minister of Foreign Affairs Park Je-sun of the Daehan Empire and envoy extraordinary and minister plenipotentiary Hayashi Gonsuke (林權助) of Japan, who were the representatives of both countries, it can be accepted that there was the authorization of the text of the Treaty. The conclusion of a treaty is carried out in a series of steps including negotiation, selection of the main text of the treaty, certification of the main text of the treaty, and the conclusion of the treaty. And, in such a case, only the steps up to the certification of the main text of the treaty were carried out.[63] People who claim that the Protectorate Treaty between Korea and Japan concluded in 1905 was lawful assert that the Emperor granted verbal approval. However, according to the fact that Prime Minister Lee Wan-yong stubbornly pressed the Emperor to affix his signature to the approval document since then, we can infer that Emperor Gojong did not authorize his signature.[64] The first line on the first page of the original text of the Protectorate Treaty between Korea and Japan concluded in 1905 stored in the Kyujanggak and the Record Office of the Japanese Ministry of Foreign Affairs is left blank. This indicates that the title was not appended, and this can also be considered as the fact that demonstrates the absence of agreement of Korea regarding the Treaty.[65] Specifically, the Protectorate Treaty between Korea and Japan concluded in 1905 is the treaty that contains an element that limits sovereignty such as the transfer of diplomatic sovereignty. Moreover, as there is no provision that specifies that ratification is omitted, the legal force of the Protectorate Treaty between Korea and Japan concluded in 1905, which was not ratified by Emperor Gojong who was the right holder to conclude a treaty, cannot be recognized. This is the evidence that Emperor Gojong did not agree to the Treaty. If this interpretation is, in fact, true, the Treaty is not legally valid.[66]

3-2. Coercion at the Time of Conclusion of the Treaty

Emperor Gojong stated as follows in his handwritten letter he intended to deliver to the United States through his presidential envoy Hulbert on November 22, 1905 right after the conclusion of the

Protectorate Treaty between Korea and Japan concluded in 1905.[67]

> "I declare that the protectorate treaty concluded between Korea and Japan recently under the force of guns and swords and coercion is invalid. I have never agreed nor will I ever agree to such a treaty in the future. Please convey my words to the US government."

Emperor Gojong sent his personally handwritten letter to the head of nine states that concluded the treaty of peace, commerce and navigation through Hulbert on June 22, 1906, asking to dispatch their respective ministers again since the Protectorate Treaty between Korea and Japan concluded in 1905 was invalid. He had expressed his will to file the petition to the international trial court. Emperor Gojong also tried to disclose and denounce the Japanese colonial rule by dispatching Eee Joon, Yi Sang-seol and Yi Wi-jong to the 2nd International Peace Conference held in Hague in June 1907. In addition, the fact that Emperor Gojong issued an order to Hwan-jik Jeong and Yong-ki Jeong to raise forces in the Gyeongsang Province also proves that the Protectorate Treaty between Korea and Japan was concluded by coercion. This is an undisputed fact that the Protectorate Treaty between Korea and Japan concluded in 1905 was not ratified by Emperor Gojong who was the head of the state according to the treaty conclusion process, and that numerous acts of coercion were applied in the conclusion process. In this way, Japan confined the ministers of the Daehan Empire and forced them to conclude the treaty by threatening their lives or bodies in the conclusion process of the Protectorate Treaty between Korea and Japan along with an armed protest. It was also accepted in the international law of those days that if there was a defect in the expression of will for the conclusion of a treaty, such a treaty became invalid even if the relevant treaty satisfied conclusion requirements, and Japan also knew of such a fact.[68]

There is also a document in Japan indicating that there was

coercion in the conclusion of the Protectorate Treaty between Korea and Japan. Circumstances at that time are specifically listed as follows using the data. However, as an unconstrained agreement cannot be found, it is necessary to pay attention to the opinion that there was coercion to a representative of a state for the conclusion of the Protectorate Treaty between Korea and Japan. For coercion to a representative of a state, it is necessary to verify whether or not the speech and behavior of Ito Hirobumi and Hayashi Gonsuke to the Emperor Gojong and the ministers, Japanese soldiers who entered the Korean imperial court, and the placement of Japanese troops in the downtown correspond to violence or a threat referred in the civil and criminal affairs of Japan and Korea. The behavior of Ito Hirobumi who pressed the Emperor to accept the protectorate treaty ("復命書," 日本外交文書, Vol. 38, Book No. 1, p. 496) comes into question. There are also records showing that they placed Korean ministers under Japanese military police or advisory police in order to prevent them from going into hiding (林權助, わが七十年を語る, 1935, 234; 中塚明, 近代日本と朝鮮, 第3版, 1994, 95), army general Yoshimichi Hasegawa (長谷川好道) imprisoned Korean ministers for a long time and forced them to express "yes" or "no" in front of each minister (戸叶薫雄-楢崎觀一, 朝鮮最近史, 1912, 22-28; 琴秉洞, "'乙巳保護條約'についての資料 2," 朝鮮研究, Issue of July 1965, 33) and participating minister Gyuseol Han who cried out grievously was taken to a separate room and Ito Hirobumi ordered others to kill him if he continued to cry out like a baby(西四辻公堯, 韓末外交秘話, 1930, pp.47-48). Such situations vividly describe the state of Gyuseol Han, who lost mental freedom and was mentally deranged, tired and daunted Korean ministers, and heavy and painful closed indoor situations.[69] In view of such a fact, the Protectorate Treaty between Korea and Japan was concluded only by the will of Japan and it cannot be concluded that such Treaty was concluded by the free will of the Daehan Empire that should be an independent state.[70]

Francis Rey pointed out in his paper "La Situation Internationale de la Coree" in 1906 that there were two defects that completely nullified the Treaty. One is that there is a defect in the indication of agreement of Korea and the other is that such Treaty was concluded due to Japan's force applied to Korea. He explains as follows.

> "The Protectorate Treaty between Korea and Japan was concluded by coercion applied to the Korean government through mental and physical violence. Ambassador plenipotentiary Ito Hirobumi and Hayashi Gonsuke obtained the signature on the Treaty by pressing the Emperor and the ministers using their Japanese troops guarding them. After resisting for two days, the council of the ministers gave up and signed on the Treaty, but the Emperor immediately dispatched an envoy to world powers, strongly claiming the invalidity of the Treaty. Since there was such a special circumstance at the time the Treaty was signed, we cannot help acknowledging that such a protectorate treaty is invalid."[71]

Francis Rey concluded that the Protectorate Treaty between Korea and Japan was the infringement of a weak state's rights by a power and Japan's political mistake. Japan had forced other people to accept the system they excluded by force and violence although they covered up the fact in the name of a treaty in order to establish the formality of protectorate's agreement. Francis Rey's claim was adopted in the draft of the Convention on the Law of Treaties prepared in 1935 which the American Society of International Law asked Harvard University to prepare in 1927, claiming that any treaty concluded by coercion was invalid and taking the Protectorate Treaty between Korea and Japan as one of the typical cases. With regard to the adoption of the Convention on the Law of Treaties, the report submitted by the United Nations International Law Commission to the UN General Assembly held in 1963 also stated the threat to the Emperor of Korea and the Minister for agreeing on the Protectorate

Treaty between Korea and Japan as a typical example of the treaty concluded by coercion in 1905, citing the Draft Convention on the Law of Treaties prepared by Harvard University.[72] Japanese scholar Tachi Sakurato focused on the process, not the protectorate system. Francis Rey also points out the aggressive act as grounds for the invalidity of the Protectorate Treaty between Korea and Japan, not the legality of colonization.[73]

With regard to the fact relevance of the coercion, Professor and historian Tae-jin Yi explains as follows. Japan concluded ⓐ a protocol dated February 23, 1904, ⓑ an agreement dated August 22, 1904, ⓒ the Protectorate Treaty between Korea and Japan dated on November 17, 1905, and ⓓ the Japan-Korea Agreement dated July 24, 1907, until the Japan-Korea Treaty of 1910. The protocol, agreements, and treaty were coerced with the main contents regarding the seizure of the right to use the territory (ⓐ), diplomatic sovereignty (ⓑ, ⓒ), and right to domestic affairs and military (ⓓ) with the purpose of seizing the national sovereignty of Korea. Japan seized the national sovereignty of Korea through the Japan-Korea Treaty of 1910 based on such a protocol, agreements, and treaty. Korea claimed that such a protocol, agreements, and treaty were invalid since these elements were concluded due to the coercion under threats from the Japanese army based on the provisions and practices under International Law that a treaty concluded through a threat to the representative of the other party could not come into force.[74] In particular, the Protectorate Treaty between Korea and Japan was concluded clearly due to the fact of coercion and threats, so it was adopted as the main subject for the claim. It was also claimed that the Japan-Korea Treaty of 1910 was invalid since it was concluded based on the Protectorate Treaty between Korea and Japan concluded in 1905 although such Treaty had no legal defect in the procedure or formality as claimed by Japan.[75] In addition, a passage in the Korean History of Pain reads that when Duk-yeong Yoon asked for the Royal Seal, the Emperor asked the Empress to stop crying. The Emperor said her crying may cause extermination and gave the royal seal to Wan-yong Lee. Japanese government appointed Duk-yeong Yoon as the viscount for such a contribution and rewarded him with four hundred thousand won.[76] This passage indicates the fact that coercion or threat was used. A Japanese scholar explains in his writing, "History of Japanese colonization of Korea," borrowing Akashi Genjiro's words, "It is certain that moving the cavalry regiment to Yongsan indicates the need of coercion for amalgamation," indicating that the Treaty was concluded by coercion.[77]

According to such relevant facts based on the Convention on the Law of Treaties, there is no doubt that the Protectorate Treaty between Korea and Japan concluded in 1905 was invalid. However, as pointed out earlier, the Convention on the Law of Treaties adopted in 1969 cannot be applied to the Japan-Korea Treaty of 1910, so it should be evaluated from the viewpoint of intertemporal law. Professor Tae-jin Yi mentioned, "It is invalid based on the provisions and practices under International Law that a treaty concluded through a threat to the representative of the other party could not come into force" in his writing, and this also should be examined in terms of international law of that time. Some say that it is the majority opinion to consider that the case of coercion to a representative of a state is invalid while the case of coercion to a state is valid at that time. Even if we accept the theory that the coercion to a state is valid as per the majority opinion of writers of international law at that time, it is questionable whether or not the expression of majority opinion can be considered evidence that it existed as the positive law which was the basis of legal positivism in the 1900s. As mentioned earlier, legal positivism focuses on what the law is through systematic research of state practice, so such a claim can be supported only when the state practice and legal conviction at that time are clearly proved by evidence. Concluding such a claim as the international law at that time due to the majority opinion of scholars cannot be regarded as a correct conclusion. This is because there were also many claims against such an opinion.

3-2-1. *Arguments of Japanese scholars*

Professor Sakamoto Shigeki points out that the legal force of a treaty concluded by coercion varies depending on whether such coercion is a threat to a representative of a state or coercion to a state according to traditional international law.[78] Sakamoto examined whether or not such legal principles were accepted as the customary international law in 1905. Concerning whether or not coercion becomes the grounds for the invalidity of a treaty, he claims "it is not wrong to conclude that the customary international law to consider that the coercion to a representative of a state becomes the grounds for the invalidity was established at that time," based on the explanation given by Oppenheim, Hall, Bluntchili, and Fiore. He also claims, "However, the coercion to a state and the coercion to a representative of a state may be divided juridically, but it is difficult to apply a dichotomy in each specific circumstance." He points out "there is no clear standard to distinguish between coercion applied to a head of a state or an official institution such as a minister in order for a power to impose its will on a weak state which is not the grounds for the invalidity of a treaty and coercion applied to an individual which is the grounds for the invalidity of a treaty" as the reason.[79] Sakamoto understands that coercion applied to a state is not grounds for the invalidity of a treaty and the coercion applied to a head of a state or an official institution is the coercion applied to a state. It is judged that this started with Oppenheim's writing.

Professor Sasakawa Norigatsu (笹川紀勝) explained the logic that a power applied coercion to a head of a state or an official institution such as a minister as a measure to force its will to a weak state did not exist in the period right before and right after the publication of Oppenheim's first edition. He explained, "Two types of coercion, including coercion to a state and coercion to a representative of a state, have been approved by customary international law and each has a different reason for its justification." He points out that to identify coercion to a representative of a state, it is important to prove the existence of violence or coercion separately. And, to identify coercion to a state, it is important to prove the relief or guarantee of rights for an illegal act to the state that applied force or coercion. His argument also intended for an inherent understanding and verification based on textbooks and history of theories regarding international law. Sasakawa made this conclusion after examining Oppenheim's 1st edition (1905), 4th edition (1927), and 9th edition (1996) of the textbook regarding international law, as well as writings by Hall (1890) and Grosch "Coercion in International Law" (1912).[80]

Professor Unno Fukuju (海野福壽) claims that the treaties were validly concluded between Japan and Korea prior to August 22, 1910, and the Japanese colonization over Korea was legitimate under international law.[81] This claim is based on the premise that a treaty concluded by coercion comes into force.

3-2-2. *Writings of international law in those days*

Grotius asserted that the observation of the principle of equality is required at the time of concluding a treaty, and equality is the concept that covers the recognition of fact as well as the freedom of choice. Therefore, the presence of fear at the time of concluding a treaty cannot be justified.[82] Vattel also takes a similar standpoint, claiming that a representative for concluding a treaty should have legitimate authority and their proper agreement should be expressed mutually.[83] Scholars in the 19th century had separate opinions regarding the validity of a treaty concluded in a war or the use of force to a weak state. However, they considered that coercion to an individual damaged the agreement which was an important element in the conclusion of a treaty.[84] For instance, Woolsey and Bernard considered that a treaty concluded by coercion was valid and personal coercion (personal duress) applied to a negotiator of a treaty damaged the agreement which was grounds for an international agreement.[85] Moore also maintains a similar opinion.[86] Some say that the standpoint to consider a treaty concluded by coercion was valid for reasons of circumstances reflected the majority opinion in the early 20th century, but there were also many opinions presenting opposite juridical grounds claiming that the treaty was invalid since a treaty concluded by coercion was illegal.

In many writings regarding traditional international law, coercion is divided into that which is inflicted on a state or on a representative of a state, and it is claimed that only the latter is invalid.[87] In the Draft Convention on the Law of Treaties prepared by Harvard University, the statements of scholars of international law regarding coercion as grounds for the nullity of a treaty under the classical international law are examined comprehensively. In particular, the position to classify coercion into two cases through the examination of a theoretical situation from the end of the 19th century to the early 20th century is taken in detail. Due to such a circumstance, the dichotomous approach to divide coercion, which is grounds for invalidating a treaty into the case of coercion to a state and the case of coercion to a representative of a state, is considered an established rule under international law.[88]

McNair premised that the description regarding coercion applied in the conclusion process of a treaty could be found from the standpoint of many literary authorities and some diplomatic authority. He describes that almost no judicial authority's standpoint could be found and further explained, "It is necessary to distinguish a law which exists and a law which should exist," and "legal and public opinion regarding coercion at the time of a conclusion of a treaty has been changed for the past half-century."[89] He explained, "A treaty concluded through the use of coercion, compulsion, violence, and force is invalid just as an agreement and such inference was not accepted in the past."[90] A traditional opinion supported by many scholars until recently explains that in the case where a state concludes a treaty under coercion to the state, such a treaty has binding force to such a state. Therefore, the case that the use of coercion invalidates a treaty should be limited to the case that coercion is applied to a representative of a state who carries out the final action according to the conclusion of the treaty (This is applicable in the case of signing a treaty that does not require ratification and ratifying a treaty which requires ratification). This is because if ratification is required even though the treaty is signed by coercion or a threat to a representative of a state, the effect of coercion or threat to the individual who signed the treaty can be remedied in case an authorized institution of the relevant state ratifies the treaty freely. McNair takes the Draft Convention on the Law of Treaties prepared by Harvard University as a specific example and explains that various literature takes the same description. However, while McNair used an expression implying that the Japan-Korea Treaty of 1910 was valid in this writing,[91] it is necessary to observe the fact that his writing did not clearly state that the Japan-Korea Treaty of 1910 was invalid. In addition, McNair's writing also indicates that the effect of coercion at the time of concluding the Treaty is found from some standpoints of the diplomatic authority (state practice). This can be counterevidence demonstrating that it did not exist as universal or general international law under the legal positivism at that time.

De Visscher indicates that the predominant view in the academic world is that the coercion applied to a representative of a state is invalid but the coercion applied to a state is valid. De Visscher also stated that when an authorized institution for the conclusion of a treaty was the subject of coercion, such coercion invalidated the treaty. This was likened to an error or fraud and the treaty was regarded the same as other agreements.[92] However, he mentioned that the treaty is valid if the coercion was applied to the state while the authorized institution held complete freedom to execute its function or the coercion was applied to the will of the state, as Westlake explained, and as a result, the state receiving coercion accepted the requirements of a stronger state.[93] Even if we follow De Visscher's claim, it is necessary to observe the fact that this description is based on the premise that coercion was applied while the authorized institution held the complete freedom to execute its function. That is, it cannot be considered that the premise claimed by De Visscher was satisfied in the case of the Japan-Korea Treaty of 1910 since the national sovereignty, that is, diplomatic sovereignty was deprived by the Protectorate Treaty between Korea and Japan concluded in 1905.

In his first edition of International Law in 1905, Oppenheim stated that as a treaty will lack binding force without real consent, absolute freedom of action on the part of the contracting parties is required.[94] It must, however, be understood that circumstances of urgent distress, such as either defeat in war or the menace of a strong State to a weak State, are, according to the rules of International Law, not regarded as excluding the freedom of action of a party consenting to the terms of a treaty.[95] He claims that the expression "freedom of action" only applies to a representative of a party state to a treaty.[96] A treaty concluded by a threat applied to a representative of a state and a treaty concluded by an abnormal representative do not have binding force, but a state forced to conclude a treaty including a submissive condition under circumstances cannot deny the obligations under the relevant treaty just because its freedom of action had been interfered with at the time of concluding the treaty. Oppenheim claimed in this explanation the case of coercion, which is divided into coercion to a state and coercion to a representative of a state. He stated that concluding the treaty under the former category could be valid for the reason of circumstances while the latter was invalid.[97] In the 8th edition amended in 1958 by Lauterpacht, it is indicated that the international law, existed prior to the Covenant of the League of Nations, the Charter of the United Nations, and the Treaty for the Renunciation of War, denied the effect of coercion which a victorious state exercised against a defeated state at the time of concluding a treaty. Since he takes the freedom of action as a state as the premise, it is significantly different from the opinion that acknowledges the effect of coercion to a state. This seems to be a consequent inference from the availability of criticism in terms of the general principle of law and the permission of war.

Wheaton explains that since an agreement made through violence is invalid according to the general principle of jurisdiction, as acknowledged by most civilized states, the freedom of agreement is essential for the validity of all agreements and an agreement obtained by coercion is invalid. Wheaton explained that this applied to all cases where a party of negotiation is personally threatened, and further evaluated that the coercion in the case of Charles IV, who was forced to abdicate the throne and the coercion applied at the time of concluding a treaty regarding Haiti in 1911, was considered sufficient personal coercion to damage the validity of the relevant agreement.[98]

Professor Frederick Smith, the former Director of Public Prosecutions, raised the issue of agreement by claiming that such inference should not be adopted too frequently on the premise that intercomparison between an agreement between states and an agreement between private individuals is useful. He further explained that since many important treaties were the results of coercion or a threat applied to a state that had no choice but to surrender, presenting such coercion as grounds for invalidating a treaty would destroy the grounds for all treaties adopted as a result of war. On the other hand, this shall not apply to cases where coercion is applied to an individual who is a party to negotiation for a treaty, classifying between coercion to a state and coercion to a representative of a state.[99] He also explained that moving troops to a conference hall for the purpose of forcing a negotiation party to agree clearly invalidates the relevant agreement. This can be applied to the historical fact of the time of the Protectorate Treaty between Korea and Japan.

The general standpoint is that it is possible to classify coercion in a treaty into coercion to a state and coercion to a representative of a state and claim the former as valid and the latter as invalid. Some scholars claim that it is impossible to classify the case of coercion or a threat into coercion to a state and coercion to a person who has the right to conclude a treaty. They claim that both cases lack unconstrained agreement in fundamental elements.[100] Some scholars claimed that force and a threat were legal measures for remedying the infringement of a right and a treaty concluded using a legal measure such as force or a threat for the purpose of remedying the infringement of a right could not be invalidated. They claimed that it was regarded that an agreement to an international treaty concluded based on the requirements in the range supposed rationally was granted voluntarily in some cases even if force was involved.[101] However, international law cannot tailor what is appropriate and what is necessary for the protection of a state claiming to be in danger in given cases. It is regarded that all agreements (compacts) are valid regardless of the use of coercion or a threat until such agreements destroy the independence of the relevant state. However, excessive coercion invalidated the relevant treaty because it could not be assumed that spontaneous suicide would be attempted by compensation or as a protective measure of another state.[102] In modern international law, the majority opinion of scholars considered that coercion to a state was valid. On the other hand, other contrasting theories existed in the period prior to 1945. Some also claim that coercion to a state should be regarded as grounds for invalidating a treaty by completely applying the principle of freedom of agreement to treaties.

The claim asserting that coercion to a state does not affect the validity of a treaty under international law in principle while coercion applied to an institution of a state causes the loss of binding force of a treaty may be supported on the premise that most or all writers provide a rational and academic argument to support such a proposition, but they criticize that it is not true.

The claim asserting that coercion to a state is not invalid is formed in a peace treaty and is applied to other treaties. The validity of a treaty concluded under international law by coercion should be adhered to according to a Roman proverb "coactus voluit, sed tamen voluit." Otherwise, all peace treaties concluded under certain coercion by a victorious country will be invalid. However, it should be noted that such a description is not a juristic demonstration.[103] As the concept of a treaty is fully unifying, the issue of coercion can be studied only by considering all treaties and it should be explained in the same definition for all treaties. However, he claims that this problem should be explained only with regard to the category of a "peace treaty" and such a solution should not be applied simply to other treaties through arbitrary inference as many scholars claim.[104] On the contrary, an opinion claiming that coercion to a state invalidates a treaty in principle is rarely supported. Scholars that support such a standpoint include Amari, Laghi, and Nippold. Pradier-Foderé also takes such a standpoint.

Weinschel presents a fundamental question of whether or not coercion to a state exists with regard to the theory to classify between coercion to a state and coercion to an institution that concludes a treaty. That is, he claims that coercion to a state cannot exist. The application of coercion to a state to conclude a treaty that would put all the citizens of the state into prison by force means that the people forming the state were subjected to coercion. However, coercion applied to a state means that the state with an authority received coercion. This, however, did not mean the people received coercion. In addition, it is possible to claim that coercion is applied to a state only in the case of imprisoning all the people who form such a state by force. However, as such a case is actually impossible, coercion to a state cannot exist accordingly. And, in most cases, as a treaty is concluded by coercion applied to a representative of a state individually, the treaty is deemed invalid. That is, a treaty concluded by coercion is invalid.[105] Weinschel's claim is in the same context as the logic of the writer of this study criticizing Wheaton's claim that a treaty concluded by coercion for social welfare should be considered as invalid.

4. CONCLUSION

On March 23, 1993, Councilor Motooka Shoji mentioned in the Japanese Parliament that Japan's colonization of the Korean Peninsula resulted from the Protectorate Treaty between Korea and Japan concluded in 1905 and that Japan's annexation of Korea was a moral violation and an illegal act under international law.[106] His comment is fully supported by historical facts already revealed and demonstrated in terms of international law. A defect in the conclusion process of the Protectorate Treaty between Korea and Japan that the Treaty was not ratified by Emperor Gojong, who was the right holder to conclude a treaty, has been confirmed. In addition, Emperor Gojong carried out various diplomatic activities to protect sovereignty through the declaration of neutralization and diplomacy using a special envoy at the end of the period of the Daehan Empire. However, the international law in the late 1800s and the early 1900s was significantly different from the international law of today and Korea was often unable to exercise freedoms due to the force of international politics. A typical case is the meaning and effect of the declaration of neutralization.

There is also an opinion in academic circles of historical studies in Korea that the declaration of neutralization without the support of self-defense capabilities for neutral diplomacy at the time of the Russo-Japanese War was Emperor Gojong's delusion and empty prayer.[107] Some criticize that the act of Emperor Gojong for appealing the injustice of the Treaty by dispatching a secret envoy to various European countries including Germany and France after the conclusion of the Protectorate Treaty between Korea and Japan was merely ignorance. That is, the Emperor is criticized for not knowing the fact that Western powers accepted or overlooked Japanese rule over Korea.[108] However, all actions including the declaration and promotion of the neutralization policy and the activities to recover sovereignty through diplomatic activities such as the delivery of a personally handwritten letter and the dispatch of a special envoy to Hague were based on international law. The problem was the idealistic expectation of Emperor Gojong that the international society would intervene in an issue of a weak state in the name of justice. We cannot deny, however, that Emperor Gojong made all possible diplomatic efforts to protect sovereignty.[109] Emperor Gojong's continuous attempts to protect sovereignty were indeed the practice of protecting sovereignty, and Japan's coercion was called into question in terms of international law. Japan assumed that the Daehan Empire was a Japanese protectorate on the grounds of the Protectorate Treaty between Korea and Japan concluded in 1905 and tried to take over Korea's diplomatic relations. In reality, such Treaty was an invalid treaty concluded by Japan's coercion without Emperor Gojong's ratification. Japan claims that a treaty concluded by coercion to a state was not invalid under international law at that time. However, according to the conclusion that can be made through the examination and analysis of writings regarding international law at that time, a treaty concluded by coercion to a representative of a state cannot come into force. Moreover, a claim that coercion to a state does not affect the validity of a treaty also cannot be considered the common view at that time. The legal principles of scholars claiming that it was the majority opinion also contain many problems. Such scholars claim that a treaty is considered an agreement between states, and when it lacks free will of a state directly involved at the time of concluding the treaty, they merely claim that it is different from a private agreement without presenting clear grounds for their claim.[110] Japan's claim based on the opinion that the coercion to a state is valid, citing a peace treaty as an example, also has a defect that the Protectorate Treaty between Korea and Japan concluded in 1905 is not a peace treaty for ending a war. In addition, the fact that Japan asked England for the validity of the Treaty of 1910 can be considered as indirect evidence showing that there was no general state practice or legal conviction that recognized the validity of the relevant Treaty.[111]

In terms of international law, the Protectorate Treaty between Korea and Japan concluded in 1905 is fundamentally invalid since Japan forced the ministers of the Daehan Empire to sign the Treaty. The Treaty is, therefore, merely an unfinished draft treaty that was not ratified by Emperor Gojong who was the right holder to conclude a treaty under the law of the Daehan Empire.

Notes

1. Sean Fern, "Tokdo or Takeshima? The International Law of Territorial Acquisition in the Japan-Korea Island Dispute," *Stanford Journal of East Asian Affairs*, Vol. 5, No. 1 (2005), p. 80.

2. Chung-hyun Paik, "Consideration of annexation of Korea by Japan in terms of international law," Study on the illegality of annexation of Korea (Seoul National University Press, 2003), Refer to pp. 218~219; Seong-eun Kang, "Forced signing process of the Japan-Korea Treaty of 1905 examined through the 1st historical record," annexation of Korea and modern times - Re-examination in terms of history and international law (Thaehaksa, 2009), pp. 198~236.

3. Alexis Dudden, *Japan's Colonization of Korea: Discourse and Power* (University of Hawaii, 2006), pp. 72~73.

4. Homer B. Hulbert, Korean Liberty Conference (1942), p. 97.

5. Tae-jin Yi, Criticism of Emperor Gojong's secret agitation theory, Northeast Asia 5 (1995); Cheol-ho Han, "Response of ruling power against the Japanese occupation," Academic symposium in commemoration of the 65th anniversary of the restoration of independence and the 23rd anniversary of opening - 100 years since the loss of sovereignty, remembrance and self-examination (Research Institute of Korean Independence Movement Studies, Independence Hall of Korea, August 5, 2010).

6. Henry Wheaton, *Elements of International Law*, The Literal Reproduction of the Edition of 1866, (Oxford, 1936), p. 27.

7. Gwang-ho Hyun, "How did the Daehan Empire try to achieve the neutralization?," History that Opens Up Tomorrow No. 17 (September 2004), pp. 204~205.

8. Rudolf L. Bindschedler, "Neutrality, Concept, and General Rules," in *Encyclopedia of Public International Law* Vol. 3 (Elsevier, 1997), p. 549.

9. Wheaton, *op. cit.*, p. 426.

10. Wheaton, *op. cit.*, p. 427.

11. L. Oppenheim, *International Law*, Vol. I Peace Second Edition (Longmans, 1912), p. 148.

12. Oppenheim, *op. cit.*, p. 149.

13. Bindschedler, *op. cit.*, p. 550.

14. Jeong-gyun Kim · Jae-ho Seong, *op. cit.*, p. 772.

15. Gwang-ho Hyun, Foreign policies of the Daehan Empire (Seo-won Shin, 2002), p. 89.

16. Gwang-ho Hyun, Foreign policies of the Daehan Empire, pp. 89~90; The government of the Daehan Empire joined 「Geneva Convention dated August 22, 1864 for the Amelioration of the Condition of the Wounded and Sick in Armed Forces in the Field」 on January 8, 1903 and 「Hague Convention of 1899」 on February 7, 1903.

17. Chan-ho Uhm, "Emperor Gojong's diplomacy using a special envoy for the protection of sovereignty," The Kangwon Historical Society No. 15 and No. 16, p. 209.

18. Gwang-ho Hyun, "How did the Daehan Empire try to achieve the neutralization?," p. 205; Emperor Gojong submitted a diplomatic document regarding the declaration of a permanently neutral nation by Korea to Secretary of State John Hay through diplomatic minister Min-hee Cho stationed in Washington on January 22, 1904, requesting for support to the United States.

19. Center for Education Research, College of Education, Seoul National University, A series of Korean educational data, Emperor Gojong's diplomacy for protecting sovereignty (1994), p. 7.

20. Chan-ho Uhm, *op. cit.*, p. 210.

21. Rudolf L. Bindschedler, "Neutrality, Concept and General Rules," in *Encyclopedia of Public International Law* Vol. 3 (Elsevier, 1997), p. 549.

22. Wheaton, *op. cit.*, p. 426.

23. Wheaton, *op. cit.*, p. 427.

24. Bindschedler, *op. cit.*, p. 550.

25. Jeong-gyun Kim · Jae-ho Seong, *op. cit.*, p. 772.

26. Emperor Gojong asked foreign countries to confirm the invalidity of the Protectorate Treaty between Korea and Japan at least 6 times from October 1905 before its conclusion to July 1907 (dispatch of secret envoys to Hague).

27. Seong-eun Kang, (Trans. Cheol-ho Han), Protectorate Treaty of Korea of 1905 and the Responsibility of Colonial Rule - Dialogue between Historical Studies and Study of International Law (Seonin, 2008), p. 148.

28. National Institute of Korean History, History of Korean Independence Movement I (1965), pp. 178~179; And, there are other references. The Emperor had diplomatic minister Min-hee Cho stationed in the United States who was returning to Korea due to the transfer to the diplomatic minister stationed in Japan in the winter of 1904 to ask the United States for cooperation in the protection of sovereignty and the United States declared to provide cooperation indirectly. Diplomatic minister Min-hee Cho had a conference with Secretary of State John Hay by the will of the Emperor, and the Emperor was very pleased with the conference result and sent a reply to express gratitude to American legation Chas W. Needam stationed in Washington. Refer to Allen to Hay, September 30, 1904, Despatches, No. 799, National Archives (M134), Center for Education Research, College of Education, Seoul National University, Emperor Gojong's diplomacy for protecting sovereignty, Re-cited from p. 7.

29. Chan-ho Uhm, *op. cit.*, p. 218.

30. Jun-man Kang, American History with Themes.

31. Emperor Gojong's diplomacy for protecting sovereignty, p. 7.

32. F.A. McKinsey, (Trans. Bong-ryong Shin), Korea's independence movements (Pyungminsa, 1986), p. 85.

33. Trans. Bong-ryong Shin, *op. cit.*, pp. 88~89.

34. Trans. Bong-ryong Shin, *op. cit.*, p. 88.

35. Chan-ho Uhm, *op. cit.*, p. 219.

36. Jun-man Kang, *op. cit.*

37. When the Protectorate Treaty between Korea and Japan was concluded by coercion in spite of the Emperor's objection, Emperor Gojong sent the following telegram to Hulbert who was carrying Emperor Gojong's personally handwritten letter to the United States urgently on November 18, 1905. "The protectorate treaty concluded recently between Japan and Korea was concluded by coercion under the threats with guns and swords, so I declare that such treaty is invalid. I have never agreed to the Treaty nor will I agree to the Treaty in the future. I ask you to deliver this fact to the US government." (Trans. Bong-ryong Shin), *op. cit.*, p. 87.

38. Emperor Gojong's diplomacy for protecting sovereignty, p. 29.

39. It shows that Emperor Gojong intended to file the petition for the issue of the Protectorate Treaty between Korea and Japan to the Permanent Court of Arbitration established by the 1st Hague Convention in 1899 through Hulbert. Chan-ho Uhm, *op. cit.*, p. 226.

40. Compiled by Tae-jin Yi, The annexation of Korea was not valid (Thaehaksa, 2001), p. 68.

41. *Yearbook of the International Law Commission* 1963, Vol. II, Documents of the fifteenth session including the reports of the Commission to the General Assembly, p. 50.

42. Professor Woomino claims that the conclusion of the former treaty was legally valid and the colonial administration was carried out through legal coercion. 海野福壽, 韓國併合の歷史認識, 世界, (1997. 7), p. 274.

43. Chung-hyun Baik, Problems of Korea-Japan Treaties in the 1900s Examined according to the International Law, Civil Lecture for Korean History, Vol. 16 (1996), Ilchokak, pp. 76~77; Professor Bae-geun Park raised a question whether or not it was sufficient to examine only some works, claiming it was generally acknowledged that coercion to a representative of a state was not grounds for invalidation. Bae-geun Park, Significance and limitations of Theory of Validity of Treaties related to the annexation of Korea, Legal Studies, Vol. 44 (Pusan National University, 2003), p. 380.

44. Sean D. Murphy, *Principles of International Law*, (West, 2006), p. 12.

45. Chung-hyun Baik, *Ibid.*, pp. 240~241.

46. Shi-hwan Do, review of problems of the Protectorate Treaty between Korea and Japan in terms of international law, Korean Journal of International Law, Vol. 60, No. 4 (2015), p. 140.

47. Oppenheim mentions by quoting many scholars that a treaty that is not ratified carries no legal binding force. See, for instance, Ullmann, § 78; Jellinek, p. 55; Nippold, p. 123; Wegmann, p. 11. recited from Oppenheim, *op cit.*, p. 553.

48. Oppenheim, *Ibid.*

49. Oppenheim, *op. cit.*, p. 546.

50. William Edward Hall, *A Treatise on International Law* (Oxford. 1895), p. 345.

51. T. J. Lawrence, *The Principles of International Law*, (Oxford, 1923), pp. 299~300.

52. Oppenheim, *op. cit.*, p. 555.

53. Oppenheim, *op. cit.*, p. 553.

54. Hall, *Ibid.*

55. Hall, *A Treatise on International Law* (Oxford, 1909), p. 323.

56. 高橋作衛, 平時國際公法, 初版, (日本法律學校, 1903), p. 561; 高橋作衛, 平時國際法論, 4訂增補9版 (日本大學校 清水書店, 1910), p. 651.

57. 立博士述, 平時國際法 大正14年東大講義 (1925), p. 373.

58. Professor Tae-jin Yi presents the fact that there has been no case that a treaty establishing a state to become a protectorate has been processed in an unofficial form as grounds. Compiled by Tae-jin Yi, *The annexation of Korea was not valid*, Thaehaksa, (2001), pp. 189~190.

59. Eo-jin Kim, *Introduction of Concept of Treaty to Korea - Commission of Full Power and Ratification*, Journal of Seoul International Law Studies, Vol. 10, No. 2 (2003), pp. 110~111.

60. 坂元茂樹, 日韓は舊條約の問題の落とし穴に陥ってはならない, 世界 第652號 (1998. 9) pp. 200~201.

61. Compiled by Tae-jin Yi, (2001), *Ibid*, p. 109.

62. In-sook Kim, *View on the ratification related to Japan-Korea Treaty of 1905*, Korean Journal of International Law, Vol. 50, No. 2 (2005), p. 81.

63. Yeong-don Rho, Issues regarding the legal force of Japan-Korea Treaty of 1905, Journal of Korean Political and Diplomatic History, Vol. 28, No. 1, p. 65.

64. Douglas Story, A secret letter from Emperor Gojong: Review of Japan-Korea Treaty of 1905 (Trans. Min-joo Kwon, Geulnameum, 2004), pp. 65~74.

65. Professor Totsuka Etsuro also claims that the Protectorate Treaty between Korea and Japan concluded in 1905 was legally invalid since there is no original document of the concluded Treaty. The Japanese government has repeatedly claimed the legitimate conclusion and valid existence of the relevant Treaty, but recent studies show that the original document of the concluded Treaty does not exist. Since the treaty should be concluded in writing, we cannot but accept the fact of legal absence that the Treaty did not exist. The Protection Treaty of 1905 the World Historical Review, Presentation of International Conference of the Academy of Korean History and Culture (2015.11.20.).

66. Compiled by Tae-jin Yi, 2001, *Ibid*, pp. 54~62.

67. National Assembly Library, Legislative Research Bureau, 1964, p. 76.

68. Totsuka Etsuro, 1995, *See* pp. 328~333.

69. 笹川紀勝, 日韓における法的な'對話'をめざして: 第二次日韓協約強制問題への視点, 世界 (1999. 7), p. 246.

70. Totsuka Etsuro, Trans. Ikhan Kim, 1995. Unlawfulness of Japan-Korea Treaty of 1905 and Responsibility of the Japanese Government, Tae-jin Yi (1995), p. 317.

71. Francis Rey, "La Situation Internationale de la Coree," *Révue Générale de Droit Internationale Public*, Tome XIII (1906), pp. 55~56.

72. Example cases including siege of Polish parliament in 773, the Protectorate Treaty between Korea and Japan concluded in 1905, siege of Haiti parliament in 1915 and forced signature of President of Czechoslovakia and minister of foreign affairs by Hitler in 1939 are presented. *Yearbook of the International Law Commission*, 1963, Vol. II, Documents of the fifteenth session including the reports of the Commission to the General Assembly, p. 50.

73. Dudden, *op. cit.*, p. 73.

74. Compiled by Tae-jin Yi, 2001, *Ibid*, p. 36.

75. Compiled by Tae-jin Yi, 2001, *Ibid*, pp. 35~36; Refer to pp. 421~451 for the detailed grounds for the coercion applied to the Protectorate Treaty between Korea and Japan.

76. 朴殷植, 1945, *Ibid*, P. 283.

77. 山邊健太郎, 日韓併合小史, (岩波書店, 1972), p. 235; With regard to coercion applied to the Treaty of 1910, Lord McNair describes it as "a treaty not unattended with acts of coercion" in this writing. Lord McNair, 1961, The Law of Treaties (Oxford, 1986), p. 209.

78. 坂元茂樹, 日韓保護條約の效力-強制における條約の觀点から, 法學論集(關西大學) 第44卷 第4・5合併號, p. 339.

79. *Ibid.*, p. 342.

80. 笹川紀勝, 日韓における法的な對話をめざして, 世界 第663號, pp. 237~246.

81. 海野福壽, 韓國併合の歷史認識-李敎授韓國併合不成立論を再檢討す, 世界 第666號, pp. 260~262.

82. Hugo Grotius, *De Jure Belli ac Pacis*, Book II, Ch. XII, Sec. X / Book II, Ch. XVII, Sec. XIX. *Classics of International Law* (Oxford, 1925).

83. Emerich de Vattel, The Law of Nations or the Principles of the Natural Law, Ch. XII. *Classics of International Law* (Carnegie Institution, 1916).

84. Stuart S. Malawer, *Imposed Treaties and International Law* (Hein, 1977), pp. 7~8.

85. T. Woolsey, 1875, Introduction to the Study of International Law 100 (4th ed.) p. 172; M. Bernard, 1868, Four Lectures on Subjects Connected with Diplomacy, p. 184, recited in Malawer, *Ibid*, p. 17.

86. J. Moore ed., 1906, *A Digest of International Law*, pp. 184~184, recited in Malawer, *Ibid*.

87. *Yearbook of the International Law Commission* (1966), p. 207.

88. C. Winfred Jenks, *The Prospects of International Adjudication* (Stevens, 1964), p. 422.

89. Lord McNair, *Law of Treaties* (Oxford, 1961), p. 207.

90. *op. cit.*, pp. 207~208.

91. *op. cit.*, pp. 208~209.

92. Fernand de Visscher, "Des traités imposès par la violence," *Recueil de droit international et legislation comparée* (1931) p. 515.

93. *Ibid.*

94. Oppenheim, International Law, First Edition (Longman, 1905), p. 525.

95. *Ibid.*

96. *Ibid.*

97. *Ibid.*; The 2nd edition in 1912 also provides the same explanation (Oppenheim, 2nd Edition (1912), p. 547), but the 8th edition amended by Lauterpacht in 1958 explains that an authentic will (agreement) of a representative of a party state to conclude a treaty is the condition for the validity of such a treaty and a treaty concluded as the result of a threat or coercion to a representative is invalid. Oppenheim, Eight Edition (1958), Edited by H. Lauterpacht, p. 891.

98. A. Berriedale Keith, Wheaton's Elements of International Law (1929), Sixth Edition, Vol. I, p. 50.

99. Sir Frederick Smith, International Law, revised by Coleman Phillipson (Dent & Sons, 1918), pp. 141~142.

100. Whitton, R.C. (1934, III), pp. 258~259, Brierly, R.C. (1936, IV), 208 in Fariborz Nozari, *Unequal Treaties in International Law* (S-Byran Stundt & Co., 1971), p. 66. Nozari's writing was published in 1971 but this writing cited Hall, Hyde, Fauchille, and Brierly who were the scholars around 1910. Some Japanese scholars also take this standpoint and claim that it is difficult to classify since there is no objective authorized organization that can classify both cases clearly and apply coercion in the reality of international society as the grounds. Sakamoto Shigaeki, Japan and Korea should fall into the trap of rescue remedy: Sekaii's one response to Tae-jin Yi's paper, Tae-jin Yi, The annexation of Korea was not valid (Thaehaksa, 2001), pp. 83~89.

101. William Edward Hall, 1917, *A Treatise on International Law* (Oxford, 1917), Edited by A. Pearce Higgins, p. 336.

102. *Ibid.*

103. Weinschel, *Zeitschrift für Völkerrecht* (1930), Band XV, S. 450.

104. *op. cit.*, SS. 450~451.

105. *op. cit.*, SS. 457~462.

106. Shi-hwan Do, *Ibid.*, p. 144.

107. Cheol-ho Han, Responses of ruling power against Japanese occupation, p. 96.

108. Cheol-ho Han, *op. cit.*, p. 98.

109. Argument of Professor Yeonghee Seo from Korea Polytechnic University who came forward as a debater against the presentation of Professor Cheol-ho Han at the academic symposium for Korea's 65th anniversary of Liberation Day and the 23rd anniversary of the opening of the Independence Hall of Korea, Institute of Korean Independence Movement Studies. Hankook Ilbo, August 9, 2010.

110. Liszt-Fleischmann, *Völkerrecht*, 12. Aufl. (1925), S. 261; Refer to Hersch Lauterpacht, *Private Law Sources and Analogies of International Law-with special reference to international arbitration* (Archon Books, 1970) Ch. IV for in-depth study regarding the relationship between a treaty and an agreement.

111. Lord McNair, *op. cit.*, p. 209.

Challenges in International Human Rights Law to Solve Issues relating to Victims of Forced Mobilization by Japan

DOH See-Hwan
Senior Research Fellow
Northeast Asian History Foundation, Seoul, Korea

Abstract

On October 30, 2018, the Korean Supreme Court reached a final verdict concerning the top court's ruling on forced labor reparation on May 24, 2012 based on the victim-centered principle according to international human rights law. In this regard, on July 1, 2019, the Japanese government officially announced export restrictions to Korea on photoresist, fluorine polyimide, and high-purity hydrogen fluoride, substances that are essential to manufacturing semiconductors and displays. Then on August 2, Japan's Abe administration decided that Korea's catch-all system was insufficient and removed Korea from its "whitelist" enabling friendly nations to be subject to simpler export procedures.

There are two backgrounds in the Korean Supreme Court ruling. About the environmental background from Japan's nationalism, first, there is the policy frame of historical distortion of the "legitimate theory of 1910 colonization" and the "completion theory of the 1965 Korea-Japan Claims Agreement" against Korea under the Japanese government's policy keynote of "breaking away from the postwar regime" and "historical revisionism," and second, the Japanese judiciary's nationalistic postwar compensation trial. About the legal background from the shift in human rights-centralism of international law, the first is the Durban Declaration toward the end of colonialism, the second is the basic principle of victims' rights toward victim-centered approach, and the third is the joint statement from Korean and Japanese intellectuals toward the nullification of the 1910 Korea-Japan Annexation Treaty.

The Korean Supreme Court decided that the victims' right to claim damages is not included in the right of the 1965 Korea-Japan claims agreement as the right to claim solarium against Japanese company of forced mobilization victims, premised upon the Japanese corporation's unlawful acts against humanity with direct links to the Japanese Government's unlawful colonial domination of the Korean Peninsula and waging of wars of aggression. Japan's export regulation is not only practically an "economic retaliation" against the Korean Supreme Court's Decision over reparation for wartime forced labor, but also Japan's export control measures amount to the typical violation concerning the norms of international trade law. In connection with the strategic material management system raised by Japan as the basis for export regulations to Korea, Korea ranked 17th has exceeded Japan ranked 36th.

We must solve the human rights issues through universal value norm of the normative system established by the international society as a peace community in the face of Japan's claim to violate international law with international law at the forefront. In relation to Japan's export regulations that the Japanese government violated international trade laws to neutralize the Korean Supreme Court's historic ruling on the relief of victims of Japan's forced labor, it is because asking us again today the meaning of international human rights laws formed due to the invasions and atrocities committed by Japan and Germany, that led to extreme contempt and violation on human dignity in World War II, is an international human rights legal challenges as a historical justice that we should answer.

Key Words

International human rights law, Forced mobilization victims, Historical distortion, Postwar compensation trials, Nationalism, Colonialism, Victim-centered approach, Individual rights of claims, Export regulation, WTO, GATT

1. INTRODUCTION

The year 2019 was not only the centennial of the March 1st Movement and the establishment of the Republic of Korea Provisional Government, but also concurrently the 80th year of the outbreak of World War II, an unprecedented tragedy of 50 million victims. However, the fact that the history of Japanese military comfort women and forced labor mobilized for Japanese invasions under Imperial Japan's colonial rule that began 110 years ago reminds us of the slew of historical tasks handed down to us today. That is the question that history poses to our generation, defined as "an unending dialogue between the present and the past" by E. H. Carr, a representative historian from the 20th century. The answer to this question comes to us through historical introspection as "challenge and response," advocated by A. J. Toynbee, which are tasks that must be illuminated from the perspective of historical justice.

On October 30, 2018, the Korean Supreme Court reached a final verdict concerning the top court's ruling on forced labor reparation on May 24, 2012 based on the victim-centered principle according to international human rights law. In this regard, on July 1, 2019, the Japanese government officially announced export restrictions to Korea on photoresist, fluorine polyimide, and high-purity hydrogen fluoride, substances that are essential to manufacturing semiconductors and displays. Then on August 2, Japan's Abe administration decided that Korea's catch-all system was insufficient and removed Korea from its "whitelist" enabling friendly nations to be subject to simpler export procedures.

This directly demonstrates that Korea and Japan are not yet free from their serious historical conflict arising from the past, a legacy of the 20th century, as a precondition of the peace community for mutual growth and prosperity in the 21st century. This is because, as the Japanese Historical Society lashed out at Abe's statement released on the 70th anniversary of the end of World War II, Japan's arrogance was expressed, becoming the provocation that breached international trade rules, namely export restrictions on key materials. This came from the mistaken belief arising from self-righteous historical awareness rather than facing up to the history under the banner of "breaking away from the postwar regime" and "historical revisionism."

Then, it will be necessary to bring to light the "legitimate theory of 1910 colonization" and the "completion theory of the 1965 Korea-Japan Claims Agreement," the twin arguments raised against Korea, and block Japan's violations of international trade rules aimed at neutralizing the Korean Supreme Court's ruling based on the principles of international law.

2. JAPAN'S NATIONALISTIC POLICY FRAME AND POSTWAR TRIALS

2-1. Japanese Government's Historical Distortion Policy Frame

The 1910 Korea-Japan Annexation Treaty, the basis of Japan's argument for the lawful colonization theory, is not a legal pact signed under the agreement by equitable sovereign states without defects in form and procedures, but rather an illegal pact compelled under pressure and aggression, which constitutes grounds for being nulled and voided. Thus, it can be said that Koreans' claim for damages caused by misdeeds directly linked to colonization, including Japan's anti-humanitarian illegal acts like Japanese military comfort women and forced labor under Japan's unlawful colonial rule, is not subject to the 1965 Korea-Japan Claims Agreement, assuming that Japan's colonial rule is legal.

The second argument – the completion theory of the 1965 Korea-Japan Claims Agreement – is that victims' individual claims became completely and ultimately extinct. But the apology for and answers to Japan's colonial rule in the Murayama statement in 1995, by Treaties Bureau director Yanai Shunji in 1991, and Japan's Foreign Minister Taro Kono on November 14, 2018 from the Diet coherently state that the right of individuals to file claims cannot be extinguished. This is because the rights of individuals, requirements that constitutes human rights in terms of international law, cannot be destroyed, and in terms of domestic law, the rights of individuals cannot be extinguished either because breaches the basic rights of a countryman. Nonetheless, unlike the answers from Japan's Diet, the Abe administration is reiterating its contention that Koreans' claim for damages was resolved with the 1965 Korea-Japan Claims Agreement.

In the regard, it is evident from the text of Agreement on the Settlement of Problem concerning Property and Claims and the Economic Cooperation between the Republic of Korea and Japan (hereinafter, "the 1965 Korea-Japan Claims Agreement") that it is an economic treaty that resolves "property" claims between the countries and does not address human rights issues. An examination of the plain language of both the 1965 Korea-Japan Claims Agreement and the earlier San Francisco Peace Treaty leads to the conclusion that the scope of those agreements was limited to matters of sovereignty over disputed territories, real properties, financial and commercial matters. There is no reference in the treaty to comfort women, forced labor as crimes against humanity, or any other atrocities committed by the Japanese against Korean civilians. Rather, the provisions in the treaty refer to property and commercial relations between the two nations.

The intentions of the Parties to the Agreements as to the generic use of the term "claims" under Article 2 of the 1965 Korea-Japan Claims Agreement must therefore be read in the context of the full factual background. Whether the funds provided by Japan under the

1965 Korea-Japan Claims Agreement were intended only for offenses relating to property matters to the exclusion of individual compensation for the victims of Japan's human rights atrocities must be assessed after a thorough examination of all the evidence available.[1] However, this much is clear, if the intent of the Parties was to extinguish the claims of the comfort women and forced labor that would have no effect. The claims of the comfort women under international law are not claims that are at the mercy of the intentions of the state parties to the 1965 Korea-Japan Claims Agreement.

2-2. Japan's Nationalistic Postwar Compensation Trials

Since the 1990s when the cold war ended, calls for 'postwar claims' escalated into lawsuits in global solidarity across Asia along amid the changes in the international situation following democratization of many Asian countries.[2] Japan only compensated for the lawsuit filed against the state through the San Francisco Peace Treaty and bilateral agreement but did not agree to personal 'reparation' at all, prompting a great number of war victims in Asia to file suit against the Japanese government.[3] Nevertheless, Japan has not recognized its responsibility for colonial rule and invasion war and only proceeded with postwar claims trials. The number of lawsuits relevant to 'postwar claims' in Japan stands at 100 as 2019.[4] Of these lawsuits, 10 were filed by former 'comfort women' with three of them made by Korean women.[5]

Meanwhile, the lawsuits filed by Korean victims over the forced labor are 'Lawsuit against Mitsubishi Heavy Industries over the Unpaid Wage' on December 11, 1995 and 'Damages for Forced Laborers in Nippon Steel & Sumitomo Metal Corporation' on December 24, 1997. However, the two suits were also dismissed by the Supreme Court of Japan for extinctive prescription and 1965 Korea-Japan Claims Agreement on November 1, 2007 and October 9, 2003 respectively.[6]

In the meantime, since 2000, the Japanese government has held a stance that individual's rights to compensation are extinguished and thus solved completely by expanding the meaning of 'waiver of claims' from 'waiver of rights to diplomatic protection.' This stance was initially devised to respond to the lawsuit[7] filed by Hwang Geum Joo and other 15 former 'Comfort women' in China, Taiwan, and the Philippines with District Court of Washington on September 18, 2000. To put it in another way, the Japanese government did so because it knew it would be difficult to have legal advantage with principles like the amount of time passed since those atrocities were committed and the lack of response or solution from the state in lawsuits filed in the US. Afterwards, the Japanese government reversed its existing claim regarding 1965 Korea-Japan Claims Agreement. It put forward as a core defense by invoking Article 2 paragraph 1[8] of the Treaty, 'the problem concerning claims...is settled completely and finally,' and Article 2 paragraph 3[9] 'No claim shall be made.'

However, the victims of forced labor by Japan filed a lawsuit with Busan District Court on May 1, 2000 against Mitsubishi Heavy Industries and Nippon Steel & Sumitomo Metal Corporation, and filed the same suit with Seoul District Court on August 26, 2005 after the suit was closed in Japan. In 2009, right before the 100th year of Japan's forced annexation of Korea, Busan High Court[10] and Seoul High Court[11] ruled against the plaintiff on February 3 and July 16 respectively in the appeals trial by upholding the 2007 Japanese Supreme Court's ruling against the plaintiff on lawsuit over international law violation and unlawful acts since 2000. At the appeal brought by the plaintiffs, the Supreme Court reversed and remanded the original judgement on May 24, 2012[12] and ruled the final decision on October 30, 2018.[13]

The verdict by the Supreme Court of Japan which well reflects the reversed standpoint of the Japanese government is no doubt nationalistic and the result of its obsession with modern impulse intended to stop the scope of justice from reaching the past. The decision to see victims' protest as "pressure that may put a great burden on the state involved" implies at the order of priority among the ruling class in Japan. They believe that the bottom-up protest against 1951 San Francisco Peace Treaty and a series of subsequent bilateral agreements on compensation and economic cooperation is nothing but a noise disturbing the gigantic postwar political order which could stir unnecessary disorder.[14]

2-3. Japan's Colonial Responsibility and Korea-Japan Treaty System

It is to be noted that even though the Japanese government has consistently denied the 'colonial responsibility' itself in the Korea-Japan Treaty in 1965 on the basis that Japan's forcible occupation of Korea for 35 years after the forced annexation of Korea and Japan in 1910 was legal.[15] The Korean court decided that Japan compensate for "Japanese corporation's unlawful acts against humanity with direct links to the Japanese Government's unlawful colonial domination of the Korean Peninsula and waging of wars of aggression." However, the Japanese government argues that 1965 Korea-Japan Basic Relations Treaty, signed as a separate postwar claims agreement, waived all the relevant rights to compensation. Japan claims that the Korean court's decision is unfair and politically motivated to nullify bilateral agreement even though the Treaty on Basic Relations between Korea and Japan voids all colonial responsibilities including those for the forced mobilization on the basis that the colonial rule was legal. The problems of the Korea-Japan Treaty System are pointed out as follows.

Professor Osamu Ota who is an expert in 'colonial responsibility' in the perspective of international treaty at Doshisha University claims that the Japanese government, which has held unclear stance toward colonial rule and war responsibility even though it forcefully mobilized labors during wartime under the colonial rule, should no longer try to conceal the truth but accept the verdicts of the Korean Supreme Court. He says that the Japanese government did not have the intention to apologize from the beginning because it believed that colonial rule blessed Korea by 'dispensation theory' and helped it modernize by 'modernization theory.'[16] He went on to point out that the 1965 Korea-Japan Claims Agreement Negotiation which was initiated based on 'property' and 'claims' stipulated in Article 4, paragraph (a) of 1951 San Francisco Peace Treaty paradoxically did not terminate 'colonial responsibility' by not holding Japan responsible for the colonial rule.[17]

Professor Lee Jong-Won, director of the Institute of Korean Studies at Waseda University, said that the Korea-Japan relationship normalization negotiation which started from 1951 should serve as an opportunity to cleanse the past history and create new ties. However, Korea-Japan Basic Relations Treaty in 1965 does not comment about Japan's colonial rule at all and 'history' appears just once in the preamble which says "the historical backgrounds and the good-neighbor relationship between the two countries," Professor Lee stresses. Korea was the only divided country during the cold war right after the Japanese colonial rule and had to make concessions and negotiations to earn economic assistance while, at the same time, raising "historical logic of colonial rule." In the meantime, Japan also considered strategic cold war request for assistance for Korea "on the free democratic side" but tried to avoid shouldering the enormous economic burden of cleansing the past. The US has shifted toward reducing its strategic burden while strengthening the Cold War system as the Vietnam was deteriorated. However, the lukewarm stance toward to colonial responsibility and putting off 'postwar compensation' are destabilizing Korea-Japan relationship even today.[18]

Professor Daniel Sneider, an expert in the Korean peninsula and

Asia at Stanford University, claims that the Japanese government completed compensation under the 1951 San Francisco Peace Treaty and 1965 Korea-Japan Claims Agreement. However, he urges compensation for victims of the 'comfort women' system and the forced labor system that started with the Sino-Japanese War in 1937. In addition he points out that the US is also responsible for Japan's incomplete postwar compensation because the cold war is partially to be blame. He says that policy makers in Washington believed for far too long that the memory about war and political issues between Korea and Japan would disappear someday. Time, however, failed to heal the wounds and individual victims of 'comfort women' and forced labor are still demanding the settlement of unpaid compensation. It is clear that the passage of the time cannot by itself cure the corrosive effect of historical injustice or dim the fires of nationalism among younger generations of Northeast Asians.[19] Therefore, consensus and practical steps should be implemented to improve this situation.

3. INTERNATIONAL LEGAL SHIFT TOWARD HUMAN RIGHTS CENTERED PEACE COMMUNITY

3-1. International Legal Shift from Nationalism to Human Rights Centralism

In the traditional international law, an individual was regarded as a citizen of a specific state. Therefore, if an individual was harmed by a foreign government, it could only be protected within the scope of determining the exercise of diplomatic protection rights in the home country. However, it is important to note that the International Human Rights Law came from the reflection that the atrocities committed by Germany and Japan right after the Second World War were derived from the traditional nationalism that despised human rights. International Human Rights Law led to the idea that an individual should be protected not as a member of a state or a group but as a human being him/herself.

At the base of the series of historic verdicts rendered by Korean courts since the 2011 Korean Constitutional Court's ruling for Japanese military 'comfort women' victims, there is the zeitgeist to build a human rights centered peace community in Northeast Asia including Korea and Japan by overcoming the bleak history of colonialism derived from nationalism in the 20th century.

In this regard, Constitutional Court of Korea[20] quotes in verdict ILC's 2006 Draft article on Diplomatic Protection which was also quoted in ICJ's Case[21] concerning Ahmadou sadio Dillo in 2007. The draft pointed out that the view that sees violation of individual rights as a violation against his/her belonging state according to international law is nothing but unfounded and agenda and should not call for sacrifice from an individual on behalf of national friendship. This is an important change in the international law in the context of the essence of diplomatic protection and individual rights to claims.

In the meantime, the individual rights to claim is the main support axis for human rights that can be remedied when human rights are violated. The individual claim rights of the forced mobilization victims for tort against humanity involving Japanese government power or colonial rule tort damages were not addressed in Claims Agreement. Thus, not only individual damages claim right has not expired due to Claims Agreement, but also ROK's diplomatic protection right was also not abandoned. Even if an individual citizen's right to claim is subject to Claims Agreement, the individual right to claim itself did not expire just based on Claims Agreement as a matter of course. With Claims Agreement, ROK's diplomatic protection right for claims was abandoned. ROK lost means to protect the pertinent right diplomatically if it expired within Japan by

Japanese measures.

There are three legal logics behind the rulings regarding 'colonial responsibility.' First, the 2001 Durban Declaration and Programme of Action which proclaimed liquidating the legacy of colonialism to be a historic mission, and the ensuing apology and compensation such as Kenya-the UK on June 7, 2013 and Netherlands-Indonesia on September 12, 2013, Second, 2005 The Basic Principles of Victims' Rights for "Victim-Centered Approach," Third, 2010 Joint Statement from Korean and Japanese intellectuals who declared the 1910 Korea-Japan Annexation Treaty "already null and void."

3-2. Durban Declaration toward the End of Colonialism

In the World Conference against Racism, Racial discrimination, Xenophobia and Related Intolerance which took place in Durban, South Africa from August 31, 2001 to September 8, it was pointed out "slavery was a crime against humanity,"[22] and "colonialism has led to racism, racial discrimination, xenophobia and related intolerance."[23] Furthermore, it was declared that eradicating slavery and colonial rule that plagued people in Asia and Africa for centuries in the past is the historical task. The declaration defined the fight against racism as a fight against colonialism in the past and in the future. In referring to the past, it mentioned the United Nations 1960 Declaration on the Grant of Independence to Colonial Countries and People; in regard to the future, it stressed the need to realize genuine equality of opportunity and treatment for all individuals and peoples.

Colonialism should be identified as a typical example of the combination of the crimes against peace and the crimes against humanity. It should further connect these two crimes to include crimes whose definition could help strengthen a different Durban anti-racist program. The criminalization of colonialism may provide a powerful basis for combating all forms of racism, racial discrimination, xenophobia, and related intolerance. The crime of colonialism, once defined as a violation of the rights to live in peace, free from fear and want, can cover new forms of neo-colonialism, including domestic colonialism directed to less developed parts of the country, cross-national colonialism exploiting migrants from less-developed countries, or colonialist relationships between indigenous peoples and multinational corporations exploiting their resources.

The forcible imposition by the Japanese Empire of a treaty that usurped the autonomous power of the Empire of Korea was illegal. This objective fact is generally discussed based on historical and legal evidence. All peoples of the world have the right to live in peace, and any infringement on this right such as the crime of colonialism is a crime against humanity and must be officially recognized by the international community.

In the meantime, the preamble of the Constitution of Japan solemnly declares that the people of Japan recognize the rights of all peoples of the world to live in peace, free from fear and want. This statement is commonly interpreted as a pacifist declaration. It is so only secondarily, since its primary purpose is to express the decision of the people of Japan not to repeat its colonialist and aggressive past that violated the right of its colonized and aggressed neighbors - beginning with Korea - to live in peace. To interpret the right to live in peace as a statement recognizing the criminality of colonialism is the only possible interpretation in view of the preceding statement. Japan is repentant and wants to become a respectable member of the international community, and the right to live in peace is formulated as an official repudiation of Japan's colonialist and aggressive past. Japan wants to join the nations of the world, all of whom should denounce colonialism and aggression. The second clause of Article 9 renounces Japan's armed forces.

If we succeed in adapting the concept of the crime of colonialism to the conditions of our age, the cases of the Japanese "annexation" of Korea and the colonial imposition of different legal, political, economic and socio-cultural standards and practices in violation of the independence of the Korean people, their cultural traditions, and political-economic interests, can provide examples that are useful for defining this crime. The criminalization of all forms of colonialism is an extremely important means to guarantee human rights and human security for minorities and weaker parties in political-economic negotiations under globalism. Criminalization could and should become part of the jurisdiction of International Criminal Court (ICC), and thus give legal authority to this concept and to the concept of the right to peace of peoples.[24]

In the regard with cases where colonial responsibility was solved, on June 6, 2013, the UK government reportedly made an official apology to Kenya over the colonial-era atrocities. The UK government said "We apologize for the armed repression and atrocities done to Mau Mau torture[25] victims in the 1950s and pay a total of £19.9 million[26] to 5,228 victims in reparations."[27] The Dutch government officially apologized for the Rawagede[28] massacre committed by the Dutch force during its rule of Indonesia from 1945 to 1949 and paid compensations to 10 widows who lost their husband to summary executions.[29]

3-3. The Basic Principles of Victims' Rights toward "Victim-Centered Approach"

What is especially noticeable in connection with the development of international human rights law is the fact that the "Basic Principles and Guidelines on the Right to a Remedy and Reparation for Victims of Gross Violations of International Humans Rights Law and Serious Violations of International Humanitarian Law" (hereinafter shortened to "Basic Principles of Victims' Rights") was adopted unanimously in the U.N. General Assembly on December 16, 2005. The principles are the fruits of efforts to create international standards concerning the rights of victims of human rights violations committed by governmental power and also to reflect the development of legal principles related to "victims' rights concerning effective relief" based on major international pacts. These principles are soft law themselves but are the "victim's bill of rights" in that they suggest principles and guidelines about the state's obligations to guarantee the acknowledged rights of human rights victims. They play the role of solving problems through the "victim-centered approach" in the development of related international norms and procedures. Victims defined in the "Basic Principles on Victims' Rights" refer to "persons who, individually or collectively, have suffered harm, including physical or mental injury, emotional suffering, economic loss or substantial impairment of their fundamental rights, through acts or omissions that constitute gross violations of international human rights law, or serious violations of international humanitarian law. Where appropriate, and in accordance with domestic law, the term 'victim' also includes the immediate family or dependents of the direct victim and persons who have suffered harm in intervening to assist victims in distress or to prevent victimization" (Article 8).

With respect to the guarantee of victims' rights, each state has the obligation to respect, ensure respect for, and implement international human rights law and international humanitarian law. The obligation emanates from, "Treaties to which a state is a party, customary international law, and the domestic law of each state" (Article 1). "If they have not already done so, States shall, as required under international law, ensure that their domestic law is consistent with their international legal obligations" (Article 2). Each state's obligation includes the duty to, "Take appropriate legislative and administrative and other appropriate measures to prevent violations, investigate violations effectively, promptly, thoroughly and impartially..." The state must also, "Provide those who claim to be victims of a human rights or humanitarian law violation with equal and effective access to justice... and provide effective remedies to victims, including reparation" (Article 3).

In cases of gross violations of international human rights law and serious violations of international humanitarian law constituting crimes under international law, States have the duty to investigate and, if there is sufficient evidence, the duty to submit to prosecution the person allegedly responsible for the violations and, if found guilty, the duty to punish her or him. Moreover, in these cases, States should, in accordance with international law, cooperate with one another and assist international judicial organs competent in the investigation and prosecution of these violations (Article 4). To that end, where so provided in an applicable treaty or under other international law obligations, States shall incorporate or otherwise implement within their domestic law appropriate provisions for universal jurisdiction. Moreover, where it is so provided for in an applicable treaty or other international legal obligations, States should facilitate extradition or surrender offenders to other States and to appropriate international judicial bodies and provide judicial assistance and other forms of cooperation in the pursuit of international justice, including assistance to, and protection of, victims and witnesses, consistent with international human rights legal standards and subject to international legal requirements such as those relating to the prohibition of torture and other forms of cruel, inhuman or degrading treatment or punishment (Article 5).

Furthermore, remedies for gross violations of international human rights law and serious violations of international humanitarian law include the victim's right to the following as provided for under international law are classified into justice, reparation, and access to relevant information (Article 11). First, a victim's rights to justice under the title of, "Equal and effective access to justice," include, "Equal access to an effective judicial remedy as provided for under international law," and, "Other remedies available to the victim include access to administrative and other bodies... in accordance with domestic law" (Article 12). Second, victims should, "As appropriate and proportional to the gravity of the violation and the circumstances of each case, be provided with full and effective reparation...which include the following forms: restitution, compensation, rehabilitation, satisfaction and guarantees of non-repetition" (Article 18). Third, "Victims and their representatives should be entitled to seek and obtain information on the causes leading to their victimization and on the causes and conditions pertaining to the gross violations of international human rights law and... international humanitarian law" (Article 24).

3-4. The 2010 Joint Statement from Korean and Japanese Intellectuals toward "1910 Korea-Japan Annexation Treaty Null and Void."

Marking the centennial anniversary of the forced Korea-Japan annexation, 2010 made us realize that it is our historic task to understand the fundamental cause of historic conflicts between Korea and Japan and find solutions for it. Getting the history right, it suggests, will lay the foundation for seeking a genuine process of historical reconciliation and establishing peace community in Northeast Asia. However, Korean high courts in February and July of 2009, upheld the effect of judgment's validity and *res judicata* of Japanese Supreme Court of 2007 that dismissed against the plaintiff in the compensation trial over forced labor filed in Japan since 1995.

Against this backdrop, scholars from Korea and Japan conducted joint studies and held international conferences to discover truth about history and establish international law justice. On June 22, 2009, they declared illegal and void the forced annexation of Korea and Japan in the perspective of international law. On July 28 prior to

the 65th Independence Day, 1,139 scholars from the two countries, an
increase from the 214 scholars on May 10, 2010, announced the joint
statement declaring "1910 Korea-Japan Annexation Treaty Already
Null and Void" on the historical justice.[30]

The 2010 Joint Statement declares unjustifiable and unlawful the
language, signing process, and annexation procedure of 1910 Korea-
Japan Annexation Treaty.[31] On top of this, with regard to the Article
2 of the Korea-Japan Basic Relations Treaty in 1965 which stipulates
that all treaty and agreement signed before August 22, 1910 are
already null and void, the scholars stressed that Korean scholars'
interpretation of the annexation treaty as being unfair and unjust
should be taken as the common opinion. The scholars also demanded
that Japan accept a variety of efforts by international law communities
regarding 'crime against humanity' and 'colonial crime' and reflect on
the history of invasion and colonial history on the very fundamental.[32]

The 2010 Joint Statement from Korean and Japanese intellectuals
as the Asian version of the 2001 Durban Declaration and Programme
of Action which proclaimed 'the historic end to the colonialism'[33]
not only sought a genuine historical reconciliation based on the right
establishment of history, but also formed the basis for the verdict on
colonial responsibility rendered by Constitutional Court of Korea in
2011 and Supreme Court of Korea in 2012 in the perspective of
history and international human rights law.[34]

4. KOREN SUPREME COURT'S DECISION ON JAPAN'S FORCED MOBILIZATION VICTIMS

4-1. Individual Rights of Claims for Japan's Forced Mobilization Victims

On May 24, 2012, the Supreme Court of Korea overturned the

original ruling that recognized the effect of a Japanese court decision which ruled that the forced mobilization of Koreans during the colonial period was lawful. The Japanese judgment directly contradicts the core values of the Korean Constitution. These were historic decisions clearly reiterating that the victims' rights to reparation and that the Japan's unlawful acts associated directly with its colonial rule were not part of the 1965 Korea-Japan Claims Agreement.

On October 30, 2018, the Supreme Court dismissed the appeal of the defendant (New Nippon Steel Corporation) and confirmed the original judgment that the defendant should pay 100 million won in solarium to the plaintiffs in a lawsuit filed by victims of forced mobilization during the Japanese colonial rule against a Japanese company.

The key issue in this case is whether the plaintiffs' claim for damages was extinguished by the 1965 Korea-Japan Claims Agreement. In regard to the Supreme Court said that the plaintiffs' right to claim damages is not included in the right of the claims agreement as the right to claim solarium against Japanese company of forced mobilization victims, premised upon the Japanese corporation's unlawful acts against humanity with direct links to the Japanese Government's unlawful colonial domination of the Korean Peninsula and waging of wars of aggression.

4-2. Rejection of Assertion for Res Judicata of Japanese Judgment

The Japanese Judgment against the Plaintiffs cannot be recognized and be given effect in Korea, even though the Plaintiffs filed a lawsuit against the Defendant in Japan prior to the litigation in the Republic of Korea and the Japanese Judgment was rendered against them and had been made final and conclusive. The reason provided for such refusal of recognition was that the Japanese Judgment was premised on a normative perception of the Japanese colonial domination over the Korean Peninsula and Koreans as lawful, and found that Imperial Japan's application of the National Mobilization Law and the National Conscription Order to the Korean Peninsula, the Plaintiffs was valid. Recognizing the Japanese Judgment containing such reasoning would go against the sound morals or other social orders of Korea.

4-3. Rejection of Assertion for Standing to be Sued

The Plaintiffs may hold the Defendant liable for the rights to claim they have against the former Nippon Steel, even though the former Nippon Steel that subjected the Plaintiffs to forced labor was dissolved pursuant to Japanese law, and a 'second company' as described in the judgment was incorporated, which was then changed to the Defendant after going through the process of a merger. It cannot be permitted as it results to debt exemption of former Mitsubishi for the Korean people on the reasons due to Japan domestic law.

4-4. Rejection of Assertion for Individual Rights to Claim expired

4-4-1. The Essence of Plaintiffs' rights to claim

The Plaintiffs' rights to claim reparations for damages at issue in this case concern the forced mobilization victims' rights to claim solatium against Japanese corporation, premised upon the Japanese corporation's unlawful acts against humanity with direct links to the Japanese Government's unlawful colonial domination of the Korean Peninsula and waging of wars of aggression (hereinafter the 'rights to claim solatium for forced mobilization').

Plaintiffs are seeking from the Defendant solatium, not any unpaid wages or other monetary compensation. In regard with Japan's Forced Annexation of the Korean Peninsula and Forced Mobilization, the following facts can be confirmed. (i) The Japanese

Government, in the process of waging unlawful wars of aggression such as the Sino-Japanese War and the Pacific War, established a long-term plan to procure necessary manpower for the Japanese steelworks, the backbone of the military industry, and mobilized manpower systematically. The former Nippon Steel, which was an integral military supplier, took a leading role in the Steel Control Association and actively cooperated with the Japanese Government's manpower mobilization policy, thereby securing additional laborers. (ⅱ) It is fair to consider that the Plaintiffs, who were not fully aware of the details of the labor they would be subjected to or the environment in which they would later be situated in Japan, were mobilized by such systematic deception of the Japanese Government and the former Nippon Steel when the Korean Peninsula and Koreans were under the unlawful and violently oppressive rule of Japan. (ⅲ) Moreover, the Plaintiffs were of a very young age and had yet to reach the age of majority when they left their families and undertook dangerous labor in a deplorable environment with a high likelihood of losing their lives or suffering bodily harm. They were forced to deposit their wages without knowing the specific amount thereof. Under the Japanese Government's harsh full-mobilization system in a state of war, they were not allowed to leave the premises and escape was impossible as they were under constant watch. If they were caught attempting to escape, they would be beaten severely.

4-4-2. *The Scope of the Claims Agreement*
According to the developments leading up to the conclusion of the Claims Agreement and the preceding and subsequent circumstances thereof, it appears that the Claims Agreement did not seek to claim damages for the unlawful colonial domination by Japan, but was basically intended for the resolution of the financial and civil credit-debt relations between Korea and Japan via a political

agreement based on Article 4 of the San Francisco Treaty.[35]

The First Korea-Japan Conference was held after the conclusion of the San Francisco Treaty (from February 15 to April 25, 1952). The Eight Items that Korea proposed at that time were also basically in relation to the financial and civil credit-debt relations between Korea and Japan. Although Item Five[36] of the Eight Items[37] uses the expression 'claim for repayment of outstanding receivables, compensations, and other rights to claim of the conscripted Koreans,'[38] no other part of the Eight Items is premised on the unlawfulness of Japan's colonial domination.[39] Therefore, it appears that the Item Five was not premised on the unlawful acts of the Japanese either.[40] Thus, it is difficult to conclude that the expression "claim for repayment of outstanding receivables, compensations, and other rights to claim of the conscripted Koreans" includes the rights to claim solatium for forced mobilization.

The 'White Paper on the Korea-Japan Conference' published by the Government of the Republic of Korea on March 20, 1965 expressly states that Article 4 of the San Francisco Treaty served as the basis of the claims issue between Korea and Japan. It further explains that "the claims against Japan specified in the aforesaid Article 4 are distinguished from the victorious nations' right to claim reparations. Since Korea was not a party to the San Francisco Treaty, its right to claim reparations for the 'damage and suffering,' which are enjoyed by the victorious nations pursuant to Article 14, was not acknowledged. The issue of claims between Korea and Japan may not encompass the claim on reparations."

Neither the text of the Claims Agreement nor its annexes, which were concluded subsequently, mention the unlawfulness of the Japanese colonial domination anywhere.[41] The Japanese Government did not admit to the unlawfulness of their colonial domination during the course of the negotiations regarding the Claims Agreement and fundamentally denied legal reparations for the losses arising from forced mobilization. Accordingly, the governments of the two countries were unable to come to an agreement with respect to the nature of the Japanese occupation of the Korean Peninsula. It is difficult to conclude under such circumstances that the rights to claim solatium for forced mobilization were included in the scope of application of the Claims Agreement.

This is more so in light of the fact that it appears highly unlikely that the Government of the Republic of Korea would have signed the Claims Agreement of its own accord, to include rights to claim solatium for forced mobilization, when the Japanese Government, a party to the Claims Agreement, was denying the existence of any unlawful activities and liability for damages arising therefrom.

4-5. Rejection of Assertion for Completion of Extinctive Prescription

Such as the circumstance that despite the normalization of the diplomatic relations between Korea and Japan in 1965, not all of the documents related to the Claims Agreement had then been publicly disclosed, and it was widely accepted in Korea that the Claims Agreement comprehensively resolved the issue of the Korean nationals' individual rights to claim against Japan and its nationals, held that, it is reasonable to conclude that the Plaintiffs had objective grounds that hindered them from exercising their rights against the Defendant up until the time they filed this lawsuit in Korea. Therefore, the Lower Court held that the Defendant's refusal to perform its obligation towards the Plaintiffs on grounds that the statute of limitations has run out is clearly unjustified and is not allowed, being an abuse of rights that contradicts the principle of good faith.

5. JAPAN'S EXPORT REGULATIONS AND CHALLENGES IN INTERNATIONAL HUMAN RIGHTS LAW

5-1. International Legal Review of Issues Raised before Export Regulations

Since the joint statement in 2010 made by 1,139 Korean and Japanese intellectuals declaring the "1910 Korea-Japan Annexation Treaty invalid," the Constitutional Court and the Supreme Court came to a final decision, based on the victim-centered principle under the "Basic Principles on Victims' Rights" adopted by the U.N. General Assembly in 2005 in the constitutional appeal in 2011 by comfort women and the lawsuit for damages in 2012 by victims of forced labor, respectively. But in relation to the Constitutional Court's decision on nonfeasance unconstitutionality in 2011, there are two issues between two countries raised that need attention such as 'composition of arbitral committee,' and 'import of Fukushima fisheries products.'

First, to resolve the status of nonfeasance unconstitutionality, the Korean government asked for Japanese government renegotiations and referral to the arbitral committee under Article 3[42] of the 1965 Korea-Japan Claims Treaty, but even the renegotiations were not realized because of the Japanese government's refusal.

Second, this is an issue regarding on the demand for the abolition of the Korean government's import restrictions on marine products contaminated on Fukushima radioactivity raised by the Japanese government at the director-level meetings of the two countries to settle the issue of comfort women in 2014. Japan then asked for withdraw of import control measures to protect people's health under (b) of Article 20 of GATT,[43] which is recognized as a general exception to the World Trade Organization (hereinafter, "the WTO"), which is based on free trade, and further filed a petition with the WTO.[44] However, Japan claimed the reform of the WTO after losing the case in the end.

5-2. Japan's Export Regulations on Korean Supreme Court's Decision

In connection with Japan's export regulations understood in the extension of this context, the Japanese government argued the violation of international law and the 1965 Korea-Japan Treaty after the Korean government rejected the arbitral committee demanded by Japan, and Japan had asked to neutralize the ruling of the Korean Supreme Court by Korean government. In relation to the Japanese administration's demands that Korea rectify the Supreme Court ruling on the forced mobilization victims issue, government interference with the judiciary is not something that is allowed in Korea as a democratic state.

Japan's Export Regulations on the Korean Supreme Court's Decision for forced mobilization are as follows. The Japanese government, on July 1, 2019, officially announced export restrictions that obligate Japanese companies to obtain government permission when they export to Korea three items that are essential in manufacturing memory chips, televisions, and smartphones. Furthermore, on August 2, 2019, it has decided to remove Korea from its "white country list" that exempts companies from having to obtain permission in order to export cutting-edge materials that could be redirected to military use. Japan's move is practically an "economic retaliation" against the Korean Supreme Court's Decision issued in October 30, 2018, over reparation for wartime forced labor.

The Japanese government released data on revised rules on export to Korea and said that it is tightening regulations on the export of materials used in TV, smartphone, and chip production. As a result, three materials including photoresist and etching gas that are crucial in manufacturing semiconductors, flexible organic light-emitting diode (OLED) used in latest smartphones, and fluorine polyimide used in manufacturing display panels were excluded from Japan's "Comprehensive Export Permission System" starting from July 4, 2019. With this rule has come in effect, Japanese companies have to obtain government permission and undergo a deliberation every time they export those three materials to Korea. The deliberation process takes 90 days and the three materials might be completely banned from exporting the materials to Korea if they do not pass the deliberation.[45]

Furthermore, on August 28, 2019, the Japanese government implemented an amended Export Trade Control Order downgrading Korea from its "Group A" (white list)[46] to "Group B." While Japanese exporters previously only had to receive one general permit every three years to export strategic goods to Korea, they are required as of now to receive case-by-case permits as a rule for all exports believed to at risk of diversion to military purposes. While the Japanese government is entitled to grant across-the-board permits with a validity period of three years through its "special general comprehensive permit" system, the possibility of its pursuing regulations during the system's implementation process has fanned uncertainties in Korea. Also, because of "catch-all" provisions for nearly all items apart from food and lumber, individual permits must be received even for non-strategic goods judged to be at risk of diversion to military uses.[47]

5-3. Japan's Export Regulations in Violation of International Trade Law

Japan defended the appropriateness of its export regulations citing alternately the confidential relationship, the forced labor ruling, and the management system of strategic goods as the reasons for its export restrictions on high-tech industrial materials. the Japanese administration claimed that our relationship of trust had been damaged by the forced labor mobilization victims issue. Then claimed 'problems' with export permit system of Korea's alleged lax control of sensitive materials potentially diverted for military use were having a negative impact on Japanese security. However, Japanese government has yet to provide concrete evidence despite repeated requests from Korean government.

Prior to that, regarding Japan's response to the Korean Supreme Court ruling of 2012 on forced mobilization victims, Japanese scholars including Yuki Asaba argued that Japan should attack Korea-Japan economic relations as a policy alternative, considering Korea's dependence on foreign trade amounting to 93 percent.[48] It is not a victim-centered solution to human rights issues, but a cross- section of the ongoing pursuit of nationalistic policy alternatives. At this point, already Japan's export regulations of Korea were scheduled. But Japan's export control measures amount to the typical violation concerning the norms of international trade law.[49]

First of all, Japan's export regulations are in violation of paragraph 1 of General Agreement of Trade and Tariffs (hereinafter, the "GATT") Article 11.[50] Export restrictions on high-tech industrial materials mean assuming arbitrary limits or bans on exports, which is a typical violation of the principle of banning quantitative restrictions.

The restrictions are also in violation of paragraph 1 of GATT Article 1.[51] The Most Favored Nation status is the most fundamental principle prohibiting discrimination against the like product. Discriminating against Korea over the three key materials for semiconductors and displays is a typical violation of the Most Favored Nation status.

Moreover, Japan violated paragraph 3 of GATT Article 10.[52] Under the GATT system, the Japanese government has enforced arbitrary export regulations, citing trust relations, forced labor rulings, and strategic material management systems, even though it has to provide uniform, impartial, and reasonable customs clearance and general administrative procedures for the contracting countries. This amounts to a typical violation of obligations to implement uniform, impartial, and reasonable customs clearance and administrative procedures.

In connection with the strategic material management system raised by Japan as the basis for export regulations to Korea, Korea has exceeded Japan in controlling trade of strategic materials, according to the Institute for Science and International Security (hereinafter, the "ISIS"). The PPI, Criteria for Evaluation of Strategic Materials Management System of ISIS, measures the effectiveness of strategic trade controls using a set of criteria relating to a country's existing laws, regulations, procedures, practices, international obligations and actions. In the PPI for 2019, released by ISIS in May 2019, the US was the top scoring country ranked No. 1, Korea ranked 17th and Japan ranked 36th.[53]

5-4. Challenges in International Human Rights Law on Japan's Export Regulations

As a response for Japan's export regulations that the Japanese government violated international trade laws to neutralize the Korean Supreme Court's historic ruling on the relief of victims of Japan's forced labor, it is necessary to review the challenges of international human rights laws based on victim-centered approach, which the international society has established toward a community of human rights, justice and peace.

First, it is necessary to reestablish legal principles to shift from nationalism, which constituted the basis for Japan's colonial rule and imperial invasion line, to human rights-centered ideology. International Human Rights Law was formed due to the invasion and atrocity committed by Japan and Germany which led to an extreme contempt and violation of human dignity. The perspective of seeing violation of human rights as violation on the relevant country under international law is merely a fiction or hypothesis, and individual sacrifices must not be forced for the amity between countries.

Second, the terrible sacrifices of mankind have been repeated when the mechanism of justice inherent in history has not worked. As elucidated by E. H. Carr, if the meaning of justice in history is a rediscovery of the truth in an 'unending dialogue between the present and the past,' International legal principles as common norms in the international community should be the last bastion of establishing, guaranteeing and protecting justice. As pointed out by Hannah Arendt, it is difficult to lead a peaceful social life in a place where there is no basic consent over what is "injustice," because "justice" is the "essence of social conditions for humans." The forced mobilization victims under the Japanese colonial rule are asking for "legal responsibility," justice as the "possibility of response" for their violated human rights.[54]

Third, it is necessary to break away from 'glorification of colonial rule as legal,' 'denial of the definition of aggression,' and 'active peace[55] for revision of peace constitution.' Moreover, at the same time take one step further from the basis 'negative peace' of international law based on apology and reparation over colonial rule and war of aggression, toward 'positive peace' based on human dignity and human rights as the universal value of mankind today, thereby seeking ways to build a true peace community. It is not a transfer to history but a task for the realization of the ongoing[56] "positive peace," unless human rights violations against forced mobilization victims during the Japanese colonial rule are realized as the right of justice and reparation.

6. CONCLUSION

The Abe administration's policy keynote of "breaking away from the postwar regime" and "historical revisionism" envisions that Japan, the war criminal of World War II, should depart from its system of peaceful constitution and return to a state that can go to war while revising history itself, rather than repenting its past misdeeds. On such a premise, the Japanese policy frame for distorting history of Korea is the "legitimate theory of 1910 colonization" and the "completion theory of the 1965 Korea-Japan Claims Agreement."

Against this backdrop, the Supreme Court's Decision on the relief of human rights for forced mobilization victims destroyed the frames of Japan's lawful colonization theory and completion theory of the Korea-Japan Treaty with just one stroke. In response, Japan should pay attention to the fact that Japan's enforcement of export regulations, a typical violation of international trade law that collapses the global value chain in an extension of its WTO complaints on forced import of Fukushima radioactive fisheries products, is no different from its colonial-imperialistic moves pursued by Japan before World War II.

Then, as a response for Japan's export regulations to Korea on the premise of violating international trade laws to neutralize the Korean Supreme Court's historic ruling on the relief of victims of Japan's forced labor, it is necessary to enhance the direction of the challenges of international human rights laws based on victim-centered approach, which the international society has established toward a community of human rights, justice and peace. It is already well-known that through Abe's statement of 70 years since the war, the assailant constantly expands and reproduces the perpetrator's logic. Thus, victims ought to solve the problems based on legal principles in accordance with international human rights law on the basis of human rights, justice and peace, and the victim-centered approach principle unanimously adopted by the U.N. General Assembly in 2005. We must solve the human rights issues through universal value norm of the normative system established by the international society as a peace community in the face of Japan's claim to violate international law with international law at the forefront. In relation to Japan's export regulations that the Japanese government violated international trade laws to neutralize the Korean Supreme Court's historic ruling on the relief of victims of Japan's forced labor, It is because asking us again today the meaning of international human rights laws formed due to the invasions and atrocities committed by Japan and Germany, that led to extreme contempt and violation on human dignity in World War II, is an international human rights legal challenges as a historical justice that we should answer.

Therefore, the Korean government should resolve the issue of victims of forced labor based on the International Human Rights Law and the principle of victim-centered approach based on human rights, justice and peace as the central axis of the victims and victimized countries. At the same time, the Japanese government and offender corporations should refrain from expanding and reproducing the perpetrator-centered logic and join in realizing historical justice through solving problems based on a victim-centered approach.

Notes

1. Gay J. Mcdougall, "Addressing State Responsibility for The Crime of Military Sexual Slavery during The Second World War: Further Attempts for Justice for The 'Comfort Women'," *The 'Comfort Women' Issue and Future - Oriented Relations between Korea and Japan*, (The 2012 KSIL International Conference, Lotte Hotel Seoul, February 17, 2012), pp. 29~32.

2. Jong-won Lee, "A Reexamination of the Policy of Post-War Compensation from the Japanese," *Reexamination Court Rulings on Colonial Responsibilities and the System of the Korea-Japan Agreement of 1965*, (Northeast Asian History Foundation, International Conference on Revisiting the fifty years of the Agreement between Korea and Japan, June 21, 2013), p. 115.

3. Won-deog Lee, "A Study on the Japan's Post-war Reparations Diplomacy : the Perspective of the International Comparisons," *North east Asian History Journal*, Vol. 22, (Northeast Asian History Foundation, December 2008), p. 32.

4. Hiroshi Tanaka·Taketoshi Nakayama·Ken Airimitsu, *Unresolved Postwar Compensation − Judgment of Japan's Past and Future* (Sousisha, 2012), pp. 208~213; Seita Yamamoto, Overview of Japan's postwar trials (http://justice.skr.jp/souran-jp-intro.html).

5. Lawsuits filed by Korean former "comfort women" are; 'Korean Victims' Claims of the Pacific War' made by Kim Hak-soon on December 6, 1991; 'Lawsuit for Official Apology for Pusan 'Comfort Women' and Comfort Women' on December 25, 1992; and 'Former Korean-Japanese 'Comfort Women' Song Sin-do's Lawsuit' on April 5, 1993. However, the judiciary solution in Japan came to an end when the Supreme Court of Japan dismissed the suits on November 19, 2004 citing the amount of time passed since those atrocities were committed and the lack of response or solution from the state. Refer to documents related to lawsuits on victims of rape by Japanese soldiers in Japan at WAM website http://wam-peace.org/ianfu-mondai/lawsuit.

6. Japanese lawyer Shuichi Adachi who led the 'postwar claim' suit in Japan analyzed the rulings rendered by the Supreme Court of Japan and presented 'four obstacles,' pointing out that the interpretation of law was justifiable nowhere but Japan. The first is Japan's failure to acknowledge the truth. The second is the 'lack of response or solution from the state' where the state is not held liable for damages under the Constitution of the Empire of Japan. Third, the amount time passed since those atrocities were committed. Fourth is political obstacle as an extinguishment of right by Korea-Japan Basic Relations Treaty in 1965 and law of property rights. Shuichi Adachi, "An Evaluation of the Limitations and Issues of the Rulings of the Supreme Court of Japan," *Revisiting the fifty years of the Agreement between Korea and Japan*, (Northeast Asian History Foundation International Conference, June 21, 2013), pp. 3~16.

7. Hwang Geum Joo et al. v. Japan, 172F. Suppp. 2d 52 (D.D.C. Oct. 4, 2001); Hwang Geum Joo et al. v. Japan, 332 F.3d 679 (C.A.D.C., 2003); Hwang Geum Joo et al. v. Japan, 413 F.3d 45 (C.A.D.C., 2005); Hwang Geum Joo et al. v.

Japan, 546 U.S. 1208, 126 S.Ct. 1418 (U.S., 2006); For more detail for this lawsuit, refer to Tae-Hyun Choi, "A Study on the Comfort Women Litigations in the United States," *New Perspectives on Historical Issues in Korean-Japanese Relations-from the Point of International Law*, Northeast Asian History Foundation, 2009, pp. 603~662.

8. The High Contracting Parties confirm that the problems concerning property, rights and interests of the two High Contracting Parties and their nationals (including juridical persons) and the claims between the High Contracting Parties and between their nationals, including those stipulated in Article IV(a) of the Peace Treaty with Japan signed at the city of San Francisco on September 8, 1951, have been settled completely and finally.

9. As a condition to comply with the provisions of paragraph 2 above, no claims shall be made with respect to the measures relating to the property, rights, and interests of either High Contracting Party and its people which were brought under the control of the other High Contracting Party on the date of the signing of the present Agreement, or to all the claims of either High Contracting Party and its people arising from the causes which occurred prior to that date.

10. Busan High Court Decision, 2007Na4288 Decided February 3, 2009.

11. Seoul High Court Decision, 2008Na49129 Decided July 16, 2009.

12. Supreme Court Decision, 2009Da22549 Decided May 24, 2012.

13. Supreme Court en banc Judgment 2013Da61381 Rendered October 30, 2018. Supreme Court en banc Judgment 2013Da61381 Rendered October 30, 2018 【Damages (Others)】 Supreme Court en banc Judgment 2013Da61381 Rendered October 30, 2018【Damages (Others)】.

14. Abe Kohki, "International Law as Memorial Sites: 'Comfort Women' Suits Revisited," *The 'Comfort Women' Issue and Future-Oriented Relations between Korea and Japan*, (The 2012 KSIL International Conference, Lotte Hotel Seoul, February 17, 2012), pp. 78~105.

15. See-hwan Doh, "Reexamination of Korea-Japan Treaty System in the Perspective of the Responsibility for the Japanese Colonial Rule on the International Law," *The Korean Journal of International Law*, Vol. 57, No. 3, (September 2012), pp. 17~45.

16. Osamu Ota, "Korea-Japan Basic Treaty Does not Address the Issue: On Postwar Compensation for Forced Labor Victims," *Sekai*, Iwanami Publishing Co., Ltd., (October 2013), pp. 189~192.

17. Osamu Ota, "Reexamination of Rights to Compensation – In the Perspective of Post-Colonialism" (Norikats Sasakawa · Tae-Jin Lee), *International Joint Study, Korea-Japan Annexation and Modern Age – Revisited through History and International Law*, (Akasi Publishing House, 2008), pp. 696~717.

18. Jong-Won Lee, "Northeast Asia in the Turbulence of Historical Transformation, Historical reconciliation needed," *Northeast Asian History Foundation News*, (September 2013), p. 7.

19. Daniel Sneider, "A dangerous stalemate between Japan and South Korea," *Washington Post*, November 1, 2013.

20. Article 19 of the Draft Articles on Diplomatic Protection adopted by the UN International Law Commission and submitted to the General Assembly in 2006 sets forth as a recommendation that a state entitled to exercise diplomatic protection should give due consideration to the possibility of exercising diplomatic protection.[23-2(A) KCCR 366, 2006Hun-Ma788, August 30, 2011]; The draft implied that it is not right to see infringements on human rights vested in individuals as the violation of rights of their state. The draft could bring a significant change in the traditional understanding of diplomatic protection that has led to the sacrifice of individual rights for the sake of nations. See-hwan Doh, "1910 annexation and remaining task," *Korea Times,* August 31, 2011, p. 9.

21. Dae-Soon Kim, "Selected Issues concerning Diplomatic Protection: centering around the UNILC's draft articles of 2006 on Diplomatic Protection," *Law Review,* Vol. 48, No. 1 (August 2007), pp. 204~205.

22. Paragraph 13. We acknowledge that slavery and the slave trade, including the transatlantic slave trade, were appalling tragedies in the history of humanity not only because of their abhorrent barbarism but also in terms of their magnitude, organized nature and especially their negation of the essence of the victims, and further acknowledge that slavery and the slave trade are a crime against humanity and should always have been so, especially the transatlantic slave trade and are among the major sources and manifestations of racism, racial discrimination, xenophobia and related intolerance, and that Africans and people of African descent, Asians and people of Asian descent and indigenous peoples were victims of these acts and continue to be victims of their consequences.

23. Paragraph 14. We recognize that colonialism has led to racism, racial discrimination, xenophobia and related intolerance, and that Africans and people of African descent, and people of Asian descent and indigenous peoples were victims of colonialism and continue to be victims of its consequences. We acknowledge the suffering caused by colonialism and affirm that, wherever and whenever it occurred, it must be condemned and its reoccurrence prevented. We further regret that the effects and persistence of these structures and practices have been among the factors contributing to lasting social and economic inequalities in many parts of the world today.

24. Kinhide Mushakoji, "Toward Recongnition of the Crime of Colonialism-The Lesson of Japan's Violent Annexation of Korea," *One Hundred Years after Japan's Forced Annexation of Korea: History and Tasks,* Peter Lang, 2015, pp. 203~210.

25. Kavita Modi, "The Mau Mau litigation; colonial era reparations in Britaina-victory against the odds," *Revisiting the fifty years of the Agreement between Korea and Japan IV,* (Northeast Asian History Foundation, 2015), pp. 147~157.

26. Then foreign affairs minister William Hague expressed regret over atrocities and pledged to set up a commemorative monument for the victims in Nairobi. The reparations is about five times the per-capita annual income of Kenya. The decision came as the appellate court ruled that plaintiff had rights to compensation in October 2012, raising the chances of losing the suit. The

Guardian analyzed that William Hague expressed ex grata out of fear about collective action over the UK's colonial rule. "UK to compensate Kenya's Mau Mau torture victims."

27. "UK Apologizes for Kenyan Atrocity in 60 years," *Dong-A Daily*, June 7, 2013; Kavita Modi, "The Mau Mau Ligitation-a victory against the odds," *Legal Policy Challenges with Compensation for Victims of Japanese Colonial Rule*, (Northeast Asian History Foundation Conference, June 20, 2014), pp. 121~136.

28. "The Netherlands apologies for Rawagede massacre, pays compensation" Dutch News. nl., December 5, 2011. <http://www.dutchnews.nl/news/archives/2011/12/the_netherlands_apologies_for.php>; Pyoung-Keun Kang, "A study on Judgment on compensation for Dutch colonial rule over Indonesia with specific reference to the Rawagede case," *Korea International Law Review*, Vol. 40, 2014.

29. "The Netherlands Follows Suit of UK, Apologizes to Kenya," *Dong-A Daily*, September 2, 2013. p. 18.

30. A book about the Joint Statement from Korean and Japanese intellectuals was published in Korea and Japan at the same time on the 68th Liberation Day. See-hwan Doh, *One Hundred Years after Japan's Forced Annexation of Kore: History and Tasks*, (Northeast Asian History Foundation, Korean version, 2013); See-hwan Doh Ed., Norikatsu Sasakawa · Young-ho Byun, et al., "International Joint Study, Korea-Japan Forced Annexation, History and Tasks of 100 Years," (Akasi Publishing Co. Ltd. 2013); See-hwan Doh, Virgil Dixon Morris, Lise Mckean, *One Hundred Years after Japan's Forced Annexation of Kore: History and Tasks*, Peter Lang GmbH, English version, 2015.

31. At 'Seoul Meeting on the 1st anniversary of 2010 Joint Statement from Korean and Japanese Intellectuals' held in Northeast Asian History Foundation on August 29, 2011 under the theme of "Void Korea-Japan Annexation and Historical Reconciliation and New Future for East Asia," Nakatuska Akira, professor emeritus at Nara Women's University criticized it as extreme fiction that the annexation treaty of rhetoric was signed under the agreement of the two countries. Korea-Japan Annexation for being ultimately untrue. "Korea-Japan Annexation as an 'Ultimate Untruth'," How to Solve the Core Issues of Korea-Japan Historical Disputes, (Jisik Sanup Publications Co, Ltd., 2013), pp. 155~165.

32. 2010 Joint Statement from Korean and Japanese intellectuals, "1910 Korea-Japan Annexation Treaty Null and Void."

33. In the Northeast Asian History Foundation session held during Jeju Forum under the theme of "Historical Reconciliation and Challenges for Establishing Peace in Northeast Asia" on May 29th, 2014, Professor Nagahara Yoko of Kyoto University emphasized in her presentation "Conceiving historical reconciliation in East Asia in the context of world history of decolonization" that the 2001 Durban Declaration was originated in the open testimony made by the former 'comfort women' Kim Hak-soon in 1991.

34. In conversation between the author and lawyer Bong-Tae Choi who took the claims lawsuit over force labor for 12 years since 2000, he did not expected

that the Supreme Court of Korea would rule in their favor. They could win the suit thanks to the efforts made by Korean and Japanese scholars such as their joint declaration, "'Japanese ruling on legalization of colonial rule cannot be approved by Korean Constitution - the Supreme Court's ruling on compensation for forced labor opens the way for historical justice'," *Northeast Asian History Foundation News*, (July 2012), pp. 6~9.

35. Gay J. McDougall, *op. cit.*, pp. 29~32.

36. It is a main argument among Japanese Professor Yuki Asaba's claims that deny the Supreme Court's Decision. Yuki Asaba, "Korean Court Turning Against Japan – Why is Resolved Issues Surfaces Again," http://webronza.asahi.com/synodos/2013082600005.html.

37. 'Eight Items of the Outline of the Claims of the Republic of Korea against Japan' are as follows. (1) claim for return of raw gold and silver Japan transferred from Korea via the Bank of Korea from 1909 to 1945; (2) request for performance regarding the Governor-General of Korea's liability payment from Aug. 9, 1945 to hereinafter; (3) claim for return of money transferred from Korea from Aug. 9, 1945; (4) claim for return concerning corporation property of corporations in Japan that presently (Aug. 9, 1945) operate main offices, main companies or major offices in Korea; (5) claim for performance regarding a Korean corporation or individual's rights to Japanese banknotes, or Korean draftees' accounts receivable, compensation and other claims; (6) a Korean individual's claims against Japan or a Japanese individual that does not constitute either (1) or (5) can be exercised individually after the ROK-Japan Negotiations are concluded; (7) claim for return of profit from property or claim right of previous period, (8) return and payment of previous period will begin immediately after the Agreement is concluded, and will be completed at least within 6 months.

38. ⌜Agreed Minutes (I) to the Agreement on the Settlement of Problem Concerning Property and Claims and on the Economic Co-operation between the Republic of Korea and Japan⌟, which was concluded on the same day as the Claims Agreement and came into force on December 18, 1965 (Treaty No. 173) provided as below with respect to Article II of the Claims Agreement. (a) It is understood that "property, rights and interests" means all kinds of substantial rights which are recognized under law to be of property value; (e) It is agreed that measures to be taken in accordance with the provisions of paragraph 3 mean the internal measures of the respective countries which would be taken for the settlement of problem concerning property, rights and interests of the two countries and their nationals and problem concerning the claims between the two countries and their nationals, referred to in paragraph 1; (g) It is confirmed that problem concerning property, rights and interests of the two countries and their nationals and concerning the claims between the two countries and their nationals, which is settled completely and finally as mentioned in paragraph 1, includes any claim falling within the scope of the "Outline of the Claims of the Republic of Korea against Japan (the so-called "Eight Items")," which was

submitted by the Korean side at the Republic of Korea-Japan negotiations and that, therefore, no contention can be made with respect to the above mentioned Outline of the Claims of the Republic of Korea against Japan.

39. See-hwan Doh, "A review of court decisions on Japan's colonial responsibility and the Korea-Japan Treaty in 1965 from the perspective of International law," *Revisiting the fifty years of the Agreement between Korea and Japan III*, (Northeast Asian History Foundation, 2014), pp. 61~62.

40. Pyoung-Keun Kang, "A Study on the Issues over Tort Claims by War-time Forced Laborers before the Courts in Korea in the Perspective of Public International Law," *Justice*, Vol. 143 (August 2014), pp. 241~247.

41. With regard to economic assistance fund and compensation issues, a look at the proceedings of the Japanese Diet reveals that Japan tried to evade not just compensation and the payment based on the rights to claims. On October 26, 1965 during the House of Representatives special committee, Lawmaker Yokomichi Sesuo of Social Party asked "Is it for addressing the rights to compensation or assistance for developing country? Or are we paying for the 35 years of colonial rule of Korea?" Then Foreign Minister Shiina Esusaburo instantly answered "Literally, it is economic assistance." House of Representatives, *The Japan-ROK Special Committee Record V*, (October 28, 1965). p. 15.

42. Article III 1. Any dispute between the High Contracting Parties concerning the interpretation or the implementation of this Agreement shall be settled primarily through diplomatic channels. 2. Any dispute which cannot be settled under the provision of paragraph 1 above shall be submitted for decision to an arbitral commission of three arbitrators; one to be appointed by the Government of each High Contracting Party within a period of thirty days from the date of receipt by the Government of either High Contracting Party from that of the other High Contracting Party of a note requesting arbitration of the dispute; and the third to be agreed upon by the two arbitrators so chosen or to be nominated by the Government of a third power as agreed upon by the two arbitrators within a further period of thirty days. However, the third arbitrator must not be a national of either High Contracting Party. 3. If, within the periods respectively referred to, the Government of either High Contracting Party fails to appoint an arbitrator, or the third arbitrator or the third nation is not agreed upon, the arbitral commission shall be composed of one arbitrator to be nominated by the Government of each of two nations respectively chosen by the Government of each High Contracting Party within a period of thirty days, and the third arbitrator to be nominated by the Government of a third power decided upon by agreement between the Governments so chosen. 4. The Governments of the High Contracting Parties shall accept decisions rendered by the arbitral commission established in accordance with the provisions of this Article.

43. (b) necessary to protect human, animal or plant life or health.

44. WTO DS495: Korea - Import Bans, and Testing and Certification Requirements for Radionuclides (https://www.wto.org/english/tratop_e/dispu_e/cases_e/ds495_e.htm).

45. "Japan takes economic retaliation against Korea for forced labor ruling," *The*

Dong-A ILBO, July 2, 2019.

46. There are currently 27 countries on the list and Korea was included in the list in 2004.

47. "Blue House expresses deep dismay over Japan removing S. Korea from 'white list'," *Hankyoreh*, August 29, 2019.

48. Yuki Asaba, *supra* note 36.

49. See-hwan Doh, "World War II and International Human Rights Law: Challenges of Historical Justice in Our Era," *Northeast Asian History Foundation News*, Vol. 154, 2019. 9, pp. 4~7.

50. No prohibitions or restrictions other than duties, taxes or other charges, whether made effective through quotas, import or export licences or other measures, shall be instituted or maintained by any contracting party on the importation of any product of the territory of any other contracting party or on the exportation or sale for export of any product destined for the territory of any other contracting party.

51. With respect to customs duties and charges of any kind imposed on or in connection with importation or exportation or imposed on the international transfer of payments for imports or exports, and with respect to the method of levying such duties and charges, and with respect to all rules and formalities in connection with importation and exportation, and with respect to all matters referred to in paragraphs 2 and 4 of Article III,* any advantage, favour, privilege or immunity granted by any contracting party to any product originating in or destined for any other country shall be accorded immediately and unconditionally to the like product originating in or destined for the territories of all other contracting parties.

52. (a) Each contracting party shall administer in a uniform, impartial and reasonable manner all its laws, regulations, decisions and rulings of the kind described in paragraph 1 of this Article.

53. David Albright, Sarah Burkhard, Andrea Stricker, *Peddling Peril Index (PPI) for 2019-Ranking National Strategic Trade Control Systems*, (Institute for Science and International Security, May 23, 2019), pp. 7~8.

54. Tetsuya Takahashi, *On the Post-War Responsibility*, (Kodansha Publishing House, 1999), pp. 23~29.

55. See-hwan Doh, "Prime Minister Abe's Negation of 'Invasion' and Colonial Responsibility," *Japan's Perception of History under the Abe Administration and Korea-Japan Relations*, (Northeast Asian History Foundation, 2013), pp. 145~193

56. Navi Pillay, "Japan's approach to the issue of 'comfort women' causing further violations of victims' human rights," *Office of the High Commissioner for Human Rights*, UN Human Rights, August 6, 2014.

So Faraway, So Close: Reparations for Victims of Wartimes Crimes before Korean and Italian Courts

Paolo Palchetti
Professor of International Law
Sorbonne Law School, University of Paris 1 Sorbonne/Panthéon, Paris, France

Abstract

In recent years, a number of cases have been submitted before Italian and Korean courts by the victims of international crimes committed during the Second World War or in the years immediately preceding it. Some of these cases have already been decided while others are still pending. The focus of the present paper is on three legal issues that have arisen, or may possibly arise, in these cases. They concern, first, the interpretation of waiver clauses contained in post-war agreements; secondly, the current status of the law of state immunity in cases concerning claims of compensation brought against a foreign State by the victims of international crimes; finally, the possible contrast between domestic constitutional principles and the international rule of State immunity.

Key Words

Domestic Courts, International Crimes, Compensation, Immunity, Treaty Interpretation, International Law and Domestic Law

1. INTRODUCTION

In the last two decades, a series of lawsuits demanding reparations for crimes committed during the Second World War, or in the years immediately preceding it, have been filed before the domestic courts of a significant number of States. Several decisions have been rendered by courts in Greece,[1] Poland,[2] Germany,[3] Slovenia,[4] France,[5] Japan.[6] A case against Germany for acts of war committed during World War II is still pending before the Supreme Federal Court of Brazil.[7] Some of these decisions have given rise to complex and still ongoing interstate disputes. This is the case, in particular, of the decisions rendered by Italian and Korean courts. For different reasons, Germany and Japan regard these decisions as constituting an infringement by, respectively, Italy and Republic of Korea (hereinafter, "Korea") of their international obligations.

The circumstances surrounding the disputes opposing Italy and Germany, on the one hand, and Korea and Japan, on the other, present some striking similarities. To highlight them, it seems useful to rapidly summarize the historical background of the two cases.

The crimes for which the Italian victims and their heirs claim reparation were committed in the period between 1943-1945 when Italy, after having surrendered to the Allies and declared war on its former ally, was occupied by the German Reich.[8] After the end of the Second World War, the 1947 Peace Treaty between Italy and the Allied Powers was concluded. Under this treaty, Italy waived "on its own behalf and on behalf of Italian nationals all claims against Germany and German nationals outstanding on May 8, 1945, except those arising out of contracts and other obligations entered into, and rights acquired, before September 1, 1939."[9] In 1961, Italy and Germany concluded two agreements relating to the consequences of the war. Under one of this agreement, Germany accepted to pay compensation for "outstanding questions of an economic nature," while Italy "declares all outstanding claims on the part of the Italian Republic or Italian natural or legal persons against the Federal Republic of Germany or German natural or legal persons to be settled to the extent that they are based on rights and circumstances which arose during the period from September 1, 1939 to May 8, 1945."[10] While these treaties seemed to have put an end to Italy's claims against Germany, the question of compensation for crimes committed during German occupation came out suddenly raised forty years later. In 2000 Germany established the "Remembrance, Responsibility and Future" Foundation to provide some form of compensation to individuals who had been subjected to forced labor by Germany during World War II. Thousands of Italian victims submitted their requests to the Foundation. However, the greatest part of such requests was rejected. These individuals sought then redress before German courts and before the European Court of Human Rights but their attempts were unsuccessful. A number of cases against Germany was finally brought before Italian courts. One of the main obstacles faced by the applicants in these cases related to the immunity enjoyed by Germany under international law. In 2004, the Italian Court of Cassation rendered its landmark decision in the *Ferrini* case.[11] By this decision, it recognized that, under international law, a State is not entitled to immunity in circumstances in which the act of the foreign State complained of amount to an international crime. Subsequent to the *Ferrini* judgment, a high number of claims for compensation against Germany was submitted before Italian courts. They were brought not only by individuals formerly employed as forced laborers but also by relatives or heirs of the victims of a number of massacres committed by the German Reich during the occupation of Italy. In 2008 Germany instituted proceedings against Italy before the International Court of Justice (hereinafter "ICJ"), asking the Court to declare that, by denying jurisdictional immunity,

Italy had breached its international obligations towards Germany. In
its 2012 judgment, the ICJ recognized, first, that under international
law, a State its entitled to immunity even if the acts complained of
amount to international crimes, and secondly, that Italy had incurred
international responsibility. As a form of reparation, the ICJ asked
Italy, "by enacting appropriate legislation, or by resorting to other
methods of its choosing, [to] ensure that the decisions of its courts
and those of other judicial authorities infringing the immunity which
the Federal Republic of Germany enjoys under international law
cease to have effect."[12] Following the ICJ's judgment, Italian courts
changed their views and recognized immunity to Germany. In
addition, in 2013, the Italian Parliament enacted a statute obliging
national judges to comply with the judgment of the ICJ. The scenario
changed again when, in October 2014, the Italian Constitutional Court,
requested by the Tribunal of Florence to assess the compatibility of
the situation created by the judgement of the ICJ with Italian
Constitution, found that the international customary rule on immunity
and the Statute adopted by the Italian Parliament in 2013 were
inconsistent with the fundamental right of access to justice provided
under Article 24 of the Italian Constitution.[13] As a consequence of
this judgement of the Constitutional Court, Italian courts are now
exercising their jurisdiction over claims for compensation brought by
Italian victims against Germany.

Taken together, the two sets of cases brought before Korean
courts – i.e. those submitted by the victims of forced labor and those
submitted by the victims of sexual slavery – raise legal issues which
are, to a significant extent, similar to those confronted by Italian
courts. First, the acts complained of, and for which the plaintiffs seek
reparation, constitute grave breaches of international law that amount
to international crimes. Secondly, like Italian courts, Korean courts
had to deal with the problem of interpreting the scope of a treaty
clause by which the State of nationality of the victims waived its

claims towards the State which committed such crimes. Under Article 2 of the 1965 Agreement of the Settlement of Problems Concerning Property and Claims and Economic Cooperation between the Republic of Korea and Japan, "the High Contracting Parties confirm that the problems concerning property, rights and interests of the two High Contracting Parties and their nationals (including juridical persons) and the claims between the High Contracting Parties and between their nationals, including those stipulated in Article IV(a) of the Treaty of Peace with Japan signed at the city of San Francisco on September 8, 1951, have been settled completely and finally."[14] In particular, the interpretation of this provision was a crucial issue in the judgments rendered in 2012 and in 2018 by the Supreme Court of Korea in the cases brought by the victims of forced labor.[15] Thirdly, the case brought by the victims of sexual slavery before the Seoul Central District Court raises the question of the immunity of Japan under international law.[16] The dilemma confronted by the Korean court will be whether to follow the *Ferrini* approach or the position held by the ICJ in its 2012 judgment. Finally, the possible impact of domestic constitutional principles should be considered. In its 2012 judgment, the Supreme Court of Korea relied on the core values of the Korean Constitution in order to justify its finding that it could not recognize previous judgments rendered by Japanese courts on the claims of the victims of forced labor.[17] The main issue now is whether, following the precedent set by the Italian Constitutional Court in 2014, core constitutional values might be taken into consideration by Korean courts when assessing the question of the immunity to be accorded to Japan.

It is not the purpose of the present study to provide a comprehensive examination of the two interstate disputes originated by the claims of compensation submitted before Italian and Korean courts. Its focus will rather be on three specific legal issues that have arisen, or may possibly arise, in the cases before these courts, both those already decided and those currently pending. They concern, first, the interpretation of the waiver clauses contained in the post-war agreements concluded, respectively, between Germany and Italy and between South Korea and Japan; secondly, the current status of the law of state immunity in cases concerning claims of compensation brought against a foreign State by the victims of international crimes; finally, the possible contrast between domestic constitutional principles and the international rule of State immunity, as well as the possible consequences stemming from the recognition of the prevalence of constitutional principles over the international law of immunity. These issues will be examined in turn in the next paragraphs.

2. INTERPRETING 'WAIVER CLAUSES': THE APPROACHES OF THE ITALIAN AND KOREAN COURTS

Both Italian and Korean courts have had to interpret the treaty clauses by which Italy and Korea had waived, also on behalf of their nationals, their claims towards, respectively, Germany and Japan for the events that occurred before the end of World War II. Both courts have retained a restrictive interpretation of the scope of such clauses. In particular, it has been excluded that these clauses cover claims of compensation arising out of the crimes complained of by the Italian and Korean victims before their respective national courts.

In its 2009 judgment in the *Milde* case, the Italian Court of Cassation mainly relied on the terms employed by the pertinent treaty clauses, as well as on the consideration of the object of these treaties, to support its interpretation. Thus, in determining the scope of the waiver clause contained in Article 2 of the 1961 Treaty between Germany and Italy on the Settlement of Certain Property-Related, Economic and Financial Questions, the Court of Cassation emphasized the fact that, by referring to "all outstanding claims," this provision could not be applied to the case before it, "which is not outstanding because it had not even been initiated at the time the Convention was entered into force between the two States."[18] Moreover, it found that the object of the 1961 Treaty was "the settlement of certain questions relating to economic and financial assets," and not "claims and applications concerning reparation for moral damage caused by international crimes committed as a result of serious infringements of inviolable human rights."[19] A partly similar reasoning was used to justify the interpretation of the waiver clause contained in Article 77 (4) of 1947 Peace Treaty, which, according to the Court of Cassation, "concerns rights *in rem* in respect of material damage and not the moral damage for which reparation must be made to the relatives of victims of war crimes."[20]

In its 2018 Judgment on the claims of compensation brought by the victims of forced labor, the Supreme Court of Korea found that Article 2 of the 1965 Agreement between Japan and the Republic of Korea does not apply to such claims, "which [are] premised on the inhumane and wrongful act of the Japanese corporation directly related to Japan's unlawful colonial rule over the Korean peninsula."[21] To support its interpretation, it relied on contextual elements, including the annexes to the 1965 Agreement, which, in its view, show that the purpose of that Agreement "was to basically resolve financial, civil debts and credit relations between Korea and Japan pursuant to Article 4 of the San Francisco Treaty through a political agreement."[22]

It has to be noted that the 2012 Judgment of the Supreme Court of Korea on the claims of the victims of forced labor had developed an additional line of reasoning to justify its conclusion about the non-applicability of the waiver clause. The argument run as follows: in the absence of any indications to the contrary, it cannot be presumed that a waiver clause, by which a State renounces its claims and the claims of its nationals, have the effect of extinguishing the individual rights of the affected individuals; the only effect is that of extinguishing the right of the State to exercise diplomatic protection on behalf of its nationals.[23]

The determination of the scope of waiver clauses formulated in generic and vague terms, such as those contained in Article 2 of the 1965 Agreement between Japan and the Republic of Korea or in Article 2 of the 1961 Treaty between Germany and Italy, does not lend itself to an easy solution. In particular, the question of whether such clauses also cover the claims of the victims of international crimes is bound to remain controversial.[24] Without pretending here to exhaust the analysis of this complex issue, it can be observed that, of the two arguments developed by Korean and Italian courts in the abovementioned decisions, the one that relies on the distinction between individual rights and rights of the State is perhaps the most controversial. This argument appears to be premised on two assumptions: first, that at the time when the crimes had been committed, international law recognized an individual right to reparation; and secondly, that the State had no power to dispose of the rights of its own nationals. Both assumptions are far from being generally accepted.[25] The other argument, which is based on the interpretation of the text of the waiver clauses in the light of contextual elements as well as the object and purpose of the treaty, appears to rely on more solid grounds. Obviously, in order to assess the plausibility of these interpretations, account must be taken of the specificity of each waiver clause and of the treaty that contains it. Two general observations can however be made. First, the distinction between 'ordinary' damage, debts and other financial issues, on the one hand, and claims arising from grave breaches of international law, on the other, found support in the views expressed by some commentators with regard to the scope of generic clauses contained in peace treaties concluded after the Second World War. Thus, for instance, in his Hague Lecture of 1948 on "The Juridical Clauses of the Peace Treaties," Gerald Fitzmaurice, at the time deputy legal advisor of the United Kingdom, observed that "[a] treaty of peace may be a settlement of the disputes which have caused the parties to go to war, but it has no inherently necessary character as a solvent of illegalities which have been committed during the course of the war"[26]; in interpreting a waiver clause included in the 1947 Peace Treaty with Italy, he then suggested that "its scope was intended to be confined to the type of claim which can only be made good against an enemy country by express provision in the Treaty of Peace, and for which no claim would exist independently on the basis of general rules of law."[27] Secondly, it can be observed that an interpretation that excludes grave breaches of international law from the scope of waiver clauses contained in post-war lump-sum agreements founds support in the principle established in the four 1949 Geneva Conventions, according to which "[n]o High Contracting Party shall be allowed to absolve itself or any other High Contracting Party of any liability incurred by itself or by another High Contracting Party in respect of breaches referred to in the preceding Article."[28] The limitation set by the Geneva Conventions constitutes an important component of the legal context which must be taken into account when interpreting the scope of waiver clauses. It strongly argues in favor of an interpretation that excludes from the scope of the waiver claims aimed arising in relation to international crimes.

The question of the interpretation to be given to waiver clauses contained in post-war agreements has not made the object, so far, of authoritative rulings by international courts. In the *Jurisdictional immunities* case, Germany and Italy held opposite views about the scope of the waiver clauses contained in the 1947 Peace Treaty and in the 1961 Treaty.[29] The ICJ did not rule upon this issue. In its 2012 judgment, it made a brief reference to the problem of the treatment accorded to individual claims of compensation in post-war lump-sum agreements. It observed that, "against the background of a century of practice in which almost every peace treaty or post-war settlement has involved either a decision not to require the payment of reparations or the use of lump sum settlements and set-offs, it is difficult to see that international law contains a rule requiring the payment of full compensation to each and every individual victim as a rule accepted by the international community of States as a whole as one from which no derogation is permitted."[30] While, by this statement, the Court appears to recognize the existence of a certain leeway for States in dealing with compensation of affected individuals in post-conflict situations, it would be hard to infer from it an indication about the interpretation to be given to waiver clauses.

3. THE LAW OF STATE IMMUNITY AFTER THE 2012 JUDGMENT OF THE ICJ

The cases submitted by the victims of forced labor before Korean courts do not raise the question of the immunity of Japan, since the claims were directed against Japanese enterprises and not against Japan. By contrast, the immunity enjoyed by Japan before Korean courts is at the heart of the case submitted by the victims of sexual slavery.

In principle, different arguments could be advanced to support the view that, under international law, Japan is not entitled to immunity for the acts complained of by the victims. First, it could be argued that since these acts, which caused grave personal injury to the victims, occurred, at least in part, on Korean territory, the rule establishing the "territorial tort exception" to immunity should apply[31]; as this exception also applies to *acta jure imperii*, it would also cover the acts committed by the Japanese armed forces during their occupation of Korea. Another argument could be that, by its conduct, Japan breached international obligations provided by *jus cogens* rule and that *jus cogens* rule must prevail over any inconsistent rule of international law, including the rule of immunity. Finally, considering that Korean victims of sexual slavery had attempted without success to secure compensation before Japanese courts, it could be argued that Korean courts would be justified in denying Japan immunity since otherwise the victims would have no other means of securing redress. Indeed, in the *Jurisdictional immunities* case, Italy relied precisely on these arguments to defend its view that Germany was not entitled to immunity for the crimes committed by the German Reich during Italy's occupation. The ICJ rejected these arguments. It found, first, that "customary international law continues to require that a State be accorded immunity in proceedings for torts allegedly committed on the territory of another State by its armed forces and other organs of State in the course of conducting an armed conflict."[32] As regards the second argument, it observed that the applicability of the customary international law on State immunity is not affected by the fact the domestic proceedings involve violations of *jus cogens* rules, since "the rules of State immunity are procedural" and "do not bear upon the question whether or not the conduct in respect of which the proceedings are brought was lawful or unlawful."[33] Finally, it found "no basis in the State practice from which customary international law is derived that international law makes the entitlement of a State to immunity dependent upon the existence of effective alternative means of securing redress."[34]

Other arguments may be put forward. It may be held that that international crimes perpetrated by States cannot be qualified as acts *jure imperii* for which a State enjoys immunity, on the assumption that committing crimes cannot be regarded as sovereign acts of the State.[35] Yet, while addressing this argument only passingly, the ICJ clearly rejected it as it considered that the illegality of the acts committed by Germany "does not alter the characterization of those acts as *acta jure imperii*."[36] Korean courts could also attempt to justify the denial of immunity as a form of countermeasure: under this argument, the denial of immunity would be a lawful response to the unlawful refusal of Japan to comply with its obligation to provide reparation to the victims of sexual slavery. Yet, this argument, which in itself would amount to an admission that the denial of immunity constitutes, in principle, a breach of an international obligation, raises complex issues relating to the respect of the conditions provided by international law for lawfully resorting to countermeasures; it would also raise the question of whether, under the domestic allocation of competences between the judiciary and the executive, domestic courts are entitled to have resort to countermeasures.

All things considered, the law of State immunity, as authoritatively interpreted by the ICJ in 2012, represents an obstacle hard to surmount in cases such as those submitted by the victims of sexual slavery. Obviously, the practice of States can evolve.[37] Domestic courts can have a major role in supporting the emergence of exceptions to immunity in case of international crimes. Indeed, in its 2014 judgment, the Italian Constitutional Court stressed the fact that a further reduction of the scope of the international rule of immunity of States from the civil jurisdiction of other States would be "a desirable – and desired by many – evolution of international law" and emphasized the role of domestic judges in the development of customary international law.[38] However, the few instances of practice subsequent to the judgment of the ICJ do not reveal the existence of a trend toward the change of law of State immunity. The prevailing attitude is rather to conform to the view affirmed by the ICJ in 2012.[39] The Italian Constitutional Court itself did not claim that, in cases of grave breaches of human rights and humanitarian law, the international law of state immunity is undergoing a change. To the contrary, it openly admitted the existence of an international rule granting immunity. In this respect, it would be hard to rely on the 2014 judgment of the Italian Constitutional Court as a precedent supporting a legal claim aimed at modifying the law of State immunity.

4. RELYING ON CONSTITUTIONAL PRINCIPLES TO PROTECT THE RIGHTS OF THE VICTIMS?

To overcome the obstacle represented by the international obligations stemming from the law of State immunity, the Italian Constitutional Court relied on the fundamental principles set out in the Italian Constitution. It found that there is a conflict between the fundamental rights of the victims to jurisdictional protection, as provided under Italian Constitution, and the law of State immunity, as defined by the ICJ. In settling this conflict, it gave prevalence to compliance with fundamental constitutional principles over compliance with international law. Since the international rule of immunity was declared unconstitutional, Italian courts have now jurisdiction to rule upon the claims of compensation brought against Germany.

The judgment of the Italian Constitutional Court has the merit of raising forcefully the question of the rights of the victims of grave breaches of human rights and of the way in which these rights are to be protected. Indeed, the judgment may be regarded as a response to the fact that, after the judgment of the ICJ, there was no political initiative aimed at addressing the situation of the victims. In such a situation, the need to afford some form of the protection to the victims may lead domestic judges to regard reliance on constitutional values as an inevitable choice. Whether Korean courts will be tempted to follow the same path is a matter of speculation.

The solution arrived at by the Italian Constitutional Court is not without drawbacks. First, Italy's defiance of its international obligations is bound to produce reputational damages. Indeed, in a dispute opposing Italy to India, India referred to the judgment of the Constitutional Court as evidence of Italy's dubious disposition towards compliance with its international obligations.[40] Secondly, the Italian Constitutional Court only recognized the incompatibility with Italian

Constitution of the international rule granting Germany immunity from jurisdiction; it did not say anything about Germany's immunity from execution.[41] This means that the judgments of Italian courts ordering Germany to pay compensation to the victims and their heirs might have little practical effects thanks to the protection which, in principle, is afforded to Germany's properties by the customary international rule on immunity from execution. Such an outcome would be extremely frustrating for the victims, who after having been told that they have a right to a judge and after having been awarded compensation would discover that they have substantially little, if any, chance of having their judgments enforced. While it cannot be excluded that the Constitutional Court may soon be called upon to assess the compatibility of the Italian Constitution with the customary international rule on immunity from execution, it is clear that the choice will be a hard one. Denying Germany immunity from execution because of the inconsistency of the international rule with the Constitution would have far reaching consequences. Finally, recognizing in general terms the prevalence of the individual right to access to a judge over the international obligation to respect immunity may entail the risk of rendering national courts an attractive forum for litigations against foreign states.[42]

It remains to be seen whether a better option was available in order to reconcile compliance with international law and respect of the fundamental rights of the victims. As I argued elsewhere,[43] an alternative solution could have been found. The Italian Constitutional Court could have established that, under Italian Constitution, the Italian government was under the obligation to assume the burden of repairing the victims. It is suggested that, in cases involving the application of the rule of immunity, the forum State could substitute itself to the foreign State. An answer of this kind has much to be praised of from a legal, moral and political perspective. Legally, not only it would permit to reconcile two conflicting values – the interest in complying with a rule of international law and the right of the individual to obtain redress. It would also have the effect of transferring on the government the risk that any attempt to obtain redress from the responsible State through interstate negotiations may be unsuccessful. In other words, this kind of solution would not imply any waiver of the claim against the responsible State. It would simply change the main actors of the dispute. Shifting the risk from the victims to the State responds also to a wider imperative: affected individuals should not be left alone in bearing the cost of complying with international law. If there is an interest of the State in complying with international law, the State should be associated with the affected individual in bearing the costs.

5. CONCLUDING REMARKS

In its judgment in the *Jurisdictional Immunities* case the ICJ noted that, while granting immunity to Germany had the effect of precluding judicial redress for the Italian victims, their claims "could be the subject of further negotiation involving the two States concerned, with a view to resolving the issue."[44] Behind these words one can easily detect an invitation to the Parties to consider the possibility of engaging in a negotiation, on the assumption that negotiation and not recourse to the domestic courts of one State is a preferable way of dealing with this matter. While the ICJ, for evident reasons, did not provide much details about the content of such negotiation, there is one point that deserves to be stressed. In referring to the possibility of negotiation, the ICJ spoke of "negotiation involving the two States" (*"négociations impliquant les deux Etats"*) and not of "negotiations between the two States." As is connoted by the word "involving," the ICJ appears to suggest that other actors should have been given a role in the negotiation. The reference seems to be to the fact that the victims themselves should have had a role. In other words, in the ICJ's view, Italy and Germany should have at least consulted the victims or the associations of victims.

The parallelism between the situation created by the decisions of Italian courts and that arising out of the decisions of Korean courts cannot be pushed too far. In both situations, however, a last common element can be detected: the absence or inadequateness of the political negotiation among the States concerned. After the 2012 judgment, and despite the ICJ's invitation, Germany and Italy failed to engage in a meaningful negotiation aimed at addressing the victims' claims. In December 2015, the Government of South Korea and Japan announced that an agreement regarding the victims of sexual slavery had been concluded. Yet, this agreement was strongly criticized by the victims and by support groups, who, among other criticism, contested the fact that the two Governments did not make any effort to take the input and opinions of the victims into account.[45] In the absence of an adequate political initiative the burden of taking a decision is shifted to domestic courts. Yet, domestic courts are unwilling to leave the claims of the victims unheard. Their decisions have the effect, in turn, of widening the scope of the dispute and of increasing the political tension in the relations between the States concerned.

In this scenario, political organs should make an attempt to govern the situation. A political initiative "involving" the States concerned and aimed at establishing a mechanism for addressing the claims of the victims, while at the same time putting to an end the proceedings instituted before domestic courts, would not only be in line with the views expressed by the ICJ in its *Jurisdictional Immunities* judgment; such an outcome would also represent the most dignified way to put an end to these long-standing disputes.

Notes

1. *See*, for instance, Areios Pagos, *Prefecture of Voiotia v. Federal Republic of Germany*, judgment of 4 May 2000, 129 International Law Reports, p. 514.

2. Supreme Court of Poland, *Natoniewski v. Federal Republic of Germany*, judgment of 29 October 2010, 30 Polish Yearbook of International Law 2010, p. 299.

3. *Bundesgerichtshof* (German Supreme Court), *Distomo*, judgment of 23 June 2003, 42 International Legal Materials 2003, p. 1030.

4. Constitutional Court of Slovenia, *Case No. Up-13/99*, judgment of 8 March 2001.

5. *Cour de Cassation* (French Court of Cassation), *Bucheron*, judgment of 2 June 2004, 158 Bulletin civil 2004, p. 132.

6. For an overview of the cases submitted before Japanese courts see Shin Hae Bong, 'Compensation for Victims of Wartime Atrocities. Recent Developments in Japan's Case Law,' 3 Journal of International Criminal Justice 2005, pp. 187-206.

7. *Supremo Tribunal Federal* (Brazilian Supreme Federal Court), *Karla Christina Azeredo Venancio da Costa e outros c. República Federal da Alemanha*.

8. For the historical and factual background of the dispute between Germany and Italy, *see also* International Court of Justice, *Jurisdictional Immunities of the State (Germany v. Italy: Greece intervening)*, judgment of 3 February 2012, ICJ Reports 2012, p. 110.

9. Article 77 (4) of the Treaty of 10 February 1947, 49 UNTS 3, No. 747.

10. Article 2 (1) of the Treaty on the Settlement of Certain Property-Related, Economic and Financial Questions, of 2 June 1961.

11. *Corte di Cassazione* (Italian Court of Cassation), *Ferrini v. Federal Republic of Germany*, decision of 11 March 2004, 87 Rivista di diritto internazionale 2004, p. 539.

12. ICJ, *supra* n. 8, p. 155.

13. *Corte Costituzionale* (Italian Constitutional Court), *Judgment n. 238*, judgment of 24 October 2014, 98 Rivista di diritto internazionale 2015, p. 237.

14. Agreement on the Settlement of Problems concerning Property and Claims and on Economic Co-operation between Japan and the Republic of Korea of 22 June 1965, 583 UNTS 173.

15. *See* Supreme Court of Korea, *Park and ors v Mitsubishi Heavy Industries Limited*, judgment of 24 May 2012, Oxford Reports on International Law, ILDC 1909 (KR 2012), and *Re New Nippon Steel Corporation*, judgment of 30 October 2018, 7 Korean Journal of International and Comparative Law 2019, p. 89. On the 2012 judgment, *see* Jang-Hie Lee, "Compensation of Victims of Japanese Forced Labor during Colonial Rule and Its International Legal Arguments & Tasks," 1 Korean Yearbook of International Law 2014, p. 5.

16. On the lawsuit filed by the victims of sexual slavery see "South Korean court begins trial over Japan's sexual slavery," The Washington Post, 13 November 2019.

17. Supreme Court of Korea, *Park and ors v Mitsubishi Heavy Industries Limited,* judgment of 24 May 2012, Oxford Reports on International Law, ILDC 1909 (KR 2012).

18. *Corte di Cassazione* (Italian Court of Cassation), *Milde,* judgment of 13 January 2009, 93 Rivista di diritto internazionale 2009, p. 618.

19. *Ibid.*

20. *Ibid.*

21. Supreme Court of Korea, *Re New Nippon Steel Corporation, supra* n. 15, p. 101.

22. *Ibid.*

23. Supreme Court of Korea, *Park and ors v Mitsubishi Heavy Industries Limited, supra* n. 15. In the 2018 judgment of the Supreme Court of Korea in *Re New Nippon Steel Corporation,* this view has been defended by Justices Kim So Young, Lee Dong Won and Roh Jeong Ho in their Separate Opinion. *Supra* n. 15, p. 109.

24. *See,* on this point, the remarks of Romain Le Boeuf, *Le traité de paix. Contribution à l'étude juridique du règlement conventionnel des différends internationaux* (Paris: Pedone, 2018), pp. 563-564.

25. On the existence of an individual right of reparation see the analysis of the pertinent practice made by Rainer Hoffmann, "Compensation for Personal Damages Suffered during World War II," in Rudiger Wolfrum (ed.) Max Planck Encyclopedia of Public International Law (Oxford: OUP, 2013), who concludes that "it is indeed difficult to argue that there was, under international law as applicable during World War II, a right to compensation for violations of the laws of war, as they stood during World War II, held by the individual victims of such violations." On the power of States to dispose of the rights and claims of their citizens see Pierre D'Argent, *Les réparations de guerre en droit international public. La responsabilité internationale des Etats à l'épreuve de la guerre* (Brussels: Bruylant 2002), pp. 761-767, and Andrea Gattini, *Le riparazioni di guerra nel diritto internazionale* (Padova: CEDAM 2003), pp. 645-653.

26. *See* Gerald G. Fitzmaurice, "The Juridical Clauses of the Peace Treaties," 73 Recueil des Cours 1948-II, pp. 255-367, p. 342.

27. *Ibid.,* p. 340, n. 1.

28. *See* Geneva Convention I, Article 51; Convention II, Article 52; Convention III, Article 131; Convention IV, Article 148. On this principle see Romain Le Boeuf, *supra* n. 24, p. 563, and Alessandro Bufalini, "On the Power of a State to Waive Reparation Claims Arising from War Crimes and Crimes against Humanity," 77 Zeitschrift fur auslaindisches öffentliches Recht und Völkerrecht 2017, pp. 465-467.

29. *See* the Memorial of Germany, 12 June 2009, para. 114, and the Counter-Memorial of Italy, 22 December 2019, para. 4.62.

30. ICJ, *supra* n. 8, p. 141, para. 94.

31. According to the territorial tort exception, as formulated by Article 12 of the United Nations Convention on the Jurisdictional Immunities of States and their Property of 2004, "a State cannot invoke immunity from jurisdiction before a court of another State which is otherwise competent in a proceeding which relates to pecuniary compensation for death or injury to the person, or damage to or loss of tangible property, caused by an act or omission which is alleged to be attributable to the State, if the act or omission occurred in whole or in part in the territory of that other State and if the author of the act or omission was present in that territory at the time of the act or omission."

32. ICJ, *supra* n. 8, p. 135, para. 78.

33. *Ibid.*, p. 140, para. 93.

34. *Ibid.*, p. 143, para. 101.

35. ICJ, *Jurisdictional Immunities of the State (Germany v. Italy: Greece intervening)*, dissenting opinion of Judge Cançado Trindade, ICJ Reports 2012, p. 228.

36. ICJ, *supra* n. 8, p. 125, para. 60.

37. As observed by Rosalyn Higgins, "Equality of States and Immunity from Suit: A Complex Relationship," 43 Netherlands Yearbook of International Law, 2012, p. 145, "it is out of kilter with the times that States are immune from process in respect of acts generally agreed to be among the most vile, and abhorred by international law. But change will have to come from the legislating and executive acts of States, and perhaps the treaties they draw up."

38. *Corte Costituzionale* (Italian Constitutional Court), *supra* n. 13, para. 3.3.

39. *See*, for instance, European Court of Human Rights, *Jones and Others v. United Kingdom*, judgment of 14 January 2014, where the European Court of Human Rights recognized that the judgment of the ICJ represented an "authoritative statement" of the content of the rule of immunity of State. *See also* Supreme Court of Canada, *Kazemi Estate v. Islamic Republic of Iran*, judgment of 19 October 2014, which rejected the view that under international law there would be an exception to immunity in case of grave breaches of *jus cogens* rules.

40. *See* the 2015 provisional measures hearing in the *"Enrica Lexie" Incident (Italy v. India)* case before the International Tribunal of the Law of the Sea, ITLOS/PV.15/C/24/2, pp. 40-42.

41. On the separateness of the regimes governing immunity from jurisdiction and immunity from execution see, among others, Ian Sinclair, "The Law of Sovereign Immunity. Recent Developments," 168 Recueil des cours 1980-II, pp. 115-284, at 218; August Reinisch, "State Immunity from Enforcement Measures," in Gerhard Hafner, Marcelo Kohen, Susan Breau (eds) State Practice Regarding State Immunity (Leiden-Boston: Martinus Njhoff, 2006), pp. 151-166; Xiaodong Yang, *State Immunity in International Law* (Cambridge: CUP, 2012), p. 347.

42. I have developed this point in "Right of Access to (Italian) Courts über alles? Legal Implications beyond Germany's Jurisdictional Immunity," in Anne Peters, Valentina Volpe, Stefano Battini (eds), Remedies against Immunity? Reconciling International and Domestic Law after Italian Constitutional Court's Sentenza 238/2014 (forthcoming).

43. *See* Paolo Palchetti, "Judgment 238/2014 of the Italian Constitutional Court: In Search of a Way Out," QIL-Questions of International Law, Zoom out II (2014), p. 44. *See also* Giorgio Gaja, "Alternative ai controlimiti rispetto a norme internazionali generali e a norme dell'Unione europea," 101 Rivista di diritto internazionale 2018, p. 1037.

44. ICJ, *supra* n. 8, p. 144, para. 104.

45. *See* Committee on the Elimination of the Discrimination against Women, 63rd Session (15 Feb - 04 Mar 2016), Written submission by The Korean Council for the Women Drafted for Military Sexual Slavery by Japan (available at https://tbinternet.ohchr.org › Treaties › CEDAW › JPN).

A Study on Environmental Impact Assessments (EIAs) under International Instruments for the Prevention of Marine Pollution: Focusing on EIAs under the Madrid Protocol and London Convention

LEE Kil-Won
Associate Professor
Chungnam National University, Law School, Daejeon, Korea

Abstract

The marine ecosystems are under the threat of pollution caused by a variety of sources. The problem is that the nature of seawater circulation makes it difficult to identify the sources of pollution; furthermore, even if measures to prevent the introduction of each source of pollution are taken, a great deal of time and effort are required for recovery. For these reasons, approaches that focus on post-pollution response are not effective. In other words, what is more important is a response based in a precautionary approach, and to accomplish this, the implementation of an environmental impact assessment regime is absolutely required.

An environmental impact assessment is the process of assessing the impact of human planned activities on the environment. Today, environmental impact assessments are recognized as a duty of a state, not only within the national legal framework but also under various international instruments related to the protection of the marine environment, such as the United Nations Convention on the Law of the Sea, the Protocol on Environmental Protection to the Antarctic Treaty (the Madrid Protocol), and the Convention on the Prevention of Marine Pollution by Dumping of Wastes and Other Matter 1972 (the London Convention). The relevant provisions under the Madrid

Protocol and the London Convention are particularly worthy of notice, as they specify the procedures of such assessments in a relatively detailed way. This study, therefore, examines the characteristics and limitations of the environmental impact assessment system under these two instruments in order to identify the factors that must be considered in the process of introducing the environmental impact assessment procedures in future negotiations.

Key Words

Environmental impact assessment, Marine pollution, United Nations Convention on the Law of the Sea, Protocol on Environmental Protection to the Antarctic Treaty (the Madrid Protocol), Convention on the Prevention of Marine Pollution by Dumping of Wastes and Other Matter 1972 (the London Convention)

1. INTRODUCTION

The world's oceans and marine ecosystems are under the threat of pollution caused by a variety of sources. The United Nations Convention on the Law of the Sea defines "pollution of the marine environment" as the "introduction by man, directly or indirectly, of substances or energy into the marine environment, including estuaries, which results or is likely to result in such deleterious effects as harm to living resources and marine life, hazards to human health, hindrance to marine activities, including fishing and other legitimate uses of the sea, impairment of quality for use of sea water and reduction of amenities."[1] There are a wide range of origins and pollution sources of marine pollution, including (1) the inflow of domestic sewage, industrial and agricultural wastewater into the seas through rivers, (2) pollutants introduced to the seas by vessels' seabed activities including vessel operation and the intentional dumping of pollutants and vessel accidents, (3) marine environment pollution caused by seabed resource exploration and harvesting activities, (4) the dumping of radioactive waste, and (5) pollution from military use of the seas.[2]

The problem is that the nature of seawater circulation makes it difficult to identify these sources of pollution; furthermore, even if measures to prevent the introduction of each source of pollution are taken, a great deal of time and effort are required in recovery from the pollution. There are also limits on the oceans' self-purification capacity to assimilate waste and make it harmless, and to regenerate natural resources. For these reasons, approaches that focus on post-pollution response are not effective, and are inefficient in terms of cost. In other words, what is more important is a response based in a precautionary approach, and to accomplish this, the implementation of an environmental impact assessment regime is absolutely required.

Environmental impact assessment is the process of assessing the impact of human planned activities on the environment. In the case concerning pulp mills on the River Uruguay, the International Court of Justice made it clear that conducting environmental impact assessments for activities that have a significant environmental impact is a requirement under general international law.[3] Today, environmental impact assessments are recognized as a duty of a state, not only within the national legal framework but also under various international instruments related to the protection of the marine environment, such as the UN Convention on the Law of the Sea, the Protocol on Environmental Protection to the Antarctic Treaty (the Madrid Protocol)[4], and the Convention on the Prevention of Marine Pollution by Dumping of Wastes and Other Matter 1972 (the London Convention).[5] The provisions of the Madrid Protocol and the London Convention on the obligation to implement environmental impact assessments are particularly worthy of notice, as they specify the procedures of such assessments in a relatively detailed way.

The UN General Assembly recently decided to develop an international legally binding instrument under the United Nations Convention on the Law of the Sea on the conservation and sustainable use of marine biological diversity of areas beyond national jurisdiction ("BBNJ instrument"). In this regard, the introduction of an environmental impact assessment system is discussed as one of major issues.[6] It is expected that in the future development of the BBNJ instrument, the Madrid Protocol and the London Convention will be reviewed as important references, as the preparatory committee of the instrument announced that it would reflect the environmental impact assessment procedures under the Madrid Protocol in the process of introducing the environmental impact assessment system, and as marine pollution caused by dumping in areas beyond national jurisdiction is subject to regulation under the London Convention and its annexes.[7] In other words, the two instruments are expected to have a great influence on the process of introducing environmental impact assessment procedures concerning marine environment protection.

This article, therefore, examines the characteristics and limitations of the environmental impact assessment system under the Madrid Protocol and the London Convention in order to identify the factors that must be considered in the process of introducing the environmental impact assessment procedures. With various forms of marine activities currently on the rise, research on environmental impact assessments, which are being conducted as a requirement for the performance of certain marine activities under international law, has significant implications.

2. KEY FEATURES OF ENVIRONMENTAL IMPACT ASSE-SSMENT SYSTEM UNDER THE MADRID PROTOCOL AND THE LONDON CONVENTION

2-1. Key Features of Environmental Impact Assessment System under the Madrid Protocol

2-1-1. *Overview*

The Madrid Protocol consists of a preamble and 27 articles that stipulate the general obligations of the contracting parties, such as the prohibition of mineral resource activities, the requirement to conduct environmental impact assessment and liability for damages.[8] The protocol aims at protecting the Antarctic environment and dependent and associated ecosystems from all human activities conducted in the Antarctic. In the Antarctic Treaty System, the Madrid Protocol complements the Antarctic Treaty, and no provision of the protocol affects the rights and obligations of the contracting parties to the protocol under other international instruments in force within the Antarctic Treaty System.[9] The Committee for Environmental Protection (CEP) was established to provide advice and consultation to the Antarctic Treaty Consultative Meeting (ATCM) regarding the implementation of the protocol, and the CEP is required to submit a report to the ATCM each session.[10]

Activities in the Antarctic Treaty area should be planned and carried out to avoid generating detrimental effects or risks to the Antarctic environment and its ecosystems.[11] To accurately determine the impact of these activities on the Antarctic environment, prior environmental impact assessment should be conducted based on a sufficient amount of information.[12] It is also required to conduct post-environmental impact assessment, including the regular monitoring of the impact of ongoing activities.[13]

Each contracting party should ensure that the environmental impact assessment procedures set out in the Madrid Protocol, Annex I, are applied to the planning process to reach decisions on activities undertaken in the Antarctic Treaty area in the categories of scientific research plans, tourism and other governmental and non-governmental activities requiring advance notification in accordance with Article 7 (5) of the Antarctic Treaty. All contracting parties should also apply the abovementioned procedures to any changes in activities caused by an increase or decrease in the scale of ongoing activities, the addition of an activity, the dismantling of a facility or other means.[14] To complement the provisions of the Madrid Protocol related to environmental impact assessment, the Guidelines for Environmental Impact Assessment in Antarctica have been adopted in accordance with the ATCM's resolution. These guidelines intend to enhance transparency and efficiency in implementing environmental impact assessments, and to establish consistent practices in relation to the fulfillment of obligations under the protocol.[15]

2-1-2. *Key Features of Environmental Impact Assessment Procedures*
The Madrid Protocol Annex I consists of eight articles under the heading "Environmental Impact Assessment," which sets out the basic principles for conducting environmental impact assessments in relation to proposed activities in the Antarctic region, and specifies detailed assessment procedures by stage. Depending on the degree of environmental impact of a proposed activity, the assessment is performed in three general stages: preliminary stage, initial environmental evaluation, and comprehensive environmental evaluation.

First, in the preliminary stage, the impact of a proposed activity on the Antarctic environment and ecosystems is examined following appropriate national procedures. If the activity is determined as "having less than a minor or transitory impact," the activity can proceed forthwith.[16]

If it is determined that the activity has more than "a minor or transitory impact" or a comprehensive environmental evaluation is not being prepared in accordance with Article 3, Annex I, an initial environmental evaluation should be conducted.[17] An initial environmental evaluation should assess the purpose, location, duration and intensity of a proposed activity; alternatives to the activity are also taken into account.[18] If an initial environmental evaluation indicates that a proposed activity has only a minor or transitory impact, the activity can be carried out, provided that appropriate measures are taken, including monitoring to assess and verify the impact of the activity.[19]

If an initial environmental evaluation shows or it is determined that a proposed activity has more than a minor or transitory impact, a comprehensive environmental evaluation should be prepared.[20] A comprehensive environmental evaluation includes a description of a proposed activity including its purpose, location, duration and intensity and a description of the methods and data used to predict the impact of the activity, and a monitoring plan.[21] While the evaluation of a proposed activity is reviewed by the contracting party concerned in the preliminary and initial environmental evaluation stages, the ATCM reviews a draft comprehensive environmental evaluation following the advice of the CEP in the corresponding stage. In this process, contracting parties to the protocol can submit comments, which are included in the final comprehensive environmental evaluation.[22]

In addition to a comprehensive environmental evaluation, an annual list of and information on an initial environmental evaluation and decisions taken as a result thereof are circulated to the contracting parties, forwarded to the CEP and made publicly available.[23] Except for urgent cases involving human life, environmental protection and other pressing factors, environmental impact assessments for all activities carried out in the Antarctic region are conducted in accordance with the procedures set out in Annex I of the Madrid Protocol.[24]

Even when a proposed activity is initiated as a result of an environmental impact assessment, the evaluation process is not terminated. A continuous review based on monitoring is required regarding the impact of the proposed activity on the environment and the effects of mitigation measures that can minimize or mitigate the impact.[25] In addition, a review of the need to change the activity or undertake a new environmental impact assessment is also implemented.[26] Specifically, Article 3(2)(d) of the protocol specifies that monitoring of the impact of ongoing activities should take place on a regular basis.[27] It is also specified that regular monitoring may be carried out to reduce or mitigate the impact of a proposed activity, and to facilitate the early detection of possible unforeseen impacts on the environment.[28] Once a proposed activity is allowed to proceed based on a comprehensive environmental assessment, it is required that procedures be prepared to assess and verify the impact of the activity, including the appropriate monitoring of key environmental indicators.[29]

When there are changes in an activity, such as alterations to the duration of the activity or materials used in the activity, or the expansion of the activity area, the environmental impact assessment may be revised or a new assessment may be performed. Any modification of an activity may result in changes in the foreseen impact and may need to be reviewed as a whole, a process which may include the identification of applicable measures to minimize its environmental impact. If the level of modification is significant, a new environmental impact assessment may be undertaken.[30]

2-2. Key Features of the Environmental Impact Assessment System under the London Convention

2-2-1. Overview

The London Convention was adopted in 1972, and was followed

by the 1996 Protocol to the Convention on the Prevention of Marine Pollution by Dumping of Wastes and Other Matter, 1972 (the London Protocol), which was prepared to modernize and eventually replace it.[31] As of March 1, 2019, 87 countries have joined the London Convention and 51 are contracting members to the London Protocol. South Korea joined the London Convention and the London Protocol in 1993 and 2009, respectively. The Convention and Protocol basically require contracting parties to take necessary measures to prevent the dumping of wastes that damage the marine environment and interfere with the legitimate use of the seas.

The London Convention is the first multilateral convention adopted to protect the marine environment from human activities. Its objective is to effectively regulate all marine pollution sources and to prevent marine pollution by dumping wastes and other matter using the best possible means.[32] The geographical jurisdiction of the London Convention covers all marine waters other than the internal waters of states.[33] Areas beyond national jurisdiction are therefore subject to regulation under the convention. The disposal of wastes or other matter directly arising from, or related to the exploration, development and associated off-shore processing of seabed mineral resources are not covered by the provisions of this convention,[34] and fall under the control of the UN International Seabed Authority.[35]

The London Protocol supersedes the London Convention as between the contracting parties to this protocol which are also parties to the convention.[36] When a state achieves the status of a contracting party to the London Protocol, it can have access to a variety of assistance related to marine pollution control activities from other contracting parties and the secretariat. Other benefits include access to the annual meetings of the contracting parties and the scientific groups, and chances to share experiences of other parties with regard to the regulation of waste dumping activities in order to enhance its level of marine water quality management.[37] The following sections will review the key points of the London Convention and the Protocol in relation to environmental impact assessment.

2-2-2. *Key Features of Environmental Impact Assessment under the London Convention*

The London Convention sets out, in its annexes, the categories of wastes and matter prohibited and permitted to be dumped. Under the convention, it is prohibited to dump wastes or other matter listed in Annex I, while the dumping of wastes such as lead, copper and zinc or other matter listed in Annex II is allowed only with a prior special permit. The dumping of all other wastes or matter not specified in Annexes I and II also requires a prior general permit.[38]

Any permit should be issued only after careful consideration of all the factors specified in Annex III, including prior studies of the characteristics of the dumping site, as set forth in sections B and C of the Annex.[39] Specifically, the conditions to be considered when establishing the criteria for determining permit issuance for the dumping of wastes or other matter include: (1) sufficient scientific basis for the nature and composition of the matter being dumped in assessing the impact of the substance on marine life and human health; (2) the characteristics of a dumping site and a disposal option including other dumping activities in the same area and its impact; (3) possible effects on marine life and fish and shellfish culture, and disposal options as alternatives that can be less harmful to the marine environment and their feasibility.[40] After such an environmental evaluation of dumping activities, a special or general permit can be issued by the appropriate authority designated by the contracting parties.

2-2-3. *Key Features of Environmental Impact Assessment under the London Protocol*

The London Protocol, which entered into force on March 24,

2006, introduces a "reverse list" approach that prohibits the dumping of all wastes or other matter except those listed in Annex I.[41] Wastes or other matter listed in Annex I that can be considered for dumping include: dredged material; sewage sludge; fish waste, or material resulting from industrial fish processing operations; vessels and platforms or other man-made structures at sea; inert, inorganic geological material; organic material of natural origin; bulky items primarily consisting of iron, steel, concrete and similarly non-harmful materials. Of course, the dumping of these substances requires a prior permit. Contracting parties should adopt administrative or legislative measures to ensure that they comply with the provisions of Annex II regarding the issuance of permits and permit conditions, and pay particular attention to opportunities to avoid dumping in favor of environmentally preferable alternatives.[42]

Annex II sets out the assessment procedures for wastes or other matter that can be considered for dumping and the practical criteria for the procedures. Specifically, it is required to evaluate the types, amounts and relative hazard of wastes and alternatives to dumping along with the feasibility of waste reduction/prevention techniques and deliberate on re-use; off-site recycling; destruction of hazardous constituents; treatment to reduce or remove the hazardous constituents; and waste management options such as disposal on land, into air and in water.[43] Contracting parties also should identify the chemical, physical and biological characteristics of wastes in detail to assess their potential impact on human health and the marine environment,[44] and develop a national Action List to provide a mechanism for screening candidate wastes on the basis of their potential effects on human health and the marine environment.[45]

In the selection of a dump site, the location of amenities, values and other uses of the sea in the area under consideration should be taken into account and the evaluation of the potential impact of dumping should be conducted. In addition, monitoring should be undertaken to ensure that a dumping activity meets the permit conditions (compliance monitoring) and that the assumptions made during the permit issuance review process and the dump site selection process are appropriate and sufficient to protect the environment and human health (field monitoring), along with the regular review of the permit based on the results of the monitoring and the purpose of the monitoring plan.[46]

2-2-4. *Key Features of Environmental Impact Assessment Regarding Ocean Fertilization Activities*

The recent escalation of climate change has led to increasing interest in "geo-engineering" activities, meaning human intervention in the climate system to mitigate global warming. "Ocean fertilization" activities to stimulate primary productivity in the ocean, such as the administration of iron and phosphorus to the ocean, is one of the most prominent of such geo-engineering activities. The Conference of the Contracting Parties to the Convention on Biological Diversity (CBD) held in 2008 recognized that the activities should be conducted in a manner consistent with the provisions of the London Convention,[47] and in the same year, resolutions adopted at the Meeting of the Contracting Parties to the London Convention and Protocol affirmed that ocean fertilization activities are also subject to regulation under the convention and protocol.[48] The ocean fertilization activity of "carbon capture and storage," one of the major geo-engineering activities, was included in the scope of activities covered by the London convention and protocol, as it easily fell under the category of dumping at sea set forth in the protocol.[49, 50]

Discussions on the regulation of ocean fertilization activities under the London Convention system began in 2007. The scientific group established under the convention advised that ocean fertilization activities be carried out in a manner consistent with the objectives of the London Convention and Protocol. The contracting parties, through the 2008 Resolution mentioned above, agreed not to permit ocean fertilization activities other than for legitimate scientific research.[51] Legitimate scientific research activities recognized as ocean fertilization activities are deemed the "placement of matter for a purpose other than the mere disposal," as set out in Article 3(1)(b) (ii) of the London Convention and Article 1(4)(2) of the London Protocol; they are therefore not regarded as dumping at sea.[52]

The 2008 Resolution requires that a research proposal be prepared before commencing the scientific research activities, which includes a case-by-case evaluation of the proposal in accordance with an assessment framework to be developed by the scientific group.[53] In addition, the resolution requires a set of mechanisms to examine whether a proposed activity is consistent with the objectives of the London Convention and Protocol, along with the use of the best available guidelines such as the agreements of the Meeting of the Contracting Parties and Annex III of the London Convention or Annex II of the London Protocol.[54] In 2010, the Meeting of the Contracting Parties to the London Convention and Protocol finally resolved to adopt the Assessment Framework for Scientific Research Involving Ocean Fertilization (The 2010 Assessment Framework).[55] The 2010 Assessment Framework prescribed that environmental impact assessment should be carried out in the two stages of initial assessment and environmental assessment. In the initial assessment stage, it is examined whether a proposed activity is an ocean fertilization activity and has scientific characteristics, and a final judgment is made on whether the activity is subject to the 2010 Assessment Framework. The results of the initial assessment are then submitted to the Secretariat of the London Convention and Protocol.[56] In the environmental assessment stage, the proposed activities are reviewed to ensure that they do not contradict the objectives of the London Convention and Protocol. Specifically, the assessment is performed through the following six steps: problem formulation, site selection and description, exposure assessment, effects assessment, risk characterization and risk management.[57]

After the completion of both the initial and environmental assessments, a final decision is made as to whether the proposed activity can proceed based on a comprehensive review to determine if the activity is a legitimate scientific research activity consistent with the objectives of the London Convention and Protocol. If an activity proceeds following the assessment result, continuous monitoring of the activity is performed and the information collected through this monitoring is used for future assessment.

In 2013, the Meeting of the Contracting Parties to the London Protocol adopted a resolution (The 2013 Resolution) related to the amendment of the protocol, which further strengthened its provisions regarding the regulation of ocean fertilization activities and other geo-engineering activities.[58] The resolution stipulated that an ocean fertilization can be considered for a permit if it is assessed as a legitimate scientific research activity as provided in Annex IV, which was added to the protocol through the amendment. It also specified the general characteristics of geo-engineering activities, and stipulated that environmental impact assessment should be carried out as a prerequisite of the implementation of the activities as set out in Article 6 bis, which was also added to the protocol through the amendment. It also specified that Annex V was adopted to specify the procedures of environmental assessment impact from consultation, assessment of potential effects, risk management to monitoring. The 2013 Resolution also confirms the relevance of the 2008 Resolution to the 2010 Assessment Framework regarding the environmental impact assessment of ocean fertilization activities; it is therefore understood that both documents should be considered together when performing an environmental impact assessment.

3. REVIEW OF EIAs UNDER THE MADRID PROTOCOL AND THE LONDON CONVENTION FROM THE PERSPECTIVE OF INTERNATIONAL LAW

3-1. More Detailed Specification of Assessment Procedures

The Madrid Protocol and the London Convention provide more detailed environmental impact assessment procedures than those set out in other international instruments. The Madrid Protocol divides environmental impact assessment procedures into the three stages of the preliminary stage, initial environmental evaluation and comprehensive environmental evaluation. Depending on the predicted degree of environmental impact of a planned activity, contracting parties should prepare an evaluation of different processes and levels, which differentiates them from uniform environmental impact assessment procedures provided in other international instruments.[59] First, under the Madrid Protocol, a proposed activity is given a permit to proceed forthwith if it is assessed as having less than a "minor or transitory" environmental impact in the preliminary stage. Each stage of the procedures is completed in a fixed period in order to ensure procedural swiftness. For instance, a period of 90 days is allowed for the receipt of comments on the draft comprehensive environmental evaluation, which is circulated to contracting parties and forwarded to the CEP for appropriate consideration 120 days before the next ATCM.[60]

Second, the environmental impact assessment under the Madrid Protocol, unlike most environmental impact assessment systems under international instruments that lack supplementary explanations or provisions for each step of assessment procedures, provides detailed guidance on what is reviewed and how it is to be reviewed in each stage based on instruments and recommendations adopted under the Antarctic Treaty, including the Guidelines for Environmental Impact

Assessment in Antarctica.[61] Although the guidelines are not a legally binding instrument, they provide a detailed evaluation method, including considerations for evaluating a proposed activity and the environment, with the aim of ensuring the stability of the assessment process and the predictability of the outcome. This is a significant difference from the UN Convention on the Law of the Sea, which is a basic international law on the sea, and the various marine environment protection agreements managed by the Regional Seas Programme of the UN Environment Programme, which only provide general guidance on environmental impact assessment.[62] In addition, guidelines for the operation of monitoring programs have also been adopted by the Council of Managers of National Antarctic Programmes (COMNAP), to provide a set of guidelines on the assessment of a monitoring program's fulfillment of the requirements set out in the Madrid Protocol and the proposed activity's compliance with the outcome of the environmental impact assessment.[63]

Under the London Convention as well, a screening to determine whether a dumping activity can be considered for a permit and a scoping to assess alternative options to the dumping activity that are less harmful to the marine environment are undertaken as assessment procedures based on the review of the characteristics of the matter to be dumped and its impact on the marine life living in the dumping site. The convention provides all the assessment procedures commonly available under international instruments. The London Convention divides wastes and other matter into two categories: those that are prohibited from being dumped, and those that can be considered for a permit. The listing method is similar to that of the Convention on Environmental Impact Assessment in a Transboundary Context, which provides the lists of activities subject to environmental impact assessment.[64]

On the other hand, it is also quite noteworthy that the convention requires assessment of the impact of a proposed activity on the environment in the two stages of initial assessment and environmental assessment in relation to the environmental impact assessment procedures provided by the 2010 Assessment Framework for ocean fertilization activities. It is deemed that actual evaluation is conducted in the environmental assessment stage only for activities that have been assessed as subject to environmental impact assessment in the initial assessment stage.

Furthermore, there are shortcomings in the environmental impact assessment procedures under the Madrid Protocol and the London Convention, respectively. As reviewed above, the environmental impact assessment set out in the Madrid Protocol and Annex I follows the three stages of preliminary stage, initial environmental evaluation and comprehensive environmental evaluation for proposed activities by dividing them into three categories depending on the intensity of their impact on the environment; that is, those with less than a minor or transitory impact, those with a minor or transitory impact and those with more than a minor or transitory impact.[65] The approach can be highly evaluated, in that it can strengthen the efforts for the conservation and protection of the environment and ecosystems related to any planned activities by subdividing their environmental impact according to intensity as part of impact analysis process.

The problem is, however, that the concepts of "minor" and "temporary" impacts have not been established under the protocol; furthermore, no agreements between contracting parties or guidelines on reviewing them have been provided. This can make it difficult for the parties to clearly understand the concepts.[66] The CEP's efforts to establish the concepts still remains at an initial stage, and thus far impact analysis has only been reviewed on a case by case basis.[67] The ambiguity of these concepts can lead to disagreement between the parties concerned, which risks expanding into disputes. This can be a very negative factor in the implementation of the overall environmental impact assessment system.[68]

A similar problem can be pointed out with the London Convention system. Regarding the procedures for reviewing the impact of a proposed activity on the environment and determining whether it can be considered for a permit, the London Convention and Protocol and other related instruments on ocean fertilization activities do not provide specific criteria or information for the assessment of the impact. With regard to the issuance of permits for the dumping of wastes, the London Convention and Protocol simply stipulate that it is determined based on the assessment of the dumping activity's potential effects on marine life, fish and shellfish culture, human health and the environment. The 2010 Assessment Framework only requires that an impact hypothesis be established to examine the possibility that a dumping activity will have a negative impact on the environment.[69] In other words, it is not clear at which level of impact on the environment a waste dumping or ocean fertilization activity may be prohibited.

In determining whether a proposed activity can be considered for a permit or accepted as an ocean fertilization activity following the environmental impact assessment procedures under the London Convention and Protocol, there is a clear need to make decisions that are mainly based on the level of the activity's impact on the environment, and establish or specify criteria for the examination of the level.

Overall, in establishing criteria for determining whether to initiate environmental impact assessment, what is important is not the choice of terms, such as "minor" or "transitory" impact. What is critical is to provide some guidelines to help correctly understand any terms used. This will ultimately establish a consistent review process with regard to whether an activity is subject to environmental impact assessment, building the confidence of contracting parties in the entire assessment procedure.[70]

3-2. Guarantee of Objectivity through Third Party Intervention

3-2-1. *Role Assignment to Internal Organizations*

As reviewed earlier, in the process of conducting an environmental impact assessment in accordance with the Madrid Protocol, internal organizations such as the ATCM and the secretariat are given certain roles to guarantee their objectivity in the environmental impact assessment and provide a forum for sharing relevant environmental information.

While the evaluation of a proposed activity is reviewed by the contracting party concerned in the preliminary and initial environmental evaluation stages, the ATCM reviews a draft comprehensive environmental evaluation following the advice of the CEP in the corresponding stage. Since the ATCM can participate in the assessment process in addition to the party concerned, the environmental impact assessment can be deemed to be carried out from a third-party perspective. Even if the party concerned has the authority to decide whether to initiate the proposed activity, it will not be easy for them to overlook an environmental impact assessment reviewed by a third party such as the ATCM, and as such they will be under intense pressure to comply with the results of the final comprehensive environmental evaluation.[71]

In addition, an annual list of environmental evaluations and decisions taken in consequence thereof is circulated to contracting parties, forwarded to the CEP and made publicly available.[72] Parties to the protocol also actively post their environmental evaluation reports that they have prepared on the official website of the Secretariat of the Antarctic Treaty System.[73]

The 2010 Assessment Framework on ocean fertilization activities also encourages the Secretariat to draw up a list of relevant information, and contracting parties submit a summary of environmental impact assessments.[74] The establishment of a publicly available database of relevant information at the secretariat level will form an important foundation for the consistency and predictability of future assessments.

3-2-2. *Establishment of Cooperative System between Contracting Parties*

The Madrid Protocol stipulates that contracting parties should mutually cooperate in planning and implementing activities in the Antarctic Treaty area, such as through providing appropriate assistance to other parties that are preparing for an environmental impact assessment, offering information on potential environmental risks at the request of other parties, and providing aid to minimize the impact of any accidents that could damage the Antarctic environment.[75]

In this context, as mentioned earlier, the ATCM encourages all contracting parties to the protocol to submit comments during the review of a draft comprehensive environmental evaluation, and publicly open the evaluation to provide the public with an opportunity to submit comments.[76] The final comprehensive environmental evaluation report is also made publicly available to all parties to the protocol.[77]

The participation of all parties and the general public as well as the party concerned in the assessment process is quite different from environmental impact assessment procedures under other existing international instruments, which require only the participation of the party concerned and the public living in the areas affected by the planned activity.[78] This third-party approach is deemed to assign common responsibilities and roles to all parties to the Protocol to comprehensively protect the Antarctic area. In that both the ATCM and all parties to the protocol can participate in the assessment process, it is considered that environmental impact assessments are managed and operated at a third-party and multilateral level under the protocol.[79]

If a planned activity is decided to be carried out based on an environmental impact assessment that reflects the opinions of all parties and the general public, the activity will be able to gain full understanding and support from the international community. The procedures seem very effective in finding ways to minimize or mitigate environmental impacts, as a wide range of opinions and information are shared between all stakeholders.

In terms of third-party intervention, the London Convention system shares commonalities with the Madrid Protocol system. The 2010 Assessment Framework system and the 2013 Resolution secure procedural objectivity in environmental impact assessments through public participation, stipulating that there should be sufficient consultation with stakeholders before adopting the results of an environmental impact assessment.[80] The 2010 evaluation system makes it clear that consultation, notification and reporting processes are part of environmental impact assessment procedures undertaken regarding ocean fertilization activities.[81] Specifically, before the decision on whether a proposed activity can be implemented, contracting parties are required to conduct consultations with all interested parties. The consultation process identifies countries affected by an activity, encourages cross-border scientific and technological cooperation, and makes publicly available the results of environmental impact assessment.[82]

Annex V to the London Protocol, which was added to it in accordance with the 2013 Resolution, also sets out procedures for consultation. If a proposed ocean fertilization activity affects waters within the jurisdiction of other countries, it is required to undertake a consultation process in order to report to regional international conventions and systems relevant to the countries, and to encourage mutual scientific and technological cooperation.[83] In addition, parties proposing an ocean fertilization activity should consult with all domestic and foreign stakeholders as soon as possible, and with relevant regional international organizations as necessary to meet relevant regional objectives and standards.[84]

4. CONCLUSIONS

This study examined the characteristics and shortcomings of the environmental impact assessment system under the Madrid Protocol and the London Convention to identify the factors that must be considered in the introduction of environmental impact assessment procedures. Today, international instruments in various forms, such as multilateral, regional, and sectoral ones, are being adopted with regard to environmental impact assessments. In the process of introducing an environmental impact assessment system, it is necessary to appropriately evaluate the characteristics and advantages of the environmental impact assessment systems introduced in accordance with the existing international instruments, and consider cooperation between different systems or problems that can arise from potential collision between them.

An environmental impact assessment, which has been confirmed by the ICJ as an obligation under international law and accepted for a long period of time as a national practice, is indispensable in preventing pollution at the source. Most importantly, assessment procedures should be established that can discourage any activities with detrimental impact on relevant environments and ecosystems.

Notes

1. United Nations Convention on the Law of the Sea, Montego Bay, December 10, 1982, 21 ILM 1261 (1982), in force November 16, 1994, Article 1(4) [hereinafter the "UN Convention on the Law of the Sea"].

2. Roe Myong-joon, "New International Environmental Law," (Beopmunsa, 2003), p. 111.

3. In the case concerning pulp mills on the River Uruguay, the ICJ confirmed that an environmental impact assessment is required for any activity by a country that may have a harmful effect on other countries under general international law. Case Concerning Pulp Mills on the River Uruguay (Arg. v. Uru.), Judgment, 2010 I.C.J. 14 (April 20), para. 204 ("the obligation to protect and preserve [the aquatic environment] ... has to be interpreted in accordance with a practice, which in recent years has gained so much acceptance that it may now be considered a requirement under general international law to undertake an environmental impact assessment where there is a risk that the proposed industrial activity may have a significant adverse impact in a transboundary context."). The International Tribunal for the Law of the Sea also confirmed that the implementation of an environmental impact assessment is a general requirement for any seabed activities under the UN Convention on the Law of the Sea and customary international law. Seabed Disputes Chamber of the International Tribunal for the Law of the Sea, Responsibilities and Obligation of States Sponsoring Persons and Entities with respect to Activities in the Area, Advisory Opinion, Case No. 17 (February 1, 2011), paras. 145 & 148.

4. Protocol on Environmental Protection to the Antarctic Treaty, Madrid, October 4, 1991, 30 I.L.M. 1455, in force January 14, 1998 [hereinafter the "Madrid Protocol"].

5. Convention on the Prevention of Marine Pollution by Dumping of Waste and Other Matter, December 29, 1972, 26 U.S.T. 2403, 1046 U.N.T.S. 138 [hereinafter the "London Convention"].

6. United Nations General Assembly, Development of an International Legally Binding Instrument under the United Nations Convention on the Law of the Sea on the Conservation and Sustainable Use of Marine Biological Diversity in Areas Beyond National Jurisdiction, G.A. Res. 69/292, U.N. Doc. A/RES/69/292 (July 6, 2015). For details of the discussion on the introduction of environmental impact assessment procedures in areas beyond national jurisdiction, see: Robin Warner, "Environmental Assessment in Marine Areas Beyond National Jurisdiction," Research Handbook on International Marine Environmental Law (Rosemary Rayfuse ed., 2015), p. 291.

7. Preparatory Committee Established by General Assembly Resolution 69/292, Chair's Streamlined Non-Paper on Elements of a Draft Text of an International Legally-Binding Instrument under the United Nations Convention on the Law of the Sea on the Conservation and Sustainable Use of Marine Biological Diversity

of Areas beyond National Jurisdiction, Fourth Session, para. 152, July 10~21, 2017, available at http://www.un.org/depts/los/biodiversity/prepcom_files/Chairs_ streamlined_non-paper_to_delegations.pdf.

8. The Antarctic Treaty, concluded in 1959, is a fundamental treaty regulating issues related to the Antarctic Region, ensuring the peaceful use of Antarctica and the freedom of scientific research. The Antarctic Treaty, December 1, 1959, 12 U.S.T. 794, 402 U.N.T.S. 71, Articles 1, 2 and 4. With the Antarctic Treaty at its heart, other agreements such as two separate conventions dealing with the Conservation of Antarctic Seals, and the Conservation of Antarctic Marine Living Resources, the Convention on the Regulation of Antarctic Mineral Resource Activities and the Madrid Protocol were adopted, forming a comprehensive system called the Antarctic Treaty System under which they operate. The Antarctic Treaty System includes the Antarctic Treaty itself, measures in force under the Antarctic Treaty, separate international instruments in force in connection with the Antarctic Treaty, and measures in force in accordance with such instruments. Madrid Protocol, Article 1(e). Basic issues such as the peaceful use of Antarctica and the conservation of biological resources are discussed in the Antarctic Treaty Consultative Meeting. At present, the Antarctic Treaty has a total of 53 state parties, including 29 consultative parties and 24 non-consultative parties. See https://www.ats.aq/dev AS/ats_parties.aspx?lang=e. The Madrid Protocol was adopted in Madrid, Spain in 1991 to complement the Antarctic Treaty, which lacks detailed provisions concerning the protection of the Antarctic environment and ecosystems. The protocol provided momentum to unify the standards for environmental protection regarding all human activities in the Antarctic. For details of the discussion on the obligations of the contracting parties to the Madrid Protocol, see: Kwon Mun-sang et al., "A Study on the Establishment of Antarctic Environment Conservation Policies in Korea," Korean Journal of International Law, No. 45 (Korean Society of International Law, 2000), pp. 3~5.

9. Madrid Protocol, Article 4.

10. Madrid Protocol, Article 11(1) and (5). The Committee for Environmental Protection (CEP) provides advice to the ATCM on:
(a) the effectiveness of measures taken pursuant to this Protocol
(b) the need to update, strengthen or otherwise improve such measures
(c) the need for additional measures, including the need for additional Annexes, where appropriate
(d) the application and implementation of the environmental impact assessment procedures set out in Article 8 and Annex I
(e) means of minimizing or mitigating environmental impacts of activities in the Antarctic Treaty area
(f) procedures for situations requiring urgent action, including response action in environmental emergencies
(g) the operation and further elaboration of the Antarctic Protected Area system
(h) inspection procedures, including formats for inspection reports and checklists for the conduct of inspections

(i) the collection, archiving, exchange and evaluation of information related to environmental protection

(j) the state of the Antarctic environment

(k) the need for scientific research, including environmental monitoring, related to the implementation of this Protocol

Madrid Protocol, Article 12(1).

11. Madrid Protocol, Article 3(2)(b).

12. Madrid Protocol, Article 3(2)(c). The considerations for a prior environmental impact assessment set out in the provision include: (i) the scope of the activity, including its area, duration and intensity; (ii) the cumulative impacts of the activity, both by itself and in combination with other activities in the Antarctic Treaty area; (iii) whether the activity will detrimentally affect any other activity in the Antarctic Treaty area; (iv) whether technology and procedures to provide for environmentally safe operations are available; (v) whether there exists the capacity to monitor key environmental parameters and ecosystem components so as to identify and provide early warning of any adverse effects of the activity, and to provide for such modification of operating procedures as may be necessary in light of the results of monitoring or increased knowledge of the Antarctic environment and dependent and associated ecosystems; and (vi) whether there exists the capacity to respond promptly and effectively to accidents, particularly those with potential environmental effects.

13. Madrid Protocol, Article 3(2)(d).

14. Madrid Protocol, Article 8. Article 7(5) of the Antarctic Treaty is as follows: Each Contracting Party shall, at the time when the present Treaty enters into force for it, inform the other Contracting Parties, and hereafter shall give them notice in advance, of:

(a) all expeditions to and within Antarctica, on the part of its ships or nationals, and all expeditions to Antarctica organized in or proceeding from its territory;

(b) all stations in Antarctica occupied by its nationals; and

(c) any military personnel or equipment intended to be introduced by it into Antarctica subject to the conditions prescribed in paragraph 2 of Article 1 of the present Treaty.

15. The Guidelines for Environmental Impact Assessment in Antarctica were initially adopted in 1999 and went through two amendments, one in 2005 and the other in 2016. Currently, the guidelines adopted in 2016 replace the previous version. Guidelines for Environmental Impact Assessment in Antarctica, Resolution 1 (2016) Annex, ATCM XXXIX ATCM XXXIX – CEP XIX, Santiago, Chile Final Report (May 23, 2016~June 1, 2016) [hereinafter the "Guidelines for Environmental Impact Assessment in Antarctica"].

16. Madrid Protocol, Annex I, Article 1.

17. Madrid Protocol, Annex I, Article 2(1).

18. *Id.*

19. Madrid Protocol, Annex I, Article 2(2).

20. Madrid Protocol, Annex I, Article 3(1).

21. The initial and comprehensive environmental evaluation as set out in Annex I of the Madrid Protocol have big differences in the evaluation methods and other details. See the Guidelines for Environmental Impact Assessment in Antarctica, p. 23.

22. Madrid Protocol, Annex I, Article 3(5) and (6).

23. Madrid Protocol, Annex I, Article 6.

24. The environmental impact assessment procedures under this annex do not apply in cases of urgent activities relating to the safety of human life or of ships, aircraft or equipment and facilities of high value, or the protection of the environment. If, however, such activities are require a comprehensive environmental evaluation, it should be reported to the parties to the protocol and the CEP, and a full explanation of the activities carried out should be provided within 90 days of those activities. Madrid Protocol, Annex I, Article 7(1) and (2).

25. In the case concerning the Gabcikovo-Nagymaros Project, Judge Weeramantry, in his separate opinion, confirmed that a monitoring process is part of an environmental impact assessment. Gabcikovo-Nagymaros Project (Hung. v. Slovk.), 1997 I.C.J. 7, at 111 (Sept. 25) ("environmental impact assessment means not merely an assessment prior to the commencement of the project, but a continuing assessment and evaluation as long as the project is in operation.").

26. Guidelines for Environmental Impact Assessment in Antarctica, p. 27. Article 5(2), Annex I, the Madrid Protocol specifies the need for monitoring; it is necessary to ensure that environmental impact assessments are implemented in a manner consistent with the Madrid Protocol, to minimize harmful effects on the environment, and to provide information on the need to suspend, cancel or modify activities where appropriate.

27. Madrid Protocol, Article 3(2)(d).

28. Madrid Protocol, Article 3(2)(e) and Madrid Protocol, Annex I, Article 3(2)(g).

29. Madrid Protocol, Annex I, Article 5(1).

30. Guidelines for Environmental Impact Assessment in Antarctica, p. 28.

31. 1996 Protocol to the Convention on the Prevention of Marine Pollution by Dumping of Wastes and Other Matter, November 7, 1996, 36 I.L.M. 1 (1997) [hereinafter the "London Protocol"]. While no provisions to regulate new kinds of activities can be added to the London Convention for no more amendment can be made to it, the London Protocol is amendable, and in 2006, carbon dioxide for underground storage was added to the list of items covered by the protocol along with seven dumping substances that had been conditionally permitted in 2006. Kim Jung-eun, "A Study on the Justification of Extension of Institutional Powers for the Management of Marine Geo-engineering under the London Convention/Protocol," Korean Journal of International Law, Vol. 58, No. 1 (2013), p. 72.

32. The London Convention and Protocol: Their Role and Contribution to Protection of the Marine Environment, International Maritime Organization, No. 4 (2012)

[hereinafter the "IMO's Summary of the London Convention and Protocol"], http://www.imo.org/en/OurWork/Environment/LCLP/Documents/22780LDC%20Le aflet%20without%2040%20Anniv%20logo2012Web1.pdf (accessed on March 1, 2019). The UN Convention on the Law of the Sea, called "the UN Charter of the sea," requires state parties to adopt laws and regulations to prevent, reduce and control pollution of the marine environment from land-based sources, including rivers, estuaries, pipelines and outfall structures, taking into account internationally agreed-upon rules, standards and recommended practices and procedures. It also stipulates that states, acting especially through competent international organizations or diplomatic conference, shall endeavor to establish global and regional rules, standards and recommended practices and procedures to prevent, reduce and control pollution of the marine environment from land-based sources. UN Convention on the Law of the Sea, Article 207 (1) and (4).

33. London Convention, Article 3(3).

34. London Convention, Article 3(1)(c).

35. Under the UN Convention on the Law of the Sea, the International Seabed Authority was established with the contracting parties to the convention as members to promote the sound development of the global economy and balanced international trade through the development of seabed resources, a common heritage of mankind. UN Convention on the Law of the Sea, Articles 156 and 157. For the details of the development and operation of seabeds under the UN Convention of the Law of the Sea, see: Kim Jeong-geon et al., "International Law" (Pakyoungsa, 2010), pp. 478~486.

36. London Protocol, Article 23.

37. The IMO's Summary of the London Convention and Protocol, *op. cit.*

38. No article in the London Convention will be construed as preventing any contracting party from prohibiting the dumping of wastes or other matter not listed in Annex I in its own country. London Convention, Article 4(3).

39. London Convention, Article 4(2).

40. See the London Convention, Annex III.

41. London Protocol, Article 1(1).

42. London Protocol, Article 4(1)(2).

43. London Protocol, Annex II, Articles 2 and 5.

44. London Protocol, Annex II, Article 7.

45. London Protocol, Annex II, Article 9.

46. London Protocol, Annex II, Articles 11, 12 and 18. In order for a national authority responsible for waste dumping regulation to conduct an impact assessment on dumping in a manner consistent with the provisions of the London Convention and Protocol, the Guidelines for the Assessment of Wastes or Other Matter that May Be Considered for Dumping were adopted. The guidelines specify the assessment procedures for wastes that may be considered for dumping as set out in Annex 2 to the London Protocol and the criteria to be reviewed in the procedures.

47. Conference of Parties to the Convention on Biodiversity, Decision Adopted by the Conference of the Parties to the Convention on Biological Diversity at Its Ninth Meeting, UNEP/CBD/COP/DEC/IX/16 (October 9, 2008), para. (C) (4).

48. London Convention and London Protocol, Resolution LC-LP.1(2008) on the Regulation of Ocean Fertilization, The Thirtieth Meeting of the Contracting Parties to the London Convention and the Third Meeting of the Contracting Parties to the London Protocol, P8, LC 30/16 (October 31, 2008), para. 1 [hereinafter the "2008 Resolution"].

49. Kim Jung-eun, *op. cit.*, pp. 75~76. "Carbon capture and storage (CCS) is a type of geo-engineering activity conducted to reduce the final amount of carbon dioxide emitted by industry or the amount of carbon dioxide emitted into the atmosphere for the purpose of mitigating climate change." *Id.*, p. 72.

50. The Article 1(4)(1) of the London Protocol defines "dumping at sea" as follows: "1. any deliberate disposal into the sea of wastes or other matter from vessels, aircraft, platforms or other man-made structures at sea;
2. any deliberate disposal into the sea of vessels, aircraft, platforms or other man-made structures at sea;
3. any storage of wastes or other matter in the seabed and the subsoil thereof from vessels, aircraft, platforms or other man-made structures at sea; and
4. any abandonment or toppling at site of platforms or other man-made structures at sea, for the sole purpose of deliberate disposal."

51. In the preamble to the 2008 Resolution, the contracting parties confirm that current knowledge of the effects and potential environmental impacts of ocean fertilization is not sufficient to justify activities other than legitimate scientific research.

52. 2008 Resolution, *op. cit.*, para. 3. Such placement should not be contrary to the objectives of the London Convention and Protocol. London Convention, Article 3(1)(b)(ii) and London Protocol, Article 1(4)(2).

53. 2008 Resolution, *op. cit.*, para. 4.

54. 2008 Resolution, *op. cit.*, paras. 5~6.

55. London Convention and London Protocol, Resolution LC-LP.2 (2010) on the Assessment Framework for Scientific Research Involving Ocean Fertilization, The Thirty-Second Consultative Meeting of the Contracting Parties to the London Convention and the Fifth Meeting of the Contracting Parties to the London Protocol, P1.2, LC 32/15 (October 14, 2010), Annex VI, p. 2 [hereinafter the "2010 Assessment Framework"]. The 2010 Assessment Framework was prepared to assess activities that fall within the scope of the activities covered by the 2008 Resolution, and was introduced as a device to examine whether such activities correspond to legitimate scientific research not contrary to the purposes of the London Convention and Protocol. 2010 Assessment Framework, *op. cit.*, paras. 1.1~1.2.

56. 2010 Assessment Framework, *op. cit.*, para. 1.7.

57. Specifically, the stage of problem formulation requires the description of a proposed activity and specification of the scope of subsequent evaluation

procedures. The site selection and description stage involves the identification of the information needed to describe the physical, geological and biological conditions of a proposed location. In the exposure assessment stage, the movement of objects added to or relocated to the relevant marine environment is described, and in the effects assessment stage, the information necessary to describe the response of the marine environment resulting from the ocean fertilization activity is collected. The risk characterization stage involves the review of the negative impact on the environment of the proposed activity. The final risk management stage requires the review of ways to minimize or manage the risk factors that were reviewed in the risk characterization stage and measures to remedy the risks or implement appropriate monitoring procedures. 2010 Assessment Framework, *op. cit.*, para. 1.3.

58. London Convention and London Protocol, Resolution LC-LP.4(8) on the Amendment to the London Protocol to Regulate the Placement of Matter for Ocean Fertilization and Other Marine Geo-engineering Activities, LC 35/15, (October 18, 2013) [hereinafter the "2013 Resolution"].

59. In general, environmental impact assessments in accordance with other existing international instruments are conducted through uniform procedures. United Nations Convention on the Law of the Sea, Montego Bay, December 10, 1982, 21 ILM 1261 (1982), in force November 16, 1994, Articles 204 to 206 [hereinafter the "UN Convention on the Law of the Sea"]; Convention on Biological Diversity, Article 14.

60. Madrid Protocol, Annex I, Article 3(3) and (4).

61. Kees Bastmeijer & Ricardo Roura, "Environmental Impact Assessment in Antarctica," in Theory and Practice of Transboundary Environmental Impact Assessment 175, 180 (Kees Bastmeijer & Timo Koivurova eds., 2008). The Guidelines for Environmental Impact Assessment in Antarctica set out in a detailed manner the process of activity and environment review carried out before analyzing the environmental impacts of the activity; impact analysis results; comparative analysis of the effects; measures to minimize or mitigate the impact; details of monitoring process; and how to prepare an environmental impact assessment report. The Guidelines for Environmental Impact Assessment in Antarctica, pp. 4~27. The Convention on Biological Diversity system also provides specific assessment procedures in accordance with the Revised Voluntary Guidelines for the Consideration of Biodiversity in Environmental Impact Assessments and Strategic Environmental Assessments in Marine and Coastal Areas, which were adopted in 2012. Conference of the Parties to the Convention on Biological Diversity, Eleventh Meeting, Hyderabad, India, Marine and Coastal Biodiversity: Revised Voluntary Guidelines for the Consideration of Biodiversity in Environmental Impact Assessments and Strategic Environmental Assessments in Marine and Coastal Areas, Note by the Executive Secretary, UNEP/CBD/COP/11/23 (August 21, 2012), pp. 3~5.

62. Lingjie Kong, "Environmental Impact Assessment under the United Nations Convention on the Law of the Sea," 10 Chinese Journal of International Law

pp. 651, 660~661 (2011). The Regional Seas Program manages 18 regional maritime conventions and action plans, which generally set out only general obligations regarding environmental impact assessment. E.g. OSPAR, OSPAR Code of Conduct for Responsible Marine Research in the Deep-Seas and High Seas of the OSPAR Maritime Area, OSPAR 08/24/1, Annex 6 (2008-1), para. 18 ("If research is planned in an area that contains features on the OSPAR List of Threatened and/or Declining Species and Habitats, a risk assessment should be completed before equipment that may have adverse effects is deployed, and where appropriate, a pre-assessment of the site should be conducted to determine possible impacts and suitable mitigation measures."); Convention for the Protection of the Natural Resources and Environment of the South Pacific Region, November 25, 1986, 26 I.L.M. 38, Article 16(2) ("Each Party shall, within its capabilities, assess the potential effects of such projects on the marine environment, so that appropriate measures can be taken to prevent any substantial pollution of, or significant and harmful changes within, the Convention Area.") [hereinafter the "SPREP Convention"].

63. Council of Managers of National Antarctic Programmes, COMNAP Practical Guidelines for Developing and Designing Environmental Monitoring Programmes in Antarctica, January 2005, https://www.comnap.aq/Publications/ Comnap%20Publications/comnap_guidelines_practicalmonitoring_2005.pdf (accessed on October 15, 2018). The COMNAP provides practical assistance in designing environmental monitoring programs, collects and manages relevant information and plays an advisory role. In addition, a guidebook on the monitoring of the environmental impact of activities carried out at Antarctic research stations was published in 2000 in collaboration with the COMNAP and the Scientific Committee on Antarctic Research (SCAR). Council of Managers of National Antarctic Programmes (COMNAP) & Scientific Committee on Antarctic Research(SCAR), Antarctic Environmental Monitoring Handbook: Standards Techniques for Monitoring in Antarctica (May 2000), https://www. comnap.aq/Publications/Comnap%20Publications/comnap-scar_env_monitoring_ha ndbook_jun2000.pdf (accessed on October 15, 2018).

64. Convention on Environmental Impact Assessment in a Transboundary Context, Feb. 25, 1991, 1989 U.N.T.S. 310, in force September 10, 1997, App. I. The environmental impact assessment procedures under the London Protocol include a screening and scoping process to examine alternative dumping options and potential impact on human health and the environment. There is also a monitoring process to determine whether a dumping activity fulfill the requirements for a permit, including regular review of the permit. Regarding ocean fertilization activities as well, the procedure includes a screening and scoping process to determine whether an activity is subject to the assessment framework in accordance with the 2010 Assessment Framework and the 2013 Resolution, along with a decision-making process to finally determine whether the proposed activity can proceed after the review of the implementation of the monitoring process.

65. Madrid Protocol, Article 8(1). In other words, assessment stages and methods

are divided according to the degree of environmental impact of a planned activity. This approach is deemed to consider the sensitive nature of the Antarctic environment and expand the range of activities covered by the assessment procedures. Under many international instruments such as the UN Environmental Programme Goals and Principles of Environmental Impact Assessment, the Convention on Biological Diversity, the UN Convention on the Law of the Sea, whether a planned activity can proceed is determined based on the review as to whether the activity has a significant impact on the environment. UNEP Goals and Principles of Environmental Impact Assessment, UNEP Res. GC14/25, 14th Sess. (1987), endorsed by GA Res. 42/184, UN GAOR, 42nd Sess., U.N. Doc. A/Res/42/184 (1987), Principle 1("... Where the extent, nature or location of a proposed activity is such that it is likely to significantly affect the environment, a comprehensive environmental impact assessment should be undertaken ...") [hereinafter the "UNEP Goals and Principles of Environmental Impact Assessment"]; Convention on Biological Diversity, Article 14(1)(a) ("[Each Contracting Party shall] introduce appropriate procedures requiring environmental impact assessment of its proposed projects that are likely to have significant adverse effects on biological diversity"); UN Convention on the Law of the Sea, Article 206 ("When States have reasonable grounds for believing that planned activities under their jurisdiction or control may cause substantial pollution of or significant and harmful changes to the marine environment, they shall, as far as practicable, assess the potential effects of such activities on the marine environment ..."). Under the UN Convention on the Law of the Sea, in addition to significant changes in the environment, the substantiality of the pollution and harmful changes in the environment are reviewed to determine whether to initiate an environmental impact assessment.

66. Antarctic Treaty Consultative Meeting XXI, Environmental Impact Assessment – The Role of EIA Guidelines in Understanding "Minor" and "Transitory," Submitted by Australia, XXII ATCM/WP19 (April, 1998); Antarctic Treaty Consultative Meeting XXI, Elements for the interpretation of Environmental Impact Assessment procedures established in Annex I of the Madrid Protocol, Submitted by Argentina, XXI ATCM/IP55 (May, 1997), p. 2.

67. Neil Craik, "The International Law of Environmental Impact Assessment: Process, Substance and Integration," 136 (2008). The difficulty in defining the concepts seems to be attributed to the dependence on many variables related to each planned activity and environmental factors.

68. In the case concerning Mox Plant, there was no disagreement about the environmental impact assessment obligations between the disputing parties, but they disputed over the interpretation of the provisions specifying the obligation in the process of fulfilling the duties due to some obscurities in the provisions. Counter-Memorial of the United Kingdom, MOX Plant (Ir. v. U.K.), (Perm. Ct. Arb. January 9, 2003), pp. 109~121, https://pcacases.com/web/sendAttach/854 (access on October 15, 2018).

69. It is stipulated that in the risk characterization stage, the proposed activity

should be reviewed for its negative impact on the environment based on the hypothesis about its effects established in the problem formulation stage. 2010 Assessment Framework, *op. cit.*, Annex 6, p. 13.

70. The Convention on Environmental Impact Assessment in a Transboundary Context (Espoo Convention) provides a list of activities that are subject to environmental impact assessment. Convention on Environmental Impact Assessment in a Transboundary Context, February 25, 1991, 1989 U.N.T.S. 310 (entered into force September 10, 1997), App. I. In addition, the International Guidelines for the Management of Deep-Sea Fisheries in the High Seas, developed by the UN Food and Agriculture Organization in 2008, designate specific regions as "vulnerable marine ecosystems" (VMEs) and require countries that seek to carry out activities to undertake environmental impact assessments. Food and Agriculture Organization, 2008 Food and Agriculture Organization (FAO) International Guidelines for the Management of Deep-Sea Fisheries in the High Seas, Adopted in Rome, Italy on 29 August 2008, paras. 42~47.

71. In the London Convention system, however, such a role is not assigned to internal organizations. To secure the procedural objectivity of an environmental impact assessment, it is necessary to consider the expansion of the roles of internal organizations such as the Secretariat and the Meeting of Contracting Parties established under the London Convention and Protocol.

72. Under the UN Convention on the Law of the Sea, state parties are required to publish reports on the results of environmental impact assessments or to submit them to relevant international organizations, which make them available to all the other state parties. UN Convention on the Law of the Sea, Article 205.

73. https://www.ats.aq/devAS/ep_eia_list.aspx?lang=e (accessed on March 1, 2019). Initial and comprehensive environmental evaluation reports posted on the official website of the Antarctic Treaty System Secretariat include a description of the planned activities, the type of environmental impact assessments, the location of the activities, and the agencies responsible for the implementation of the environmental impact assessments. Guidelines for Environmental Impact Assessment in Antarctica, Resolution 1 (2016) Annex, ATCM XXXIX ATCM XXXIX – CEP XIX, Santiago, Chile Final Report (May 23, 2016~June 1, 2016), p. 6.

74. 2010 Resolution, *op. cit.*, para. 1.10. It seems that there is no system as of yet to induce the implementation of these recommendations.

75. Madrid Protocol, Article 6(1)(b) and (c).

76. Madrid Protocol, Annex I, Article 3(3).

77. Madrid Protocol, Annex I, Article 3(6).

78. SPREP Convention, Article 16(3). For instance, under the Espoo Convention, only the involvement of the public living in the areas where a planned activity has a significant impact and the parties concerned is required in the environmental impact assessment process. Espoo Convention, Article 3(8). For reference, under the Espoo Convetion system, guidelines on public participation in the environmental impact assessment procedures have been adopted.

Guidance on Public Participation in Environmental Impact Assessment in a Transboundary Context, Meeting of the Parties to the Convention on Environmental Impact Assessment in a Transboundary Context, Report of the Third Meeting, UN Doc. ECE/MP.EIA/6, September 13, 2004, Decision III/8.

79. However, the ATCM and contracting parties to the protocol do not participate in any post environmental impact assessment stages, including monitoring. Multilateral monitoring can put considerable pressure on the parties concerned, and can be very effective in inducing compliance with the assessment results. Regarding the implementation of the results of an environmental impact assessment, it is suggested that the issue be put on the agenda of the ATCM and remain on it until the termination of the activity, and that the parties concerned report progress in the implementation of the environmental impact assessment to the ATCM in written form. This will put considerable pressure on them to implement the assessment results. For reference, in the WTO dispute settlement process, a dispute settlement organization monitors the implementation of the decision made regarding the dispute while the issue is put on the agenda of the organization and remains on it until the dispute is completely settled. In addition, member states concerned are required to report on progress in the implementation of decisions made with regard to the dispute to the organization in written form. Understanding on Rules and Procedures Governing the Settlement of Disputes, 15 April 1994, Marrakesh Agreement Establishing the World Trade Organization, Legal Instruments – Results of the Uruguay Round, 33 I.L.M. 1125, Annex 2 (1994), Article 21(6).

80. Under the Convention on Environmental Impact Assessment in a Transboundary Context, parties have adopted guidelines on public participation in environmental impact assessment procedures. Guidance on Public Participation in Environmental Impact Assessment in a Transboundary Context, Meeting of the Parties to the Convention on Environmental Impact Assessment in a Transbounday Context, Report of the Third Meeting, U.N. Doc. ECE/MP.EIA/6. September 13, 2004, Decision III/8.

81. 2010 Assessment Framework, *op. cit.*, para. 4.

82. 2010 Assessment Framework, *op. cit.*, paras. 1.8~1.9.

83. 2013 Resolution, *op. cit.*, para. 10.

84. 2013 Resolution, *op. cit.*, para. 11.

Current Status and Future Outlook of the Implementation of the Convention Relating to the Status of Refugees in Korea

CHOE Seoji
Lecturer
University of Seoul Law School, Seoul, Korea

Abstract

Beginning with the Yemen refugee incident in Jeju Island in 2018, there has been a lot of discussion regarding refugees in Korea, which has previously not been a significant issue. The people, who have been living in a traditional mono-ethnic nation, have demanded high standards regarding the recognition of the status of refugees while recalling the adverse effects that have affected some Western nations, and in response, some lawmakers have proposed the abolition of the Refugee Act. It is imperative that Korea recognizes its low refugee recognition rate and takes a more proactive stance to accommodating refugees if it is to maintain its status as an advanced nation in the world, and the country urgently needs to establish reasonable plans to resolve confusion in this situation in which there is a mixture of vague anxiety regarding its inexperience in handling such situations.

Based on such domestic sentiments, the Ministry of Justice is preparing amendments to the Refugee Act, and issues relating to such areas as the refugee screening system, refugee screening at ports of entry, force repatriation, and expedited screening are being discussed among experts. We intend to establish the direction of improvement moving forward based on the matters that need to be considered regarding the accommodation of refugee applicants.

Key Words

Amendment to the Refugee Act, Forced repatriation system, Expedited screening system, Refugee screening, Port of entry refugee screening system, Domestic implementation of the Refugee Act

1. INTRODUCTION

In 2013, the Republic of Korea (hereinafter, "Korea") became the first country in Asia to establish the Refugee Act to determine whether refugees can be legally recognized as such, thereby laying the groundwork for adhering to the International Convention Relating to the Status of Refugees. In addition to refugees generally recognized under the Convention Relating to the Status of Refugees, Korea recognizes 'humanitarian sojourners' and 'refugees seeking resettlement,' thereby extending the scale of recognition of refugees than set forth by the International Convention Relating to the Status of Refugees within Korea.

However, due to the sudden influx of refugee applications from Yemen on Jeju Island, Korea in 2018, new discussions on the recognition of refugee status have been underway in Korea. Such discussions are linked with the existing revisions to the Refugee Act, which now has been amended by the National Assembly a total of fourteen times, and the Ministry of Justice is also preparing amendments to the Refugee Act. The main issues in the amendments of the Refugee Act include the conditions for exclusion from application of the Refugee Act and forced repatriation, the conditions of refusal of refugee recognition for domestically made applications and applications made at an entry and departure port, the definitions of humanitarian sojourners and resettled refugees, applications for refugee reimbursement without changes in circumstances, and improving procedural speed and accuracy.

This paper examines the status of refugees in domestic law and related domestic precedents with a focus on amendments to the Refugee Act in Korea, and compares and analyzes the main contents of the amendments to the Refugee Act pending in the National Assembly, with the aim of forecasting the future direction of the Refugee Act in Korea.

2. LEGAL STATUS OF REFUGEES IN KOREA AND STATUS OF REFUGEES

2-1. Legal Status of Refugees in Korea

The legal status of refugees in Korea has changed considerably since 2013 when the status of refugees recognized based on the procedures regarding the recognition of refugees set forth in the Immigration Control Act were reinforced through the enactment of the Refugee Act in 2012. This was the result of policy in Korea that aims for more effective national enforcement of international human rights norms, such as the '1951 Convention Related to the Status of Refugees' and the '1967 Protocol Relating to the Status of Refugees.' The enactment of the Refugee Act not only made Korea the first country in Asia to establish an independent Refugee Act, but also includes recognized refugees,[1] humanitarian sojourners,[2] and refugees seeking to resettle,[3] so it is evaluated to be compliant with the basic principles of the International Convention Related to the Status of Refugees.

2-2. Recent Status of Refugee Applications

Since the enactment of the Refugee Act in 2013, refugee applicants have increased rapidly every year until recently. In 2018,

16,173 people applied for refugee status, and between January and November 2019, 14,065 people applied.[4] Among the applicants, there were three times more men than women, with Pakistani and Chinese nationalities accounting for the majority.[5]

[Table 1] Refugee Status Applications (by year, by gender, by nationality) Statistical Table   [Unit: persons]

Classification		2011	2012	2013	2014	2015	2016	2017	2018
Gender	Male	909	1,039	1,366	2,403	4,814	6,147	7,825	12,126
	Female	102	104	208	493	897	1,395	2,117	4,047
Nationality	Pakistan	434	242	275	396	1,143	809	667	1,120
	Egypt	4	7	97	568	812	1,002	741	870
	China	8	3	45	360	401	1,061	1,413	1,199
	Syria	2	146	295	204	404	171	103	64
	Nigeria	39	102	207	201	264	324	486	390
	Other	524	643	655	1,167	2,687	4,175	6,532	12,530
		1,011	1,143	1,574	2,896	5,711	7,542	9,942	16,173

Source: Statistical Yearbook of Immigration and Foreigner Policy, Ministry of Justice[6]

In contrast with this, the refugee recognition rate has been just 3.7% among all refugee applicants between 1994 and November 2019. In addition, the refugee protection rate (refugee recognition rate and humanitarian stay rate), which includes humanitarian sojourners who are not refugees but are also eligible to stay in the country, is 11.7%.[7]

[Table 2] Results of Refugee Application Examinations   [Unit: cases]

Classification Year	Examination completed	Refugee Recognition (Protection)					Denied
		Subtotal	Approved	Humanitarian stay	Approval rate	Protection rate	
Sum	27,154	3,163	997	2,166	3.7%	11.7%	23,991
1994~2012	2,646	495	324	171	12.2%	18.7%	2,151
2013	523	63	57	6	10.9%	1.2%	460
2014	1,574	627	94	533	6%	40%	947
2015	2,755	303	105	198	3.8%	11%	2,452
2016	5,665	350	98	252	1.7%	62%	5,315
2017	5,876	438	121	317	2.1%	7.4%	5,438
2018	3,964	652	144	508	3.6%	16.4%	3,312
Jan. ~ Nov. 2019	4,151	235	54	181	1.3%	4.4%	3,916

Source: Monthly Report on the Statistics of Immigration and Foreigner Policy[8]

This shows that although the number of refugee status applicants has significantly increased since this enactment of the Refugee Act, it seems that there are various reasons for applications. In other words, as the legal status of refugees in Korea is strengthened, the number of so-called 'false refugees' seeking to stay legally by obtaining refugee status in Korea is increasing.[9] For example, there have been many cases where people have applied for refugee status as illegal immigrants in order to take advantage of the fact that refugee examinations can take several years with the aim of extending their stay in the country. In particular, the fact that the vast majority of refugee applicants are young men[10] is naturally reminiscent of the problems associated with refugees previously in Western society. It is true that the 'genuine refugees' who can be granted refugee status under the Refugee Act will be disadvantaged due to these 'false refugee' applicants. As a result, those false refugee applicants are recognized as a potential threat in Korea, and this movement has been expressed in the way of making petitions to Blue House.[11]

This seems to be due to confusion of the meanings of refugee, refugee applicant and illegal immigrant. The Convention Related to the Status of Refugees defines refugees in long sentences, but these can be divided into four parts as follows. i) The person must be outside of his/her country of nationality, ii) if the person returns to his/her country of nationality, he/she may be persecuted for race, nationality or ethnicity, religion, political views, membership in a particular social group, iii) the person must have a well-founded fear, iv) and protection against such matters from the person's country of nationality may not be reasonably expected. This can be interpreted as protecting the human rights not only of those who have been persecuted in the past, but also of those who are likely to be persecuted in the future, for the protection of human rights, which is the core purpose of the Convention Related to the Status of Refugees. On the other hand, the term illegal immigrants refers to cases where the refugee application system is abused to increase the length of stay in Korea. It mainly refers to those who have illegally immigrated to a foreign country while violating the immigration control laws of the country to which they are immigrating, and they generally migrate for economic reasons.[12] Unless exact standards and regulations related to the status of refugees are established, as I have seen in previous European precedents, it is difficult to erase the image of refugees as being illegal immigrants staying to engage in economic activities only.

3. STANDARDS RELATING TO THE RECOGNITION OF REFUGEES IN KOREAN COURT CASES

In Korea, the policy recognizing the status of refugees has not only taken a long time to be established, but has the distinct characteristic of being dependent on the judicial judgment of a single country. Nevertheless, it is not easy to gather and analyze the procedures and contents related to refugee status recognition, and there are limitations with regards to accessing precedents. The criteria for refugee recognition are described based on cases related to refugee recognition in Korea.

3-1. Possibility of Persecution

The term persecution mainly refers to 'serious violation of human rights,' not just discrimination, considering the purpose and intent of the Convention Related to the Status of Refugees and the nature of alternative protection described by the Convention. This can be inferred from the status of execution of the judiciary[13] as the criteria for judging the degree of infringement differ according to the type of human rights violated. In addition paragraph 51 of the

Manual on Refugees[14] also states that "threat to the life or freedom of an individual always falls under persecution. Other serious human rights violations are considered to be persecution for the same reason."[15]

First, there is a ruling[16] that recognizes that female circumcision for being a member of a particular social group violates human dignity and constitutes 'persecution.' In other words, it was ruled that there was a risk of a repatriated refugee being circumcised against his/her will, and it was recognized that it would be unreasonable to expect sufficient protection from the person's country of nationality, so the case fell under the condition of there being 'reasonable evidence that the refugee would be persecuted' as defined by the Refugee Act.[17]

There is a ruling in which 'homosexuality' does not fall under persecution requiring international protection.[18] In other words, if the homosexual orientation or gender identity of the person is disclosed to the outside, it may be contrary to the moral code of the person's country of origin, and the person may be subjected to hostility and condemnation from family, neighbors, and the general public; however, the 'decision to conceal one's sexual orientation to avoid such social stigma, dishonor, and humiliation' may be an unfair social constraint, but it does not correspond to 'persecution' as described in the Convention, that is, persecution of a refugee applicant requiring international protection.[19]

In contrast, there was a ruling that determined that if serious violation of human dignity or discrimination occurs, such as threats to life, body, or freedom, beyond the usual social stigma due to the sexual orientation of the refugee applicant, this falls under persecution as described in the Convention.[20]

In addition, there was a ruling that determined that having to conceal one's religion due to the possibility of being discriminated against by the state, thereby resulting in "deprivation of freedom to conduct religious events" does not constitute persecution.[21]

3-2. Well-Founded Fear

A well-founded fear in the Convention Related to the Status of Refugees basically means 'fear that has a sufficient basis.' There are such problems as the expression of the word 'fear' and 'sufficient basis.' It means that it is not only judgment regarding the possibility of the refugee applicant being subjected to persecution, but the person's subjective feelings are also included as criteria, and with regards to recognition of refugee status, not only the person's psychological state is considered, but that psychological state must be backed by objective circumstances.[22] This is composed of the subjective element of 'fear' and the object element of 'sufficient basis' in accordance with the Paragraph 37 and Paragraph 38 of the United Nations High Commissioner for Refugees (UNHCR) Manual (hereinafter "UNHCR Manual")[23], and with regards to recognition of refugee status, taking the two elements into full consideration is in line with traditional views.[24]

In response, the Supreme Court ruled that the "foreigner" applying for recognition as a refugee must prove that there is 'well-founded fear' that he/she will be subject to 'persecution' required for recognition as a refugee.[25]

There is also a ruling in which it was determined that, given the special circumstances of refugees whose evidence is not readily available, proof should be considered complete when it is reasonable to accept the matters claimed by the foreigner based on objective evidence.[26] In addition, there is a ruling in which a foreigner who entered the country using another person's passport had a 'well-founded fear of persecution' by the government of his/her country of origin due to having been actively engaged in activities to improve human rights in his/her country of origin while in Korea.[27]

3-3. Degree of Proof

A well-founded fear regards persecution, which leads to the question of how likely the possibility of persecution must be in order to be considered reasonable, and this is related to the degree of proof. However, considering the unique characteristics of refugees, it is the opinion of most courts and the mainstream of academic society that, in light of the purpose and intent of protecting the human rights of refugees, the required degree of proof should only be that there is a reasonable possibility that persecution may occur.[28] In addition, unde Paragraph 196 of the UNHCR Manual, where there is a question of credibility, the principle of 'benefit of the doubt' for the refugee applicant is the rule of thumb. Unlike what is indicated in the manual credibility is not a matter of truth, meaning that even if a refugee applicant's statement is unlikely to be true, the credibility of the statement can be acknowledged, and this is due to the special circumstances of the refugee, such as the social and psychological vulnerability of refugee applicants (such as memory limitations, language and cultural barriers) and the potential distressthat could be experienced by the refugee as a consequence of misjudgment.[29]

Firstly, there is a case in which the degree of proof to be provided by the refugee is "simple possibility."[30] In Myanmar, for example, it is 'possible' that refugee applicants may be arrested and tortured if they are forcibly returned. there is a case where it was recognized that if a person who had returned without appropriate documents such as a valid passport made an application for refugee status but was refused, because there is a 'possibility' that such person could be sentenced to extremely severe punishment for illegal departure/ entry, such 'simple possibility' was found to satisfy refugee justice.[31]

In contrast, there have been cases in which a "relatively high degree of proof" has been required. For example, there was a case[32] in which a refugee applicant from near the Northwestern border of

Pakistan, bordering Afghanistan, claimed that he had been persecuted in ways such as the Taliban bombing his home due to the fact that he had provided the Pakistani government with information on the Taliban; however, the refugee applicant had never been abducted by the Taliban, and it was ruled that there was no evidence to support the claim that the Taliban had bombed his house.[33]

4. KEY ISSUES RELATED TO THE AMENDMENT OF THE REFUGEE ACT IN 2013

4-1. Discussions on Amendments to the Refugee Act in 2013

In addition to the enactment of the Refugee Act in 2013, the entry barrier for refugee applicants has been lowered due to the visa waiver entry system operated in Jeju Special Self-Governing Province. However, despite the provisions of Korea's progressive Refugee Act, the large number of refugee applications by Yemeni refugees on Jeju Island in 2018 has raised various problems in Korean society. In order to cope with such problems, the National Assembly and the Ministry of Justice have been preparing amendments to the Refugee Act 2013. In particular, the Ministry of Justice increased the number of refugee screening officers at the Jeju Immigration and Foreign Affairs Office from four to ten on June 29, 2018 to prepare for the amendments to the Refugee Act and increase the speed of refugee applicant screening process.[34] In addition, various opinions have been raised in domestic public opinion regarding the amendments to the Refugee Act. Regarding the revision of the Refugee Act as it relates to the Jeju refugee crisis, the Ministry of Justice expressed on August 1, 2018 its position to maintain the current Refugee Act through efforts to prevent entry examination of 'false refugees.'[35] As such, the domestic impact caused by the surge in refugee applicants since the enactment of the Refugee Act in 2013 is rather large.

4-2. Exclusion from Application of the Refugee Act and Forced Repatriation

Article 3 of the Refugee Act states that "No recognized refugee, humanitarian sojourner, nor refugee applicant shall be repatriated compulsorily against his/her will under Article 39 of the Refugee Convention and Article 3 of the Convention against Torture and Other Cruel, Inhuman or Degrading Treatment or Punishment." In the planned amendment thereto, i) persons who have good reason to be considered a threat to national security or who are convicted of a serious crime prescribed by Presidential Decree and who are dangerous to the national community, and ii) recognized refugees, humanitarian sojourners and refugee applicants may be repatriated in accordance with Article 32 of the Refugee Convention for reasons of national security or public order, in which case, due process must be made in accordance with the law, and procedures for making an appeal shall be recognized except where inevitable for national security.[36]

Although the principle of prohibition of forced repatriation applies, the way in which this principle is implemented can be chosen by each country. The adoption of summary procedure, which differs from formal procedure, is not in itself a violation of the principle of prohibition of force repatriation. The problem is that if the review process is simplified and the procedural guarantees are weakened, the possibility of false repatriation will be realistically increased.[37] Although it is necessary to systematically overhaul the refugee screening standards for the continuously increasing number of refugee applications, there is the opinion that it seems undesirable to discuss domestic measures to neutralize the principle of prohibiting forced repatriation,[38] which is a peremptory norm and not just international customary law.

4-3. Refugee Screening Requirements

Before the Refugee Act was enacted, refugee application procedures at ports of entry were not recognized. Therefore, persons who sought to apply for refugee status had to apply for temporary landing permission first, and after entering Korea with the temporary landing permission, they were able to then apply for refugee status. However, the Refugee Act currently permits people to make refugee applications at entry ports.[39]

The original intention of the system that allows for refugee application at the port of entry was for the purpose of protecting refugee applicants through prompt recognition of their refugee status; however, in the case of the Refugee Act in Korea, there is constant criticism regarding the insufficient guarantee of human rights such as difficult to claim right, lack of external assistance, unfair treatment, and problems with examination practices. According to the current operation of the Ministry of Justice, foreigners who have applied for refugee status at the port of entry are made to wait in a designated location, and there have been many legal debates and amendments to the law regarding whether accommodation in the designated location is actually detainment, what the basis for it is, and who is operating the designated location.[40]

If the Minister of Justice decides not to refer the reflicant for recognition screening, that is, in the case of there being a decision to refuse to conduct the refugee recognition screening, the question is what to do next. There are those who are of the opinion that it should be clearly stipulated in the Act or the Enforcement Decree of the Act to enable those who disagree with the refusal decision to be included as 'applicants for refugee recognition' under Article 2 (4) of the Refugee Act, so that the regulations on the treatment of refugee applicants.[41] Despite the long history of implementing the refugee screening system, expanding informal procedures can compromise the guarantee of fairness. In addition, there are concerns that under the current conditions, where the number of personnel dedicated to screening refugee applicants is insufficient it will not contribute positively to the protection of refugee applicants.

4-4. Refugee Application without Change of Circumstances

Article 8 of the Refugee Act provides for a prompt process for screening that can omit parts of the screening procedure if certain requirements[42] are met. This has been criticized for severely limiting the right to fair refugee screening, and there is a problem in that there are no precise standards for 'change of circumstances' in the case of a person applying for refugee status again without material change of circumstances. However, the change of circumstances cannot be identified without a detailed interview or investigation of facts, so it is important to provide refugee applicants with sufficient opportunity to prove his or her change of circumstances. In fact, many of the reapplicants who requested consultation with the UNHCR were deemed to be 'false' applicants and were refused permission to stay despite the reasons for reapplying due to changes in the situation in their respective countries.[43]

With regards to this, under 'Decision to Disqualify from Refugee Screening' in Article 5 (2) of the amended Act proposed by the Ministry of Justice, if a person who has previously been disqualified from making an application for refugee status, a person who has been refused recognition as a refugee, or a person for whom the decision to grant recognition as a refugee has been canceled/revoked expresses his or her intention to obtain refugee status such as by reapplying, etc., and there is objective evidence resulting in the person being disqualified from refugee screening, there should be no further review and the case should be dismissed.[44] In this case, if the refugee himself/herself proves that there is material change in circumstances or that refugee screening is necessary, there is room for discretionary interpretation to prevent the decision to disqualify. There is room for criticism as to whether the burden of proof on refugee applicants is excessive.

4-5. Acceleration and Accuracy of Procedures

In 2018, there was a partial amendment of the Enforcement Decree of the Refugee Act by the Ministry of Justice. Such amendments were not made for the purpose of guaranteeing the rights of refugee applicants, but rather for procedural convenience. The changes made were: i) the decision to issue a notification of refusal to provide refugee recognition screening in cases where it has been decided not to grant refugee recognition screening for refugee applicants at a port of entry by establishing the grounds for issuing a notification of refusal to grant refugee screening,[45] ii) establishment of the grounds for issuance of receipts for appeal applications to applicants when an application for appeal has been submitted to the chief of the local Immigration and Foreign Affairs Office regarding an appeal to a decision to refuse refugee recognition to a person who has applied for refugee status,[46] iii) to delegate the authority for the operation of refugee support facilities to the Director of the Immigration and Foreign Resident Support Center in order to efficiently carry out support services for refugee applicants.[47]

5. CONCLUSION

I have examined some of the problems that have been consistently raised in Korea for the last six years since the enactment of the Refugee Act, and I have reviewed where improvements can be made through amendments to the Act. Some provisions in the amendments proposed by the Ministry of Justice set a positive direction for ensuring procedural fairness and efficiency while also enhancing the protection of refugees. Examples of positive proposed amendments include the proposal to establish a basic plan to support refugees every five years, the proposal to provide notification of the reasons for refusal to grant recognition of refugee status in a language that the applicant can understand, the proposal to establish the grounds for making an appeal application regarding a decision to refuse recognition of refugee status, and the proposal of a plan to provide the opportunity to applicants to provide a written opinion at the committee level.

In particular, it may seem at first glance that the denial of refugee status by the court due to hearings on cases brought forth by individuals without a lawyer and accumulated cases, is becoming more prominent; however, as can be seen in cases of the District Court described above in which the opinions of the refugee applicant are considered, it is possible to expect healthy development of procedures. The qualitative development of court cases that can present the administrative office with the screening standards, and the fact that discussions among the relevant institutions regarding the amendment of the Refugee Act are underway, will inevitably lead to conflict, but can be expected to lay the foundation for development in a desirable direction.

As the number of refugee applicants continues to increase, discussions that have previously not been made continue to progress. Although sufficient discussion and understanding are necessary as they directly affect the real life of the people, there are also problems properly understanding refugee applicants due to over-reporting on just a few negative phenomena. It is hoped that through reasonable discussion based on understanding refugees, Korea will have the opportunity to develop into a more mature society that can accommodate persons from other countries.

Notes

1. Article 2 (2) of the Refugee Act.
2. Article 2 (3) of the Refugee Act.
3. Article 2 (5) of the Refugee Act.
4. Annual Report, Korea Immigration Service 2019, http://www.moj.go.kr/moj/2411/subview.do (Last visit on January 20, 2020).
5. Ministry of Justice, Immigration Statistics, http://www.moj.go.kr/moj/2417/subview.do (Last visit on January 20, 2020).
6. Korea Policy Briefing, Statistical Yearbook of Immigration and Foreigner Policy 2018, http://www.korea.kr/archive/expDocView.do?docId=38725 (Last visit on January 14, 2020).
7. Recognition of Refugees a Pie in the Sky... Only 1.9% of Applicants Accepted Last Year, *The Hankyoreh*, June 15, 2019, http://www.hani.co.kr/arti/society/rights/898027.html (Last visit on January 14, 2020).
8. Monthly Report on the Statistics of Immigration and Foreigner Policy Nov. 2019, Immigration and Foreigner Policy Division http://www.korea.kr/archive/expDocView.do?docId=38764 (Last visit on January 14, 2020).
9. South Korea Is Going Crazy Over a Handful of Refugees, August 6, 2018, https://foreignpolicy.com/2018/08/06/south-korea-is-going-crazy-over-a-handful-of-refugees/.
10. Ministry of Justice, Immigration Statistics, http://www.moj.go.kr/moj/2417/subview.do (Last visit on January 20, 2020).
11. Petitions to Blue House, The National Petition of South Korea is a political communication effort to address citizen concerns in South Korea.
12. Minyeong Kim, Research on international migration according to the dispatch activities of the International Organization for Migration (IMO) and on the direction of refugee policy in Korea, Immigration and Foreigner Policy Division of the Ministry of Justice, 2018.8, p. 106.
13. Il Lee, Critical Analysis of Conditions for Refugee Status in Korean Cases, Private Law 2019 Vol. 47, 2019.2, p. 47.
14. Handbook on Procedures and criteria for Determining Refugee Status under the 1951 Convention and the 1967 Protocol relating to the Status of Refugees.
15. Paragraph 51, Manual on Refugees.
16. Supreme Court 2017.12.5. Ruling 2016Du42913.
17. Inseop Jeong, Judgment on international law in our court, Seoul International Law Research Vol. 25 Edition 2 (2018), p. 301.
18. Seoul High Court 2016.10.6. Ruling 2016Nu38619.
19. Seoul High Court 2016.10.6. Ruling 2016Nu38619.
20. Supreme Court 2017.1.11. Ruling 2016Du56080.
21. Announced on 2018.1.18. Ruling 2017Nu74803.

22. Bokhui Jang, "Well-founded fear of persecution" as defined by the Convention Related to the Status of Refugees, Korean Journal of Humanitarian Law (24), Korean Red Cross Institute for Human Rights, 2004.7, p. 112.

23. Handbook on Procedures and criteria for Determining Refugee Status under the 1951 Convention and the 1967 Protocol relating to the Status of Refugees.

24. Yeonghwa Moon, Unique characteristics of refugee litigation and burden of proof regarding 'well-founded fear of persecution' – Supreme Court 2013.12.12. Ruling 2011Du12689 -, Sungkyunkwan University Law Vol. 30 Edition 1, 2018.3, p. 50.

25. Supreme Court 2013.4.25. Ruling 2012Du14378.

26. Supreme Court 2008.7.24. Ruling 2007Du3930.

27. Supreme Court 2017.3.9. Ruling 2013Du16852.

28. [Notes] Understanding the degree and methods of proof and passing judgment on credibility in refugee cases, Appeal to the Public Interest Law Center, http://apil.or.kr/?p=3008 (Last visit on January 14, 2020).

29. Jongcheol Kim, Critical review of cases of refugee justice in Korea, Seoul International Law Research Vol. 21, Edition 2, 2014.12, p. 61.

30. UNHCR Manual.

31. Seoul Administrative Court 2010.11.11. Ruling 2010Gu-hap21624.

32. Seoul Administrative Court 2010.4.8. Ruling 2009Gu-hap49619.

33. The Kyunghyang Shinmun, November 23, 2017, http://news.khan.co.kr/kh_news/khan_art_view.html?art_id=201711232146015.

34. The Hankyoreh, "Ministry of Justice cuts Yemen refugee screening time from 8 months to 2 to 3 months," 2018.6.29. http://www.hani.co.kr/arti/society/society_general/851201.html#csidx2ccd1fadddd13fb9b0e1b5245fc1885 (Last visit on January 14, 2020).

35. Ministry of Justice, http://www.immigration.go.kr/immigration/1567/subview.do.

36. The Ministry of Justice's amendments to the Refugee Act have not yet been submitted to the National Assembly and have not been made public. The planned amendments above are cited from the Symposium on the Refugee Act Amendment, co-hosted by the Korean Bar Association and UNHCR Korea in November 2019. Dongyeong Noh, Symposium on the Direction of Amendment of the Refugee Act, Principle of Prohibition of Repatriation, and Archives from the Symposium on the Direction of Amendment of the Refugee Act, P. 15.

37. Gyeyeong Choi, "Due Process of Refugee Application Procedures at Immigration Ports," 'Status and Tasks of the Refugee Act' (Public Interest and Human Rights 30), 2019, 9-10, p. 13.

38. Dongyeong Noh, Direction of Amendments to the Refugee Act and the Principle of Prohibiting Forced Repatriation, Research on Law and Policy, 2019.9, p. 483.

39. Article 6 of the Refugee Act.

40. Korean Bar Association, 2018 Human Rights Report p. 190, (Last visit on January 14, 2020).

41. Hyeon Lim, Evaluation and Tasks Related to the Refugee Act, The Legislative System Edition 1, Office of Legislation 2014, p. 42.

42. It is prescribed in the Refugee Act Article 8. https://elaw.klri.re.kr/kor_service/lawView.do?hseq=43622&lang=ENG.

43. Hyeonyeong Chae, "Direction of Improvement for Refugee Applications and Recognition Procedures in the Republic of Korea," 「Refugee Human Rights and Justice」 Seminar, Korea Institute of International Law (2017), pp. 41~42.

44. Dongyeong Noh, Direction of Amendment to the Refugee Act and the Principle of Prohibition of Forced Repatriation, Archives from the Symposium on the Direction of Improvement for the Refugee Act, P. 22.

45. Article 5 of the Enforcement Decree of the Refugee Act.

46. Article 9 (2) of the Enforcement Decree of the Refugee Act.

47. Article 24 (2) of the Enforcement Decree of the Refugee Act.

SPECIAL REPORTS

Trade and Politics in Recent Trade Measures by the United States and Japan: An Effect on Korea

LEE Yong–Shik
Director and Professorial Fellow
The Law and Development Institute, USA
Visiting Professor of Law
Georgia State University School of Law, USA

Key Words

Trade and Politics, GATT Article XXI, National Security, United States, Japan

1. INTRODUCTION

Since President Trump came into power, the United States administration has introduced the use of national security arguments to restrict imports from its trade partners for commercial reasons. I recently warned that the U.S. use of security arguments to justify its additional tariffs on steel and aluminum imports would create a dangerous precedent,[1] and shortly after that Japan - another major trading nation indeed followed this precedent.

This special report introduces the U.S. trade measures that invoked the national security argument and explains their inconsistency with the rules of international trade law under the auspices of the

World Trade Organization (WTO). In the second part, the report discusses the subsequent trade measure by Japan against imports from the Republic of Korea (hereinafter, "Korea") and its implications for the bilateral trade relations between Korea and Japan and for the international trade order beyond the two countries. The report warns the danger of using the national security argument to justify trade measures adopted for commercial purposes and the (mis)use of trade measures to impose political agenda.

2. U.S. STEEL AND ALUMINUM TARIFFS[2]

On March 8, 2018, President Trump announced the 25 percent and 10 percent increases in tariffs on steel and aluminum products, respectively, to be effective as of March 23, 2018.[3] The U.S. Department of Commerce had conducted investigations into the effect of imports of steel and aluminum products on the national security of the United States under section 232 of the Trade Expansion Act of 1962,[4] generating two reports by January of 2018.[5] The investigation reports found that steel and aluminum are essential to U.S. national security, but domestic industries producing these products have been weakened due to increases in imports.[6] Based on these findings, the reports concluded that it was necessary to adopt measures that will reduce imports of these steel and aluminum products to strengthen two industries deemed essential to national security.[7] Pursuant to this conclusion, the Secretary of Commerce recommended tariffs or quotas on steel and aluminum, and President Trump subsequently imposed the tariffs.[8]

The U.S. tariffs are among the largest trade measures in history – affecting $29 billion of steel trade and $17 billion of aluminum trade. The products subject to these measures are also extensive, including all imported products of iron or steel[9] as well as all entries of aluminum products.[10] These extensive U.S. measures invoked worldwide criticism and challenges from major steel and aluminum exporting countries, including the European Union (EU), China, Japan, Mexico, Canada, India, Norway, Russia, Switzerland, and Turkey.[11] Several of the affected WTO Members (Members), including the EU, China, Mexico, Canada, Russia, India, and Turkey, adopted retaliatory measures in the form of their own tariff increases on imports from the United States.[12] These countries did not agree that the U.S. measures were justified by its national security concerns, but instead concluded that they were a disguised trade protection inconsistent with WTO rules.[13]

GATT Article XXI, which authorizes trade measures to protect essential national security interests, is designed to cover situations in which Members feel that they need to adopt trade-restrictive measures necessary to protect national security interests.[14] This type of trade restrictions to protect national security, such as a war-time trade restriction imposed on materials that are used to build weapons, trade control of fissionable material that could be made into dangerous nuclear devices, and trade sanctions adopted according to a United Nations resolution, is well justifiable. However, the inherent difficulty with an exception of this nature is the possibility of abuse. There was a suggestion to limit the use of any national security exception to a decision by the United Nations Security Council.[15] There is indeed a risk that Article XXI measures might be applied unilaterally and arbitrarily without any consensus and thus undermine the multilateral trading system in the absence of such a joint decision or resolution.[16]

The United States invoked Article XXI to justify its trade measures and argued that the justification under Article XXI is self-judging.[17] This view is supported by some academic literature,[18] but this proposition is predicated on the presumption that it will be exercised with wisdom and in good faith,[19] which is questionable in the U.S. tariff case. Obviously, the WTO system will not be sustainable if a Member is authorized to do anything that it claims necessary to protect an identified essential security interest, and several WTO members have criticized the U.S. steel and aluminum tariffs as being unjustified under GATT Article XXI and rather being adopted as a disguised trade protection.[20] The United States has attempted to protect the declining domestic steel and aluminum industries for decades, imposing a number of trade measures;[21] thus, given the history of trade protection, switching to Article XXI under the umbrella of national security has not inspired much credibility to the other Members.[22]

The U.S. investigations leading to the Steel and Aluminum Reports have demonstrated neither the existence of essential security interests in the protection of a broad range of infrastructural needs, nor a reasoned explanation of the necessity of said tariffs to protect essential security interests. The Reports did not consider all relevant factors, such as the availability of less-trade restrictive measures. There is no provision in the DSU to support the U.S. claim that its tariffs are a self-judging matter, unreviewable by the WTO, and WTO jurisprudence also does not support the U.S. claim that the question of national security is not reviewable by the DSB.[23] The questionable U.S. (mis)use of the national security argument is a concerning precedent that could be followed by other trading nations, which further disrupts the international trading system. The danger is illustrated by the following export restraint measure adopted by Japan.

3. MIMICKING PRESIDENT TRUMP? – JAPAN'S EXPORT RESTRAINT MEASURES AGAINST KOREA[24]

On July 1, 2019, the Japanese government announced the exclusion of Korea from a group of countries ("the white list") that benefited from a simpler approval process for the exportation of materials and items that Japan considers "strategic," because they can be converted into military use. Initially this exclusion covered three items that are essential to produce Korea's key export product: semiconductors, namely, photo resists, hydrogen fluoride (HF) and fluorinated polyimides.[25] Japan's measure does not prohibit the exportation of the said items *per se*, but it requires a tighter approval process for each export request, which may take up to 90 days, at the end of which there is no guarantee of approval. This measure creates substantial uncertainty from the perspective of both exporters and importers. In the worst scenario, IT industries worldwide could have been devastated if the supply of semiconductors from Korea, which supplies up 70 percent of the global market, were to be disrupted.

Despite these concerns, the Japanese government escalated the situation. On August 2, it decided to expand on its earlier measure and exclude Korea from the white list with respect to all the other strategic export items beyond the initial three.[26] The Japanese government justified its measure in terms of its security concern over the exportation of such items, but it is widely considered to be an act of retribution to the supreme court decision in Korea that ordered the Japanese companies to provide compensation for the Koreans who were forced to work by the Japanese government during the Second World War.[27] The Japanese government protested against this decision claiming that it had already offered compensation in the treaty made between Korea and Japan in 1965. The Korean court found, however, that the treaty did not exclude the claim of a private person for the compensation.

It is also possible, however, that Japan's measure had a commercial objective – as many suspect the same of President Trump's use of tariffs on steel and aluminum and his threat to use them on automobiles. Japan's measure may have been motivated by its desire to keep Korea in check; Korea has become a major competitor to Japan in important product categories that Japan once dominated, such as home electronics and semiconductors.[28] Korean manufacturers, such as Samsung, plan to expand their production into new areas, such as the next generation of systems semiconductors which use new production technologies that require materials from Japan. The Korean semiconductor manufacturers rely on the supply of these items from Japan,[29] and finding alternative suppliers might prove to be difficult, if not impossible.

Irrespective of its motives, Japan's export measure is unprecedented: it is Japan's first use of the national security argument for a trade restriction, and it is the first trade measure since the establishment of the WTO system in which a high income country specifically targeted another such country and tightened exports over a security concern. Prior to the U.S. steel and aluminum tariffs, WTO members had rarely used national security as a justification for a trade measure, without there being a resolution by the United Nations.[30] Thus it is highly plausible that Japan felt that those tariffs offered cover for its own measure. It is true that the U.S. measure is an import measure while Japan's an export one, but this distinction is immaterial: both use the national security argument to restrict the trade of their trading partners to meet their own economic and political interests.

Even more concerning, Japan has gone beyond the U.S. precedent. President Trump used national security as a cover for his tariffs, but he did not single out a particular country under this measure.[31] Similarly, while the United States and many other countries also have export control regimes in place for products that could be used for military purposes, none has removed a country from a group that had simplified approval processes, other than for obviously security-related reasons.

Given the concerns, the compatibility of Japan's measure with

WTO rules requires an examination. Japan argues that its measure does not breach WTO rules, as it does not restrict exports to Korea but merely moves Korea from one administrative group of countries to another.[32] However, this "reclassification" constitutes a discriminatory trade practice against Korea vis-à-vis the other exempted countries; thus, it is a prima facie violation of GATT Article I that requires the Most Favored Nation (MFN) treatment and prohibits discriminatory trade practice, unless there is a defense under other WTO provisions. Since Japan argues the national security justification, the relevant provision is GATT Article XXI. Article XXI authorizes a WTO member to take "any action which it considers necessary for *the protection of its essential security interests,*" [emphasis added] including measures that would otherwise be in breach of Article I.

The question is whether an exporting country may move one country from a favored group to another less-favored group in absence of a genuine security concern. Arguably, Article XXI does not cover this. Moreover, recent case law suggests that the determination of the legitimacy of using Article XXI is not at the sole discretion of the exporting country. The U.S. has claimed that measures taken under Article XXI are self-judging, rendering them unreviewable by the WTO, but no provision under the WTO Dispute Settlement Understanding (DSU) supports such an exclusion, and a recent WTO panel has found that it has jurisdiction to review Article XXI matters.[33] Previous panels and the Appellate Body have clarified the applicable standard of review (i.e., they will not conduct a *de novo* review of the national authorities' investigations), but they will nevertheless require the WTO member to evaluate all relevant factors and provide a reasoned and adequate explanation of how the facts support their determinations. Arguably, Japan has not offered such an explanation as to why trade with Korea poses a security concern that necessitates the country's reclassification into the group requiring a tighter review.

As of June 3, 2020, the dispute has not been resolved. As announced, the Japanese government excluded Korea from its white list on August 28, 2019, and Korea responded by excluding Japan from its own white list. Considerable concerns have been raised by businesses, policy makers, scholars, and the general public in both countries and around the world. Japan has reportedly declined U.S. mediation and a request to put the planned exclusion of Korea from the white list on hold. Both countries have failed to come to a resolution, and Korea has resumed the WTO proceedings against Japan's measure that it had suspended for talks. Regardless of the ultimate outcome, the dispute illustrates the dangers of weaponizing trade for political reasons.

4. CONCLUDING REMARKS

The U.S. steel and aluminum tariffs and Japan's export restraint measures are concerning examples of using trade measures to promote a commercial objective and to impose a political agenda, respectively, both disguised as a security interest. Such misuses of trade measures and the subsequent retaliatory responses by the affected trading nations escalate trade protections and restrain international trade, which is directly in conflict with the objective of the current multilateral trading system under the WTO, the promotion of freer and open trade. The preceding discussion has also pointed out the inconsistencies of their measures with the requirements under WTO law.

In this increasingly interdependent and interconnected world, national governments are tempted to use trade measures to promote their own commercial and political interests at the expense of their trade partners, and the cited measures are not the first cases of this kind. However, the weight and the adverse impact of such measures on the world trading system are truly critical when they are applied by some of the largest trading nations in the world, such as the United States and Japan. As the world's major exporters, both are among the largest beneficiary of the open trading system. This means that the damage that their measures inflict on world trade can be turned into a significant cost to their own trade. It is why caution and moderation is necessary in applying trade measures, which both countries failed to do with respect to their measures.

Notes

This report is based on the author's contribution to U.K. Trade Policy Observatory Blog, "Mimicking President Trump? - Trade and Politics in Japan's Recent Export Measure," (September 5, 2019) and the author's recent article, "Three Wrongs Do Not Make a Right: The Conundrum of the U.S. Steel and Aluminum Tariffs," 13(3), World Trade Review, (July 2019), pp. 481-501. A previous version of Section 3 of this report has also been published in "Mimicking President Trump? - Trade and Politics in Japan's Recent Export Measure," 14(1), Review of Institution and Economics, (February 2020), pp. 1-5.

1. Yong-Shik Lee, "Three Wrongs Do Not Make a Right: The Conundrum of the U.S. Steel and Aluminum Tariffs," 13(3), World Trade Review, (July 2019), pp. 481-501.

2. This section is comprised of excerpts from Lee (July 2019), *ibid.*, pp. 481-483, 485-486, 500.

3. Proclamation 9705 of March 8, 2018 "Adjusting Imports of Steel into the United States," 83 *Federal Register* 11625 (March 15, 2018); and Proclamation 9704 of March 8, 2018 "Adjusting Imports of Aluminum Into the United States," 83 *Federal Register* 11619 (March 15, 2018).

4. As amended 19 U.S.C. 1862.

5. U.S. Department of Commerce, *The Effect of Imports of Steel on the National Security: An Investigation Conducted under Section 232 of the Trade Expansion Act of 1962, as amended* (January 11, 2018) ("Steel Report") and *The Effect of Imports of Aluminum on the National Security: An Investigation Conducted under Section 232 of the Trade Expansion Act of 1962, as amended* (January 17, 2018) ("Aluminum Report").

6. *Ibid.*

7. *Ibid.*

8. The president acted on the secretary's counsel that steel and aluminum products were "being imported into the United States in such quantities and under such circumstances as to threaten to impair the national security of the United States" and that actions to adjust the imports of steel articles and aluminum were necessary "so that such imports will not threaten to impair the national security." *Supra* note 3.

9. HTS heading 9903.80.01.

10. HTS heading 9903.85.01.

11. World Trade Organization, *Disputes by Member, available at* https://www.wto.org/english/ tratop_e/dispu_e/dispu_by_country_e.htm, [Accessed on December 13, 2018]; *United States - Certain Measures on U.S. Steel and Aluminum Products*, DS550, DS563, DS548, DS547, DS551, DS552, DS554, DS556, DS564.

12. WTO docs. G/SG/N/12/EU/1 (May 18, 2018); G/SG/N/12/RUS/2 (May 22, 2018); G/SG/N/12/CHN/1 (April 3, 2018); G/SG/N/12/TUR/6 (May 22, 2018);

G/SG/N/12/IND/1/Rev.1 (June 14, 2018), *Customs Notice 18-08: Surtaxes Imposed on Certain Products Originating in the United States* (June 29, 2018, Revised July 11, 2018) (Canada); *Decree Modifying the Tariff Schedule of the Law of General Import and Export Taxes, the Decree establishing the General Import Tax Rate applicable during 2003 for goods originating in North America, and the Decree establishing Various Sectoral Promotion Programs* (enacted June 5, 2018; effective June 5, 2018) (Mexico).

13. *United States – Certain Measures on U.S. Steel and Aluminum Products, supra* note 11.

14. *Ibid.*

15. A view raised by the representative of India at the GATT's forty-seventh session in December 1991 concerning trade measures for non-economic purposes against Yugoslavia. GATT, SR.47/3 (1991), at 5.

16. *Ibid.*

17. *See Communication from the United States,* WT/DS548/13 (July 6, 2018).

18. *See* Roger P. Alford, "The Self-Judging WTO Security Exception," Utah Law Review (2011), pp. 697-759.

19. *Ibid.,* at 758.

20. WTO, *Disputes by Member,* available online at: https://www.wto.org/english/tratop_e/dispu_e/dispu_by_country_e.htm (last visited January 21, 2019); *United States – Certain Measures on U.S. Steel and Aluminum Products* (*United States – Steel and Aluminum Products*), DS550, DS563, DS548, DS547, DS551, DS552, DS554, DS556, DS564.

21. For the imposition of anti-dumping measures, see WTO, *Anti-dumping Sectoral Distribution of Measures: By Reporting Member* 01/01/1995 – 31/12/2017, https://www.wto.org/english/tratop_e/adp_e/AD_Sectoral_MeasuresByRepMem.pdf (last visited January 21, 2019).

22. *Supra* note 20.

23. A recent WTO panel has found that it has jurisdiction to review Article XXI matters. WTO, *Russia–Measures Concerning Traffic in Transit,* Report of the Panel, WT/DS512/R (April 5, 2019), paras. 7.53-7.58.

24. This section has been published in U.K. Trade Observatory Blog by the University of Sussex (September 5, 2019) and in "Mimicking President Trump? – Trade and Politics in Japan's Recent Export Measure," 14(1), Review of Institution and Economics, (February 2020), pp. 1-5.

25. Makiko Yamazaki, Ju-min Park, "Japan to tighten tech material exports to South Korea in wartime labor row," Reuters, July 1, 2019, *available at* https://www.reuters.com/article/us-southkorea-japan-laborers/japan-to-tighten-tech-material-exports-to-south-korea-in-wartime-labor-row-idUSKCN1TW144, [Accessed on July 25, 2019], cited in Yong-Shik Lee, "South Korean Economy at the Crossroads: Structure Issues under External Pressure – An Report from a Law and Development Perspective," 12(3), Law and Development Review, (2019), pp. 865-885.

26. "Japan-South Korea Rift: Japan to decide to remove South Korea from 'whitelist' on Aug 2," Nikkei Asian Review, July 26, 2019, *available at* https://asia.nikkei.com/Spotlight/Japan-South-Korea-rift/Japan-to-decide-to-remove-South-Korea-from-whitelist-on-Aug-2, [Accessed on July 28, 2019].

27. *See supra* note 25.

28. Jae-Ha Hwang, "Japan's Export Restraints – Could Have Been Implemented to Keep Korea's Semiconductor Industry in Check," Yonhap News, July 12, 2019 (in Korean), *available at* https://www.yna.co.kr/view/AKR20190712026700008, [Accessed on July 28, 2019].

29. Korea relies on the supply of materials from Japan for the production of its key products such as semiconductors (e.g., 90 percent of resists, 43.9 percent of hydrogen fluoride (etching gas), and 93.7 percent of fluorinated polyimides for the production of semiconductors). Chang Sung Ku, "Japan's Three Items Subject to Export Restraint Measures, Import Dependency up to the Maximum of 94 Percent," MK News, July 1, 2019, *available at* https://www.mk.co.kr/news/business/view/2019/07/476728/, [Accessed on July 25, 2019].

30. *Ibid.*

31. Lee (2019), *supra* note 1.

32. Tom Miles, "Japan, South Korea clash at WTO over trade dispute," Japan Today, July 25, 2018, *available at* https://japantoday.com/category/politics/update-2-japan-and-south-korea-clash-at-wto-over-trade-row, [Accessed on August 13, 2019].

33. WTO, *Russia−Measures Concerning Traffic in Transit, Report of the Panel*, WT/DS512/R (5 April 2019), paras. 7.53-7.58 and Lee (2019), *supra* note 1, pp. 490-491.

Silhouette of Korean Legal Service Market Opening*

KIM Dae-Won
Professor
Seoul City University, School of Law, Seoul, Korea

1. INTRODUCTION

This report covers meaningful changes of Korean legal service market opening mainly based on Korea-EU Free Trade Agreement (FTA) and Korea-US FTA. As is well acknowledged, there are distinct characteristics of legal services compared to other service fields. The most prominent point is that, because of their positive role for managing public order as it forms the basis of the order of a state, it is difficult to regulate the legal services area just like other commercial markets opening approach. For example, while 'the activity related to law enforcement' is included in the definition of legal service, it is common that such activity will be excluded from the object of legal service market opening due to its public nature according to Article 1.3(c) of WTO/GATS. Moreover, due to the different legal systems and unique legal occupations of each country, it is also difficult to generalize the opening of legal service.

2. CLASSIFICATIONS AND MEANING OF LEGAL SERVICE

The classification and definition of legal service under WTO are based on the 'Service Sectoral Classification List'[1] distributed by the WTO Secretariat at the time of Uruguay Round(UR) negotiation from 1986 to 1993. This classification was made according to the "United Nations Provisional Central Product Classification" (UN Provisional CPC)[2] No.861 in 1991. The legal service in the UN Provisional CPC No.861 is subclassified as follows: (i) legal advice and litigation service related to criminal Law (86111), (ii) legal advice regarding other legal procedure of other legal areas and legal service (86119), (iii) legal advice and litigation service for the legal procedure of quasi-judicial agency and committee, *etc.* (86120), (iv) legal documents preparation and certification service (86130), (v) other legal and consultation service (8619) and (vi) arbitration and mediation service which was added after 1998 (86602).[3] However, as shown in the WTO Secretariat's materials in 1998, it can be found that the classification such as (i) legal advice and litigation service regarding host country law, home country law, international law and (ii) legal document preparation and certification service and other legal and advice service, *etc.* were preferred over UN Provisional CPC.[4] From this criteria, WTO Member countries such as Korea, US, Japan prefer legal market opening through 'Foreign Legal Consultants' (FLC) who provide legal service for home country law, third country law and international law.[5]

As stated above, some Member countries that were of the position that the UN Provisional CPC did not reflect the trade reality enough at WTO negotiation, started to suggest the classifications of legal service among home country law, third country law international law, and the providers based on the jurisdiction as the FLC.[6] Considering the fact that there has been an increasing demand for more professional and international legal services reflecting trade and investment-related transactions, it appears a substantial rationale for functional existence of FLC as more appropriate classification of legal professionals who are working with multiple jurisdictions.

3. STATE OF PLAY IN KOREAN LEGAL SERVICE MARKET OPENING

3-1. WTO Dimension

Discussion about the Korean legal service opening at WTO started to be regularized after 2000 when the additional concessions negotiation, according to Article 19 of GATS, was proceeded (*built-in agenda*). On top of it, Korea has been combined some bilateral results with the DDA negotiation process. Thus the 4 columns and contents of Korea's DDA Schedule in 2005 need to be reviewed in the details as it will form the foundation of Korean legal market opening. Firstly, the 'sector or sub-sector of opening,' different from other service areas, defines the areas to be excluded in the definition of services. In other words, the following four sectors or sub-sectors are excluded in the definition of legal services itself: (i) representation of judicial proceedings or legal procedures of court and other governmental agencies and preparation of legal documents for such processes; (ii) legal representation for preparation and consignment of notarial deed; (iii) those activities concerning a legal case whose objective is the acquisition or loss or change of rights concerning real property in Korea, intellectual property rights, mining rights or other rights arising upon registration thereof with government agencies in Korea; and (iv) activities regarding legal cases about family relationship or inheritance when the concerned party is a Korean citizen or the relevant property is in Korea. Secondly, in connection with 'MA' (market access) column, Mode 1 (cross-border trade) and Mode 2 (consumption abroad) were presented for 'unlimited opening (None)' and Mode 3 (commercial presence) and Mode 4 (temporary movement of natural persons) suggested for limited opening: this is tantamount to the stage 1 opening of the legal service market according to the later schedules such as Korea-EU FTA; Thirdly, for the 'NT' (national treatment), Mode 1 and Mode 2 were presented as unlimited opening (None) and Mode 3 and Mode 4 were shown as limited opening as well. More detailed, Foreign Legal Consultants are required to have at least 3 years of work experience in the countries where they acquired legal licenses, and minimum 180 days of stay in Korea, unlike Korean lawyers. These rules are also equivalent to stage 1 legal service opening; Fourthly, in the 'additional commitments' column, Korea additionally inserted 2 limitations, that is, (i) Representation in international commercial arbitration is permitted, provided that the applicable procedural and substantive laws in the arbitration are the laws which the foreign legal consultant is qualified to practice in Korea; (ii) Use of firm name is permitted, provided that it is used with reference to 'Foreign Legal Consultants Office.'

3-2. FTA Dimension

Along with the DDA negotiation commenced in 2001, Korea has also been opening the legal service market through several FTAs: Starting with 2003 Korea-Chile FTA, as of January 2020, 16 FTAs are in effect with 56 countries.[7] Among them, Korea-EU and Korea US FTA have been assessed as the highest opening level in connection with legal services. Korean legal service market opening has been conducted in 3 stages: establishment of the foreign legal consultant office (stage 1); special cooperation agreement between domestic and foreign law firms (stage 2); and establishment of a joint firm between domestic and foreign law firms (stage 3). And the stage 3 was achieved by taking effect of the Korea-EU and Korea-US FTA in 2017. Such establishment has been domestically supported by the amendment of *Foreign Legal Consultant Act* in 2016. Looking into the two FTAs more closely, first of all, the Korea-EU FTA Chapter 7 ('Establishment of service and e-commerce' sector) is dealing service sectors, which regulates cross-border trade of service sector, investment, movement of natural persons, and the investment for non-service sector. Reviewing its Annex [Annex 7-A-4 (Republic of Korea)], sectors such as quasi-judicial occupations, judicial scrivener, patent lawyer, *etc.* are excluded like the DDA concessions of Korea in 2005. Secondly, regarding 'MA,' (a) in service Mode 1, 2, 3, restrictions on qualification of service supplier and supply form are stated,[8] and in Mode 4, the concession only allows matters which are related with commercial presence of Mode 3.[9] This is evaluated to be similar to the DDA concession in 2005. In (b), the content of 3 stages of legal market opening is specified. Stage 1 of the market opening is about the permission of 'establishment of the foreign legal consultant office' for 'Foreign Legal Consultants' whose original licensed countries in the EU before July 1, 2011. Stage 2 is about market opening through the cooperation of a certain business between foreign legal consultant office and a Korean law firm. In stage 3, law firms from EU member countries can establish a joint company with Korean law firms and such joint law firms can employee Korean lawyers. Specific matters regarding this is regulated in the 'Foreign Legal Consultant Act.' Thirdly, regarding 'NT,' some restrictions in connection with 'MA' are to be applied, and its content is specified in 'Foreign Legal Consultant Act.' For example, Foreign Legal Consultants are required at least 3 years of work experience from the country where they acquired their licenses and minimum 180 days of stay in Korea. Fourthly, 'additional commitments' contains similar contents seen in the 2005 DDA concessions.

In the Korea-US FTA, Chapter 11 ('investments') and Chapter 12 ('cross-border service trade') are related to legal services with their opening method: If the sectors are not mentioned in *Annex I (present reservation)* or *Annex II (future reservation)*, the relevant measures are considered that the four obligations - 'national treatment,' 'most-favored-nation treatment,' 'prohibition of restriction on market access,' and 'prohibition of imposition of local presence' - are applied (*negative approach*). Therefore, the contents of *present reservation list* of Annex I in the reservation lists, which means "the list of present measures that cannot be squared with the FTA obligations but is not to be applied by retreating previous liberalization level," and "the contents included in Annex II of *future reservation list* which dictates the present measures not being squared with the FAT obligations and can be more strongly restricted in the future,"[10] are the key elements to understand Korean legal service market opening.[11]

4. SOME ISSUES LEFT

Reviewing the present situation of the Korean legal market opening through amended Foreign Legal Consultant Act, I think that it favors bigger law firms relatively. The market opening is acknowledged to be an unavoidable task considering the Korean situation as a second mover who aims advanced legal service. However, at the same time, for future purposes, ways of improving smaller law firms and more specializing quasi-judicial occupations should be considered as well. In this context, it is necessary to reduce the exclusion sectors from the definitions of legal services in the Korea's Schedules. The significance of such exclusion to protect the Korean quasi-judicial occupations, which would not be found in other countries, was recognizable. However, in the long-term, in order to specialize the quasi-judicial occupations and strengthen their competitiveness, it seems necessary to consider the opening of such sectors prospectively. It is more persuasive if domestic-foreign joint ventures can provide relevant services eventually. In conclusion, as acknowledging that the legal market opening is in the process of optimization between strengthening competitiveness of the legal market and protection of domestic legal service, Korean government needs to strike a subtle balance between the two factors.

Notes

* This Report is a summarized version previously published in Daewon Kim, *A Critical Review of Korea's Foreign Legal Consultant Act*, Korean Journal of International Economic Law (2016.03), pp. 7~25 and its English version by Korea Legislation Research Institute in 2017.

1. WTO documents, MTN.GNS/W/120 (1991).
2. Department of International Economic and Social Affairs, "Statistical Office of the United Nations, Statistical Papers Series M No. 77, Provisional Central Product Classification" (New York, 1991).
3. WTO, S/CSC/W/6/Add.10 (1998).
4. WTO, S/C/W/43 (1998), p. 5.
5. Whereas, most countries such as EU, Canada, etc. insisted to keep 1991 Service Sector Classification. However, it is known that there are lots of cases that such countries did not follow such classification.
6. WTO, S/C/W/43, paras. 16~18.
7. http://www.fta.go.kr/main/situation/kfta/ov/.
8. "(a) Only the lawyers who registered in Korean Bar Association can provide legal service. The office of lawyer or judicial scrivener opened in Korea should be in the jurisdiction of local court where such lawyer or judicial scrivener starts their business. The office of notary should be in the district under jurisdiction of local district public prosecutor's office where such notary starts his business. Only lawyers can establish law office, law firm, law firm (limited) or lawyers union. To make things clearer, a person who does not have Korean lawyer license cannot invest such legal entity."
9. "[Stage 1 Opening] (i) Before the effective date of this agreement, Korea allows law firms from EU member countries to establish its representative office in Korea (foreign legal consultant office) under certain requirements, and allow lawyers from EU member countries to provide legal consultant service as a Foreign Legal Consultants regarding the law of the country where they acquired their lawyers' licenses and public international law in Korea. Moreover [Stage 2] (ii) Within 2 years from the effective date of this agreement, Korea will allow foreign legal consultant office to jointly handle cases the issues of which are related to domestic and foreign law jointly by making special cooperation agreement with Korean law firms and receive profit from such cases under certain requirements which meet this agreement. [Stage 3] (iii) Within 5 years from the effective date of this agreement, Korea will allow law firms from EU member countries to establish a joint venture firm with Korean law firms under certain requirements which meet this agreement. Korean firms can restrict on the voting right and ratio of shares of such joint venture firm. To make things clearer, such joint-venture firms can hire Korean lawyers as partners or associates under certain requirements." (Emphases added).

10. Explanatory material of 'Korea-US FTA' (2012.06), p. 104.

11. "1. Korea will reserve rights to take or keep any measures including but not limited to followings. A. Restriction on legal professional holding foreign license or foreign law firm to be granted license, approved, registered, permitted or supervised in providing legal service in any form and other requirements B. Restriction on legal professional holding foreign license or foreign law firm to make any kind of relationship such as partnership, alliance, association, etc. with Korean lawyer, law firm, judicial scrivener, CPA, tax account or licensed customs agent C. Restriction on legal professional holding foreign license or foreign law firm to employ Korean lawyer, law firm, judicial scrivener, CPA, tax account or licensed customs agent in Korea D. Restriction on upper management and board of directors including chairman of board of directors of legal entity which provide foreign legal consultant. 2. Despite of paragraph 1, [Stage 1 Opening] A. Before the effective date of this agreement, Korea allows law firms from the US to establish its representative office in Korea (foreign legal consultant office) under certain requirements, and allow lawyers from the US to provide legal consultant service as a Foreign Legal Consultants regarding the law of the country where they acquired their lawyers' licenses and public international law in Korea. [Stage 2] B. Within 2 years from the effective date of this agreement, Korea will allow foreign legal consultant office to handle cases the issues of which are related to domestic and foreign law jointly by making special cooperation agreement with Korean law firms and receive profit from such cases under certain requirements which meet this agreement. [Stage 3] C. Within 5 years from the effective date of this agreement, Korea will allow law firms from the US to establish a joint venture firm with Korean law firms under certain requirements which meet this agreement. Korean can restrict on the voting right and ratio of shares of such joint venture firm. To make things clearer, such joint-venture firms can hire Korean lawyers as partners or associates under certain requirements. 3. Korea shall keep the measures to be taken to fulfill the commitment of paragraph 2." (Emphases added).

KYIL

'Comfort Women' Lawsuits against Japan before the Korean Courts: Legal Issues from the Perspective of Private International Law

LEE Jong Hyeok
Assistant Professor
Hanyang University, School of Law, Seoul, Korea

Key Words

Comfort women, Restrictive theory of sovereign immunity, Inter-temporal law, Applicable law, Inter-hierarchical law, Recognition and enforcement of foreign judgments

1. INTRODUCTION

As of March 2020, there are two pending lawsuits before the Korean Courts which were filed by so-called 'comfort women' against the Japanese Government. First one was brought by twelve former Korean 'comfort women' on August 13, 2013 in the form of court mediation claiming for 100,000,000 KRW per person in compensation for psychiatric harm[1] and, as the court decided on December 30, 2015 not to proceed to mediation procedure, it was converted to ordinary litigation.[2] Another lawsuit was directly brought as ordinary civil litigation by twenty former Korean 'comfort women' on December 28, 2016,[3] but as the defendant, Japanese Government, refused two times to receive a copy of the plaintiffs' application which was delivered through the process promulgated in the Hague Convention on the Service Abroad of Judicial and Extrajudicial Documents in Civil or Commercial Matters, the court ordered service by publication on March 5, 2019 and the conveyance was effectuated on May 9, 2019.

Two lawsuits mentioned above seem to provoke a number of private international law issues that this article aims to provide an overview in chronological sequence: (i) whether the Japanese Government enjoys jurisdictional immunity from Korean courts; (ii) whether foreign judgments from Japan and the United States denying the compensation for the former Korean 'comfort women' should be recognized in Korea; (iii) in terms of inter-temporal law, which conflict rules and substantive rules should be applied to the above mentioned two cases; (iv) how to decide the law applicable to the Japanese Government's liability; (v) the impacts of the Agreement on the Settlement of Problems Concerning Property and Claim and Economic Co-operation between Japan and the Republic Korea (hereinafter the "Korea-Japan Claims Agreement") and the Hague Convention respecting the Laws and Customs of War on Land of 1907 (hereinafter the "1907 Hague Convention") for the determination of the applicable law; and (vi) a possibility of the enforcement of Korean judgment ordering compensation by Japanese Government in Korea and abroad including Japan.

2. RESTRICTIVE DOCTRINE OF JURISDICTIONAL IMMUNITY OF THE STATE

The Korean Supreme Court has already adopted the restrictive theory of sovereign immunity by a judgment of 1998,[4] abandoning the absolute theory of sovereign immunity declared by a judgment of 1975.[5] The 1998 judgment ruled as follows: "According to the rule of customary international law, sovereign acts (*acta jure imperii*) of the State are exempted from the jurisdiction of other States in principle, but it cannot be regarded as international law or international customs that private law acts or non-sovereign acts (*acta jure gestionis*) of the State are exempted from the jurisdiction of other States." The Korean Supreme Court held that in the absence of exceptional circumstances, Korean courts may exercise jurisdiction with respect to non-sovereign acts of a foreign State conducted in Korea. This corresponds with the Jurisdictional Immunities of the State Case rendered in 2012 by the International Court of Justice.[6] However, some Korean scholars and practitioners, influenced by the Italian Constitutional Court decision in 2014 which denied the above mentioned ICJ judgment within the scope of excluding the adjudicatory jurisdiction to the violation of human rights, have argued that the Korean Constitutional Court may render a decision on the constitutionality of customary international law[7] and declare that the rule of customary international law which grants the Japanese Government a privilege of jurisdiction immunity is unconstitutional and cannot be applied at the ordinary courts.[8]

Whatever the nature or objective of the State's acts which is the criteria for the distinction between sovereign acts and non-sovereign acts of the State, the law applicable to the distinction is *lex fori*.[9] Both the Japanese Government and individuals, not only legal persons but natural persons having operated or supported the 'comfort house,' were engaged in sexual slavery in the Japanese Military, i.e. seduction and/or coercion to execute employment agreement and to have sex trafficking, and violence or duress. In 2000, Tokyo High Court held that in some cases, the Japanese Government was a party to the contracts with, or a business partner of, the employers of the 'comfort women.'[10] If the acts of the Japanese Military and the Japanese Government were united with those of employers of the 'comfort women,' it is not needed to consider the acts of the

Japanese Military and the Japanese Government as sovereign acts in that those were non-sovereign acts by itself or closely related to non-sovereign acts which are not subject to jurisdictional immunity.

3. RECOGNITION OF JAPANESE AND U.S. JUDGMENTS IN KOREA

Korean 'comfort women' had already filed a tort claim for their damage during the Japanese colonial period at Japanese and U.S. courts. However, Japanese courts, save some district court decisions, dismissed those claims mainly based on the State Immunity Doctrine (*Kokka Mutouseki no Hori*) and Article 2(1), (3) of the Korea-Japan Claims Agreement,[11] and the U.S. courts dismissed the case as well based on the Jurisdictional Immunity Doctrine and Political Question Doctrine.[12] The plaintiffs of the current Korean lawsuits seem to be different from those at the previous Japanese and U.S. lawsuits. However, if the bereaved family member(s) of the former Korean 'comfort women' who had already raised claims at Japanese or U.S. courts are included in the plaintiffs of current Korean lawsuits, recognition of foreign judgments and the subjective scope of *res judicata* (Article 218(1) of the Korean Civil Procedure Law) would become a problem. If so, the recognition of the foreign judgments based on the State Immunity Doctrine or Jurisdictional Immunity Doctrine will be refused on the ground, which the Korean Supreme Court already declared in the forced labor victim cases in 2012, that if those judgments are recognized, public policy (*ordre public*) of Korea would be infringed.

4. INTER-TEMPORAL LAW OF CONFLICT RULES AND SUBSTANTIVE RULES

Even though private international law primarily functions to indicate the limits of different domestic laws between one another, conflict of laws in time, i.e. inter-temporal law, may also arise if there is (i) a change in the conflict rules of the forum or (ii) a change in the domestic rules of *lex causae* that is applicable under the choice-of-rules of the forum.[13]

4-1. Inter-temporal Law of Conflict Rules

The possible conflict rules that Korean courts may apply to the 'comfort women' cases pending before them vary as follows: (i) the *Horei* (Japanese Statute on Applicable Law) carried into effect over the Korean peninsula by the Japanese Imperial Edict No. 21 on March 28, 1912 until the end of the Second World War; (ii) the *Horei* temporarily incorporated into Korean legal system during the immediate postwar period by the Decree No. 21 of the U.S. military government and Article 100, one of the supplementary provisions, of the first Korean Constitution, both having recognized the effectiveness of existing law at the time; (iii) the *Seopoesabeop* (former Korean Private International Law Act) promulgated and entered into force on January 15, 1962; or (iv) the *Gukjesabeop* (current Korean Private International Law Act) promulgated on April 7, 2001 and entered into force as of July 1, 2001. Despite the possible intervention of inter-temporal public policy (*ordre public*) to rectify the consequence of applying the *Horei*, it is considered inevitable to apply the *Horei* to the 'comfort women' cases, namely as the above mentioned (i) for the periods before August 9, 1945 and as the above mentioned (ii) for the periods on and after August 9, 1945. If the *Gukjesabeop* is applied on the ground of inter-temporal public policy,[14] the State immunity doctrine denying liability for the State's acts of a highly public character would not be a problem as the *Gukjesabeop* abandoned the principle of cumulative which were promulgated in the *Horei* and the *Seopoesabeop*.

4-2. Inter-temporal Law of Substantive Rules

Given the temporal changes of substantive Korean law chosen by the conflict rules, inter-temporal law of substantive rules should be given some attention. This is an internal problem of the substantive law and usually resolved by a transitional rule provided in the relevant statute in itself. When it comes to the 'comfort women' cases, the possible applicable substantive rules in Korean legal history are as follows: (i) the Former Japanese Civil Code carried into effect over the Korean peninsula by the Japanese Imperial Edict No. 7 on March 18, 1912; (ii) the Former Japanese Civil Code temporarily incorporated into Korean legal system during the immediate postwar period by the Decree No. 21 of the U.S. military government and Article 100 of the first Korean Constitution; or (iii) the Korean Civil Code promulgated and entered into force on January 1, 1960. Article 2 of the Addendum of the Korean Civil Code of 1960 provided under the title of "Retroactive Effect of This Act" that "unless otherwise provided, this Act shall also apply to matters before the date of enforcement of this Act: provided that no effect taken already under the previous Act shall be affected by this Act." In the forced labor cases, the Korean Supreme Court held that not the Former Japanese Civil Code but the Korean Civil Code of 1960 apply to the questions of whether cases before January 1, 1960 constitute torts and whether the right to claim for damages is subject to the statutory limitation.[15]

5. LAW APPLICABLE TO GOVERNMENTAL LIABILITY

As previously analyzed from the perspective of inter-temporal law of conflict rules, the *Horei* should apply to the tort claims filed by the former Korean 'comfort women' and as such, under Article 11(1) of the *Horei*, the establishment and effects of the right to claim damages in tort are determined by *lex loci delicti*, i.e. the law of place where the tort occurred, namely (i) the law of Japan, (ii) the law of Korea, i.e. the Korean Civil Code, not the Former Japanese Civil Code, from the perspective of inter-temporal law of substantive rules according to the Korean Supreme Court's interpretation of Article 2 of the Addendum of the Korean Civil Code of 1960, (iii) the law of the Republic of China which had existed in the mainland of China before the People's Republic of China or (iv) the law of Manchukuo. Even though some cases may account for scattered tort (Streudelikt/ Multi-State-Delikt), it is hard to divide respective torts and determine the applicable law for each and as such, inevitable to concentrate on one single law to govern the tort as a whole. In addition, due to the fact that Manchukuo was a puppet government of Japan and the League of Nations did not recognize it as an independent State, it is arguable whether the law of Manchukuo should be applied as *lex loci delicti*.[16]

If the law applicable to a liability of the Japanese Government is determined as Japanese law, the liability might be denied on the basis of Article 11(2) of the *Horei* which provided the principle of cumulative application as follows: "As to unlawful acts, the preceding paragraph shall not apply where the facts occurring abroad are not unlawful under Japanese law." As such, the liability of the Japanese Government might be denied under the State immunity doctrine meaning that if the alleged offenses are characterized as acts of a highly public character (*acta jure imperii*), liability of the State to pay compensation for the offenses should be denied. However, there exists an intra-systemic limitation for the application of the State immunity doctrine: there did not exist a dominant-subordinate relationship between the Japanese Government and the former Korean 'comfort women' which justifies the application of the questioned doctrine. There is also a possibility of applying Korean law on the basis of inter-temporal public policy.

6. INTER-HIERARCHICAL LAW ISSUES

It is useful to analyze the former Korean 'comfort women' cases from the perspective of inter-hierarchical law or conflict of laws of hierarchy (Rang-Kollisionsrecht) which regulates the relationship between the systems of law with different rank[17]: the relationship between (i) the Korea-Japan Claims Agreement of 1965 and the general civil law rules and (ii) the Hague Convention of 1907 and the general civil law rules.

6-1. Korea-Japan Claims Agreement of 1965

Article 2(1) of the Korea-Japan Claims Agreement provides that "the Contracting Parties confirm that problem concerning property, rights, and interests of the two Contracting Parties and their nationals (including juridical persons) and concerning claims between the Contracting Parties and their nationals, including those provided for in Article IV, paragraph (a) of the Treaty of Peace with Japan signed at the city of San Francisco on September 8, 1951, is settled completely and finally." While the Japanese Government has been contending that Korean enforced labor victims against Japanese companies and Korean 'comfort women' against the Japanese Government are not entitled to claim tort since their rights to claim tort are included in 'completely and finally settled rights of the Contracting Party's nationals,'[18] the Korean Supreme Court held in historic judgments for restorative justice that those rights of enforced labor victims are not included in the scope of application of Article 2(1) of the Korea-Japan Claims Agreement due to the fact that those were not dealt with during the negotiation process of the Claims Agreement.[19] The Korean Supreme Court affirmed the same conclusion in the decision of 2018,[20] even though there were some arguments among the Justices concerning whether the diplomatic protection rights have been abandoned by the Claims Agreement. The same rationale may apply to the rights to claim by 'comfort women' against the Japanese Government. As such, the Korea-Japan Claims Agreement has no role in the perspective of inter-hierarchical law, in that the Claims Agreement does not prohibit for former Korean 'comfort women' to exercise the rights to claim for compensation against the Japanese Government.

6-2. Hague Convention of 1907

Article 3 of the 1907 Hague Convention provides as follows: "A belligerent party which violates the provisions of the said Regulations shall, if the case demands, be liable to pay compensation. It shall be responsible for all acts committed by persons forming part of its armed forces." While Japan ratified the 1907 Hague Convention in 1911 and the Convention was entered into force in 1912, Korea - the Korean Empire at the time - only ratified the Convention with respect to the Laws and Customs of War on Land of 1899 (hereinafter the "1899 Hague Convention"),[21] and has not ratified the 1907 Hague Convention. Even though Korea is not a Contracting State to the 1907 Hague Convention, it is generally recognized that most of the content for both the 1899 Hague Convention and the 1907 Hague Convention constitute customary international law which, under Article 6(1) of the Korean Constitution, has the same effect with domestic statutory law.[22]

Whereas Japanese courts have held that the above mentioned Article does not provide whether individuals hold a right to claim compensation against an offending State and most of the Japanese scholars also describe that the Article only stipulates reparations between the States,[23] it should be interpreted that an individual is the subject of a claim for compensation and an individual can bring a lawsuit against an offending State. If there is a *lacuna* concerning the contents of a right to claim compensation against Japan save the existence itself, the loophole should be filled by analogy with the governing law.

7. ENFORCEMENT OF KOREAN JUDGMENTS

Even though the Korean courts render judgment for the torts compensation of the Japanese Government to the former Korean 'comfort women,' the Japanese Government's property located in Korea used for the sovereign, public or non-commercial purposes – for example, embassy, diplomatic offices or residence – are not allowed to be subject to enforcement and only the property for the commercial purposes is allowed to be enforced. On the other hand, it is highly predictable that the Japanese courts would not allow the recognition and enforcement of the above mentioned Korean judgments on the ground of the public policy of Japan. It is controversial that the Korean judgment could be recognized and enforced in the third country where the Japanese Government has its property.

8. CONCLUSION

This article has analyzed the possible private international law issues briefly and reached the following conclusion: (i) the Japanese Government is not privileged to enjoy a jurisdictional immunity from the Korean courts, (ii) Japanese and U.S. judgments denying liability of the Japanese Government would not be recognized in Korea, (iii) the Japanese *Horei* would be applied as conflict rules, save a possibility of applying Korean *Gukjesabeop* on the ground of inter-temporal public policy, and if Korean law is designated as applicable law, the Korean Civil Code of 1960, not the former Japanese Civil Code, would be applied, as a mean for filling the gap in the Hague Convention of 1907; (iv) even though the principle of cumulative application under the *Horei* should be applied, the State immunity doctrine cannot govern the relationship between the Japanese Government and the former Korean 'comfort women'; and (v) the judgment recognizing the Japanese Government's liability could be enforced for the Government's property for the commercial uses.

Notes

1. Seoul Central District Court, Docket No. 2013Meo50479.

2. Seoul Central District Court, Docket No. 2016Ga-hap505092.

3. Seoul District Court, Docket No. 2016Ga-hap580239.

4. Docket No. 97Da39216, rendered on December 17, 1998.

5. Docket No. 74Ma281, rendered on May 23, 1975.

6. Jurisdictional Immunities of the State (Germany v. Italy: Greece Intervening).

7. A decision of the Korean Constitutional Court rendered on March 21, 2013 (Docket No. 2010Heon-ba70, 132, 170) recognized a possible constitutional review on customary international law; and a historic decision of the same Court rendered on August 30, 2011 (Docket No. 2006Heon-ma788) declared that enforcement of sexual slavery by the Japanese forces accounts for a crime against humanity.

8. *See* Young Hwa Moon, "Exercise of Jurisdiction to adjudicate on the Case of Japanese Military Comfort Women's Trial," *The Justice*, Vol. 174, Korean Legal Center, 2019, pp. 131~137; Young Jin Lee, "A Study on "State Immunity": In re the claim for damages of the "Comfort Women" victims," *Study on the American Constitution*, Vol. 25, No. 3, Institution of American Constitution, 2014, pp. 396~402 (both in Korean language).

9. Kwang Hyun Suk, *International Civil Procedure Law*, Pakyoungsa, 2012, pp. 40~41 (in Korean language).

10. Docket No. 5333Ne, 1999 rendered on November 30, 2000. For details, *see* Yasuhiro Okuda, "The Law Applicable to Governmental Liability for Injuries to Foreign Individuals during World War II: Questions of Private International Law in the Ongoing Legal Proceedings before Japanese Courts," *Yearbook of Private International Law*, Vol. 3, Kluwer Law International & Swiss Institute of Comparative Law, 2001, p. 130.

11. For details on the decisions of Japanese courts and the doctrine, *see* Okuda, *supra*, p. 116 *et seq.*

12. For example, Hwang Geum Joo, *et al. v. Japan.* 367 U.S. App. D.C. 45; 413 F.3d 45. For both Japanese and U.S. judgments, the database of the Center for Korean Legal Studies at Columbia Law School is quite helpful: https://kls.law.columbia.edu/content/lawsuits-brought-against-japan-former-korean-comfort -women.

13. For details, *see* Jan K. Grodecki, "Chapter 8. Intertemporal Conflict of Laws," in Kurt Lipstein et al. (ed.), *International Encyclopedia of Comparative Law*, Vol. III, Private International Law, Part 1, Mohr Siebeck, 2011, para. 8-1.

14. For details on the rules determining the applicable law of torts under the *Gukjesabeop* in English language, *see* Kwang Hyun Suk, "The New Conflict of Laws Act of the Republic of Korea," *Yearbook of Private International Law*, Vol. 5, Kluwer Law International & Swiss Institute of Comparative Law, 2003, pp.

127~128; Hong Sik Chung, "Private International Law," in Korea Legislation Research Institute (ed.), *Introduction to Korean Law*, Springer, 2012, pp. 294~296.

15. Docket No. 2009Da22549 and 2009Da22549 both render on May 24, 2012. However, another authoritative opinion says that under Article 2 of the Addendum of the Korean Civil Code of 1960, the Former Japanese Civil Code should apply to the above mentioned questions. *See* Kwang Hyun Suk, "Compensation of Damage resulting from Forced Labor during Japanese Colonial Era," in Hyo Soon Nam *et al.*, *A Comprehensive Study on the Forced Labor Cases during Japanese Colonial Era*, Pakyoungsa, 2014, pp. 105~106 (in Korean language).

16. *See* Okuda, *supra*, p. 128.

17. Gerhard Kegel/Klaus Schurig, Internationales Privatrecht, 9. Auflage, Verlag C.H. Beck, 2004, S. 46 f.

18. *See* https://www.mofa.go.jp/press/release/press4e_002204.html (press releases from the Japanese Ministry of Foreign Affairs).

19. Docket No. 2009Da22549 and 2009Da22549 both render on May 24, 2012. The judgment of the Korean Supreme Court showed that the Korea-Japan Claims Agreement has not affected the rights to claims by Korean victims: "The Claims Agreement did not negotiate for compensation for Japanese colonial rule. Based on Article 4 of the San Francisco Treaty, it attempts to solve financial and civil debt relations between Korea and Japan with a political agreement. Under Article 1 of the Claims Agreement, the Japanese Government's economic cooperation fund to the Korean Government is not related legally to a solution of the rights-related issues under Article 2. In the negotiation process of the Claims Agreement, the Japanese Government did not acknowledge colonial rule's unlawfulness and denied legal compensation for forced labor victims. Korean and Japanese Governments did not agree on the nature of Japanese rule over the Korean peninsula. In this circumstance, rights to claim for tort against humanity involving the Japanese Government or colonial rule tort damages were not addressed in the Claims Agreement. Thus, individual damages claim right has not expired due to the Claims Agreement. Diplomatic protection right of Korea was also not abandoned. Further, a country may not expire a citizen's individual right to claim without the consent of an individual citizen by treaty where a diplomatic protection right is abandoned. It is against the principle of modern law. If a country may expire citizen's individual right to claim by treaty under international law, unless explicitly expressed in the treaty, citizen's individual right to claim cannot be seen as expired together with the country's diplomatic protection right since the country and individual citizen are separate legal entity. The Claims Agreement does not have a sufficient basis to show agreement between Korean and Japanese Governments as to whether an individual right to claim expired. Japan enacted and enforced the Property Right Settlement Act after the Claims Agreement in order to expire Korean citizen's right against Japan and her citizens within Japan under the premise that the Claims Agreement alone did not expire Korean citizen's individual right to claim. Even if an individual citizen's right to claim is subject to the Claims

Agreement, the individual right to claim itself did not expire just based on the Claims Agreement as a matter of course. With the Claims Agreement, Korea's diplomatic protection right for claims was abandoned. Korea lost means to protect the pertinent right diplomatically if it expired within Japan by Japanese measures."

20. Docket No. 2013Da61381 rendered on October 30, 2018.

21. The Government of the Republic of Korea declared on August 8 of 1986 that the 1899 Hague Convention is one of the treaties which had been ratified by the Korean Empire and still had effects to the Republic of Korea, and published those treaties in the Official Gazette.

22. In Seop Chung, *International Law*, 10th Edition, Pakyoungsa, 2020, p. 1178 *et seq.* (in Korean language).

23. For the detailed information about Japanese judgments and Japanese scholarly writings, *see* Okuda, *supra*, pp. 122~123, nn. 23~25.

Development of Fintech Regulation in Korea from an International Perspective: Focusing on Crowdfunding Regulation

CHUN Changmin
Assistant Professor
Seoul National University of Science and Technology, Seoul, Korea

Key Words

Fintech Regulation, Crowdfunding Regulation, Securities-based Crowdfunding, P2P Lending, Private International Law

1. INTRODUCTION

Fintech is a compound word of finance and technology and thus the business areas of fintech services quite vary as much wide as those of finance. Fintech business areas include, for instance, crowdfunding, money transfer, payments, billing, insurance, wealth management, etc. Among fintech areas, crowdfunding is one of the most well-known areas of fintech services. Crowdfunding refers to an alternative financing practice where those in need of money publicize their ideas and/or initial products commonly via the internet to the general public who will then use "wisdom of crowds" to chip in and post their opinions. Crowdfunding has proliferated and grown exponentially since the emergence of web 2.0 which enables two-way communication gave rise to the companies who began tapping in the technology to connect the public with those in need of capital (e.g., individuals, start-ups, and venture firms) in the late 2000s.

In January 2016, the Republic of Korea ("Korea") implemented securities-based crowdfunding regulation. Further, in October 2019 the National Assembly of Korea passed the Act on P2P Lending and it is expected that the P2P Lending Act will be implemented, at least, at the end of August 2020.[1] This paper overviews international aspects of securities-based crowdfunding regulation under the Korean capital market law *i.e.*, the Financial Services and Capital Markets Act ("FSCMA") since the full regulatory regime of the Korean P2P Lending regulation has yet to be completed due to the fact that the enforcement decree and other implementing supervisory rules in accordance with the P2P Lending Act should be prepared.

In this regard, this paper, first, briefly explains the types of crowdfunding and regulatory intervention to crowdfunding practices. Second, this paper overviews the general procedure for foreign investors to invest in domestic securities in Korea, and then applies the procedure to securities-based crowdfunding, which will help identify the obstacles foreign investors face before investing in crowdfunding projects. Next, by exploring issues related to the international securities disclosure law, this paper tries to provide important prolegomena to a future framework that will enable cross-border securities-based crowdfunding.

2. TYPES OF CROWDFUNDING AND OVERVIEW OF SECURITIES-BASED CROWDFUNDING REGULATION IN KOREA

2-1. Types of Crowdfunding and Regulation

Crowdfunding can be broadly categorized into two types: non-investment type and investment type. The non-investment type includes donation-based and reward-based, while the investment-type consists of lending-based (or widely known as P2P lending) and securities-based.[2] Why was there a legislative measure for securities-based crowdfunding only in 2016, not for other types of crowdfunding? This is because securities-based crowdfunding is *de facto* banned under the rule of the FSCMA before the amendment thereto. This was a common denominator also observed in other countries: The U.S., the EU, Japan, and almost all countries impose the rigid securities regulation on the act of raising capital in exchange for securities, for the sake of investor protection. More specifically, the primary reason behind the ban stems from the regulation on public offering and securities firm regulation included in the securities regulation. Soliciting investments online is regarded as public offering, which requires either the compliance with the small-scale public offering procedure or the filing of a registration statement. In addition, any entity which engages in dealing or brokering in securities offering must acquire the investment dealing or brokerage licenses. Engaging in those services without a proper license is subject to prosecution or penalty. In short, before 2016, securities-based crowdfunding was impossible in Korea because the securities regulation forced companies in need for cash to bear the burdensome procedure and high costs, and crowdfunding platform providers to face the financial securities firm regulation.

Based on this legislative background and following successful funding story though Makestar, a Korean rewards-based crowdfunding platform specialized for Korean Wave contents, some of the crowdfunding market participants have had such an idea that Korean fintech firms may solicit foreign capital providers so that capital formation of Korean companies can be more facilitated. However, financial services are one of the highly regulated industries due to investor protection, market stabilization, etc. Fintech services including profit-seeking crowdfunding are not exemption to such a fact because fintech is also a branch of financial services.

First let us look at the successful funding story via Makestar. Makestar successfully ran a single album production project for a Korean idol singer, *Jeongmin* from September 19 to October 31, 2019. Although the initial funding target was KRW 1 million, the project was successfully received by a total of 152 supporters who put about KRW 20 million or 2,000% of the target.[3] Not to mention that the funding target was beaten without a hitch, also notable was the formidable presence of foreigners from Japan, China, Southeast Asia, Americas, etc.[4] This shed light on two features of crowdfunding: First, crowdfunding enables cross-border online financing and second, it gives Korea's competitive products abundant opportunities for global publicity.

However, cross-border crowdfunding is available in only limited types of crowdfunding, more specifically, donation-based and rewards-based types that have non-investment or non-profit characteristics seeking no profits in exchange for funding. Typically, crowdfunding based on donation and rewards provide no or low counter-performance for the funds provided; and thus there is virtually no need for investor protection. Accordingly, it is a global standard that donation-based and reward-based crowdfunding sit outside almost all financial regulations, except for anti-money laundering regulation.

By contrast, security-based crowdfunding, as mentioned above, one of the classic examples of investment-type or profit-seeking crowdfunding, raises funds via securities issuance; and therefore is subject to securities laws and regulations, unless otherwise stated. This is why the FSCMA came to adopt the securities-based crowdfunding system by placing special rules considered an exception to the securities regulation. However, the securities-based crowdfunding system under the FSCMA is basically designed for Korean firms and investors, without any consideration on foreign investors. Hence, any foreign investor who wishes to participate in a project on Korea's securities-based crowdfunding platform is subject to Korea's general securities regulation governing foreigners' securities investments. Furthermore, any securities issuance via crowdfunding is in effect an international solicitation; and thus subject to international securities disclosure law. Expanding the investor base for securities-based crowdfunding to foreign investors, hence, requires much more than a domestic regulatory overhaul.

2-2. Overview of Securities-based Crowdfunding Regulation in Korea

Before digging into the international regulatory aspect of securities-based crowdfunding, this section overviews the current securities-based crowdfunding regulation in Korea. From the issuers' perspective, the FSCMA Enforcement Decree limits the annual issuance amount up to KRW 1.5 billion per annum. This appears to reflect that crowdfunding is a tool for small-sized financing. Among others, the legislator though that financing up to KRW 1.5 billion per year would seem sufficient for issuers subject to securities-based crowdfunding regulation that should be in principle startups with less than 7-year business history.[5] But the KRW 1.5 billion restriction may be an obstacle to large-scale financing from professional investors, such as angel investors. Taking into account this, the FSCMA Enforcement Decree places an exception: If securities acquired via crowdfunding by professional investors are locked up or deposited not to be resold for one year, the acquired amount is excluded from the KRW 1.5 billion limit. This purports to induce wider participation by professional investors and to help issuers raise more capital. On top of this, the FSCMA Enforcement Decree also excludes the amount raised via private placement during the previous year from the KRW 1.5 billion limit. Simply put, issuers can raise capital via private placement as freely as before.[6] Hence, innovative startups making their name known to the public via crowdfunding will be able to tap into private placement to raise large-scale capital from venture capitals or angel investors.

From the investors' perspective, the FSCMA places the per-investor and per-issuer annual investment cap for ordinary investors at KRW 10 million, and KRW 5 million, respectively. The per-investor limit intends to prevent catastrophic losses given the risk inherent in crowdfunding. Ordinary investors lacking investment experience may not be able to handle unexpected losses from excessive investments in crowdfunding. On the other hand, the per-issuer limit tries to induce portfolio diversification. In addition, the annual investment limits for high income earners are KRW 20 million, and KRW 10 million, respectively. And professional investors have no limit in their investment as in the U.S. Under the FSCMA Enforcement Decree, high income earners are defined as any individual whose annual labor income for the previous year exceeds KRW 100 million or who is subject to composite income tax, and any legal entity whose own capital for the most recent business year exceeds KRW 1 billion.

At the same time, the FSCMA bans all securities issued via crowdfunding from being resold for 6 months,[7] except for the cases where the purchaser is a professional investor or any person meeting the conditions stipulated in the FSCMA Enforcement Decree. In order to induce investment exits and re-investments, and take into account the investor protection issue for prospective investors, the FSCMA Enforcement Decree expands the range of investors who can buy the resold securities from professional investors only to professional investors as well as issuers and their major shareholders. Especially, the resale restriction was substantially relaxed to allow all investors to sell their securities regardless of the resale restriction or six-month resale ban in the cases that the securities at issue are listed on exchanges such as the KOSDAQ or KONEX, or traded on the K-OTC market operated by KOFIA.

3. SECURITIES INVESTMENT PROCEDURE FOR FOREIGNER INVESTORS AND CROWDFUNDING[8]

Under the FSCMA, a foreign investor means a foreign individual[9] or corporation[10] investing in financial investment products.[11] For the sake of investor protection and fair trade order, the FSCMA sets out detailed regulations on foreign investors' trading of securities or exchange-traded products, unlike that of domestic investors. Other than the regulations prescribed under the FSCMA, the Regulation on Foreign Exchange Transactions ("RFET") places stringent rules on foreign investors' acquisition of KRW-denominated securities or related fund transfers. While the FSCMA regulation on securities investments by foreign investors mostly focuses on trading of listed securities, the RFET is applicable, regardless of whether transactions are for listed securities or not. This is the biggest difference between the two regulations.

First and foremost, the FSCMA mandates any foreign investor to open a securities account before investing in domestic securities. But the Regulations on Financial Investment Business ("RFIB") prescribes that a foreign investor shall open a trading account with a securities firm shall open such account for each type of securities, and present his or her investment registration certificate to the securities firm.[12] Actually, the use of the investment registration certificate is restricted to an acquisition or disposal of listed or IPO securities.[13] However, the aforementioned clause related to the opening of a trading account can be interpreted as requiring the investment registration certificate for any trading of non-listed securities. Although it is also possible to view "securities investment" under the context of relevant regulations as limited to listed securities, securities firms, in practice, conform to the RFIB by requiring foreign investors to present their investment registration certificate as one of the documents necessary for opening an account. For registration, a foreign investor shall register with the Financial Supervisory Service ("FSS") in person or through a legal representative, or appoint the Korea Securities Depository ("KSD") or other financial institutions as a standing proxy for electronic registration.[14] Because most foreign investors reside in or are based on foreign countries, it is general for them to establish a standing proxy agreement before trading securities issued by Korean companies in Korea. Aside from the procedural regulation related to the opening of accounts, foreign investors shall enter into a contract with a custodian (e.g., KSD), a foreign exchange bank, a securities firm, etc. to deposit the acquired securities.[15] Foreign investors are not allowed to directly hold the acquired securities.

The Korea's RFET places a provision that mandates monitoring of any foreign exchange transaction between foreign investors[16] or foreign investors and residents with regard to an acquisition of securities. Any foreign investor who intends to trade KRW-denominated securities shall open both "investment-only foreign currency account" and "investment-only non-resident Korean won account" in his or her name in a foreign exchange bank.[17] The RFET sets out strict requirements for depositing or disposing money in both accounts, adopting a positive list approach.

In applying the FSCMA and the FETA provisions on securities investments by foreign investors to the investment procedure of securities-based crowdfunding, one would easily find out that it is nearly impossible for foreign investors to participate in Korea's securities-based crowdfunding projects. As described above, a foreign investor shall establish a standing proxy agreement to appoint a standing proxy agent, apply for an investment registration certificate via the agent, and then present the certificate to open a trading account for small-sum securities investments. It is no exaggeration to say that there would be no foreign investor willing to go through such ordeals for a petty sum of investments, not to mention that not many financial institutions would want to provide standing proxy services for such small-sized investments. Usually, financial institutions link standing proxy and custodian services, but providing such services for securities-based crowdfunding projects will generate nothing more than very low securities custody or currency exchange fees. In terms of banking accounts, a foreign investor shall open an investment-only foreign currency account as well as an investment-only non-resident Korean won account via a standing proxy in order to qualify himself or herself to apply for an account in a crowdfunding platform.

4. INTERNATIONAL SECURITIES DISCLOSURE LAW AND CROWDFUNDING

The aforementioned FSCMA and RFET provisions on securities investments by foreign investors lack sufficient considerations on securities-based crowdfunding because establishing an institutional framework for domestic investors was a more pressing need. Hence, a reform on relevant provisions in the FSCMA and RFET could address the domestic regulation issues. But the act of posting specific issuance conditions for general solicitation of securities is in effect a cross-border solicitation of securities for domestic as well as foreign investors who have online access. In particular, offering translations of the content into foreign languages such as English, Chinese, and Japanese is highly probable to fall under a public offering 'directed' at the investors in the jurisdictions using those languages. The crowdfunding system under the FSCMA is a Korean scheme, not a foreign one. Hence, a Korean crowdfunding project soliciting foreign investors may be interpreted as an illicit public offering without the filing of a securities registration statement from the regulatory perspective in relevant jurisdictions. For this reason, the UK's two largest securities-based crowdfunding platforms Crowdcube and

Seedrs use disclaimer stating that any investment solicitation offered via the platforms shall not be directed at persons located in the U.S., Canada, or Japan, and at any investor resident in the regions where such solicitation is unlawful.

As such, any act of publishing information, via Crowdfunding platforms, related to securities offering in any foreign language, especially in English, means much more than mere information provision. Such act has a risk of altering the domestic nature of a project into an international one, which is prone to a problem related to international securities disclosure law. Offering securities of a startup with high investment risks can be deemed as a public offering requiring the filing of a securities registration statement. And any breach in this area may lead to liability claims under the law of relevant jurisdictions. Moreover, it is worth bearing in mind that such act can be interpreted as a financial intermediary role in securities issuance without a proper license or authorization.

5. CLOSING REMARKS: PROLEGOMENA FOR IMPROVEMENT

"The Age of Shadows (*Miljeong*)" released on September 7, 2016 is the first Korean movie invested and produced by global distributor Warner Bros. and the "Parasite (*Kisaengchung*)," the first Korean movie nominated for six Oscars in the 92nd Academy Awards in January 13, 2020, which evidence keen interests of the global market in Korea's cultural contents. If those contents are made easily accessible by overseas investors and met by securities-based crowdfunding, this will give the Korean capital markets with golden opportunities to export the Korean Wave contents to the global markets. However, the FSCMA and RFET regulations *de facto* disqualify foreign investors from participating in securities-based crowdfunding projects. To address this issue, it is wise to carry out bold deregulation given that crowdfunding mostly deals with small-sized investments. More precisely, it is necessary to devise a special rule for crowdfunding in which foreign investors may participate. Although the rule may take many different shapes, the most realistic and effective approach should be an integrated system where a custodian or the Central Archive Agent manages foreign investors who then will not have to open separate trading, custodian, and bank accounts as before.

Although Korea fully would overhaul its foreign investor laws and regulations, it is hard to cross over the threshold of international securities disclosure law.[18] Because the international nature of Internet and other online activities are applicable to securities issuance, securities-based crowdfunding may fall under the act of cross-border securities issuance.

Tackling the issue related to international securities disclosure law certainly requires more than domestic efforts. It is welcome that special securities-based crowdfunding regimes have been widely adopted in several Asian countries including Japan, Taiwan, Singapore, Malaysia, Thailand, etc. In the North America, the U.S. and Canada have also introduced this type of crowdfunding scheme, and so have Germany, Austria, Spain, France and Portugal in Europe. A desirable approach is to forge an international convention with selected few countries whose regulations are similar to the Korean one so that the financial authorities may exempt crowdfunding projects offered to investors in their jurisdictions from the general solicitation rule. This means introducing a "crowdfunding passport system" among countries with similar regulatory levels. Because the economies of scale in crowdfunding, a larger pool of prospective investors increases the chance of successful fundraising. Hence, more and more countries adopting similar crowdfunding regulatory schemes are expected to positively review joining the crowdfunding passport agreement in order to facilitate financing for startups and ventures. It is especially worth considering a tentative crowdfunding passport system limited to neighboring Asian countries that are familiar with the Korean Wave before expanding it to a wider range of countries. However, startups and securities-based crowdfunding platforms should bear in mind that their soliciting activities towards foreign investors are not a mere information provision but the activities are subject to securities regulation of the jurisdiction where the foreign investors reside before forging out such an international or regional convention for securities crowdfunding. Further, it also needs to be mindful that P2P lending is also highly regulated in most countries; thus soliciting foreign investors in P2P lending projects could be subject to foreign regulation.

Notes

1. After finalizing this paper, the enforcement date of the P2P Lending Act was confirmed as August 27, 2020. For more details of the Act, refer to Changmin Chun, "Arrival of the Novel P2P Lending Act: Main Issues and Legal Challenges," Commercial Law Journal, Vol. 39 Issue 1, 2020 at 55~123.

2. In general, securities-based crowdfunding is also referred to as equity-based crowdfunding meaning the receipt of equity securities in exchange for cash. But technically speaking, the backer of securities-based crowdfunding can receive not only equity securities, but also debt or other types of securities. Hence, using the two terms interchangeably is inaccurate.

3. Refer to the following website to check the details on the Stellar's crowdfunding project on *Jeongmin*: https://www.makestar.co/projects/singer_jeongmin_01?locale=ko.

4. Makestar is a rewards-based crowdfunding platform offering its project pitch in Korean, English, Chinese and Japanese.

5. Exceptionally, the FSCMA Enforcement Decree allows venture firms and technology innovation-type SMEs to be exempt from the 7-year restriction, which *de facto* eliminates the business history restriction for almost all innovative companies.

6. However, the FSCMA Enforcement Decree regards any offering targeting a total of more than 50 ordinary investors for the previous six-month as a public offering, and includes such an offering in the KRW 1.5 billion limit. This intends to curb any ill-intended effort to circumvent the KRW 1.5 billion limit.

7. Originally, it was 1 year but it has been revised into 6 months, in order to boost crowdfunding and economy in the long run.

8. Hereinafter is drawn on this author's short memo published through the Korea Capital Market Institute. *See* Changmin Chun, "Cross-Border Solicitation of Securities through Crowdfunding and its Limitation under Korean Law," KCMI Capital Market Opinion, September 20, 2016.

9. Under §168 (1) of the FSCMA, foreigners refer to individuals with no domicile or residence for at least six months in Korea.

10. Under §9 (16) of the FSCMA, a foreign corporation, etc. refers to any person who is a foreign government, a foreign local government, a foreign public institution, a foreign company established pursuant to the laws and rules of a foreign country, or any international organization specified by the Enforcement Decree.

11. While the FSCMA adopts the terms "foreigner" and "foreign corporation," the RFIB, for convenience, uses the single term "foreigner" referring to any foreign legal entity or a private individual of foreign nationality without his/her domicile or abode in Korea for six months or longer (§6-1-1). In this paper, this author uses "foreign investors" instead of foreigners.

12. §6-14-1, RFIB.

13. §6-10, RFIB.

14. According to the FSS, foreign investors are not allowed to directly apply for electronic investment registration without a standing proxy agent (FAQ, Can a Foreigner Directly Apply for Electronic Investment Registration without Appointing a Standing Proxy Agent?).

15. §6-21, RFIB. Such custody is not mandatory in the case of bonds issued by registration; thus no physical bond certificates are issued.

16. The RFET uses the term "non-resident" instead of "foreign investor." The FETA defines an individual and a legal entity other than residents as a non-resident, while the term "resident" refers to an individual who has a domicile or residence in Korea and a legal entity whose main office is located in Korea (§3 (1), §14, and §15). And foreigners who engage in business activities in Korea or stay in Korea for not less than six months are regarded as residents (§10 (1) 4, Enforcement Decree). Hence, it is understood that the definitions on foreign investors under the FSCMA and FETA are not accurately equivalent, but analogous for the sake of convenience.

17. §7-37, RFET. In practice, a standing proxy is also required to open bank accounts for securities investments.

18. For more details of international disclosure law issues, *see* Jonghyeok Lee, Prospectus Liability in Cross-border securities Offering: Focusing on the Choice-of-law Rules, Doctoral Dissertation of the Seoul National University, 2019.

Legal Framework for Secured Transactions in Korea* **

LEE Jae Sung
Legal Officer
United Nations Commission on International Trade Law (UNCITRAL), Vienna, Austria

PARK Issey
Associate Expert
United Nations Commission on International Trade Law (UNCITRAL), Vienna, Austria

Key Words

Mortgage, Movable Property, Pledge, Receivable, Security Right, UNCITRAL Model Law on Secured Transactions

1. INTRODUCTION

The Republic of Korea ("Korea") ranked fifth in the World Bank's Doing Business 2020 report.[1] While this is the ninth successive year in which Korea ranked in the top 10 overall for providing an attractive business environment, its ranking in the area of getting credit has fallen from eighth in the 2012 report to

---

* The views expressed herein are those of the authors and do not necessarily reflect the views of the United Nations.
** Unless otherwise specified, the unofficial English translation of the legislation is as provided by the Korea Legislation Research Institute at http://elaw.klri.re.kr/ eng_service/main.do and the National Law Information Center at http://www. law.go.kr/LSW/eng/engMain.do.

sixty-seventh. As one of the 12 areas of the Doing Business report, getting credit measures the legal rights of borrowers and lenders with respect to secured transactions, and the reporting of credit information. It captures two aspects of access to credit, the effectiveness of movable collateral and insolvency laws in facilitating lending to businesses and the coverage, scope, and accessibility of credit information systems in the economy.

The fall in rankings over the last eight years does not mean that the Korean government has done little to expand access to credit or otherwise to improve the business environment. In 2012, the Act on Security over Movable Property, Receivable, and Others (the "Act on Security over Movables") entered into force.[2] In practice, efforts to enhance the availability of credit by promoting the use of movable assets as collateral have continued to date. The Financial Services Commission in 2018 announced a strategy to "facilitate the use of movable assets as collateral,"[3] and more recently in support of the 2020 Economic Policies,[4] mentioned as one of its key tasks attaining "financing movable asset-based loans (including intellectual property) in the amount of KRW 3 trillion[5] by the end of 2020."[6] The Ministry of Justice is also in the course of preparing a bill to revise the Act on Security over Movables to make it possible to take security rights in different types of assets (movable property, receivables, and intellectual property rights) with a single agreement.[7]

This paper provides a brief introduction to the legal framework for using movable assets as collateral in Korea (Section 2) and makes a comparison with the UNCITRAL Model Law on Secured Transactions (the "Model Law"),[8] which was adopted by the United Nations Commission on International Trade Law (UNCITRAL) in 2016 as a tool for States to modernise their secured transactions laws (Section 3).[9] It should be noted that the Model Law addresses, among others, the rights and obligations of debtors and creditors in secured transactions, which is captured by the getting credit indicator of the Doing Business reports. This paper concludes with some recommendations on the way forward to reforms (Section 4).

2. LEGAL FRAMEWORK IN KOREA FOR USING MOVABLE ASSETS AS COLLATERAL

In Korea, the term 'security right' refers to right in rem, i.e., a right in property granted to a creditor to secure payment or other performance of an obligation.[10] Article 185 of the Civil Act of Korea stipulates that no rights in rem "can be created at will other than ones provided for by law or customary law." This representation of numerus clausus restricts the kinds and terms of rights in rem.

The Civil Act provides for consensual security rights, which include pledge of movable property (Articles 329-344), pledge of rights (Articles 345-355), and mortgage on immovable property (Articles 356-372). In addition, courts have acknowledged and developed the notion of assignment for the purpose of establishment of security interests, i.e., fiduciary transfers of title in tangible assets and those of receivables for security purposes. Retention of title and financial leases are other examples of security devices in Korea. The Act on Security over Movables, which entered into force on 11 June 2012, is the latest addition to the secured transactions legal framework and establishes security rights in movable property, receivables, and intellectual property rights.

2-1. Pledge

The pledge of movable property under the Civil Act is a possessory security right in that the pledgee takes possession of the movable property offered as security by the debtor or a third party.[11] In addition to a security agreement, the transfer of possession is required for such pledge to be created.[12]

The pledge of rights under the Civil Act is a non-possessory security right. A pledgor may offer as security any assignable property right other than a right to use or receive profit from immovable property.[13] Unless otherwise provided, the creation of such pledge requires an assignment of the property right.[14] Where a receivable is the subject matter of the pledge, the pledge may not be asserted against third parties, including the debtor of the receivable, unless notice of the creation is given to the debtor of the receivable or such debtor acknowledges the same.[15]

Upon default, a pledgee can enforce its security right through a public auction, which is the principal method, while if a justifiable ground exists, a pledgee may request from a court immediate appropriation of the encumbered movable property with the evaluation of an appraiser, in satisfaction of the secured obligation.[16] The parties can agree that the pledgee would acquire the movable property in satisfaction of the secured obligation or that the pledgee would dispose of it without applying to a court, but only after the secured obligation becomes due.[17] In the case of receivables, the pledgee may directly seek payment.[18]

2-2. Mortgage

A mortgage under the Civil Act is a security right in immovable property provided by the debtor or a third party to secure an obligation.[19] Unlike a pledge, transfer of possession is not required for the creation of a mortgage, but registration is required.[20]

While a mortgage also covers fixtures to and appurtenances in the immovable property,[21] movables cannot be the object of a mortgage under the Civil Act. However, the provisions of the Civil Act on mortgages apply mutatis mutandis to mortgages created by other laws that cover movables.[22]

For example, the Commercial Act provides for ship mortgages.[23] The Act on Mortgage on Motor Vehicles and Other Specific Movables, as its name indicates, provides for mortgages over automobiles, construction machinery, small ships, and certain aircrafts, all of which are subject to registration under the respective laws.[24] Movables that constitute a factory foundation or a mining foundation can be the object of a mortgage under the Factory and Mining Assets Mortgage Act upon registration.[25]

In general, the enforcement of a mortgage is through public auction, and a third-party acquirer of the mortgaged property may bid and purchase it at such auction.[26]

2-3. Assignment for Security

Although there are no clear rules in Korean legislation that provide for the assignment of movables for security purposes, the demand in the market for a non-possessory security right catalysed its development through court precedents.[27] While such an assignment may be used to encumber different types of asset, including immovable property, the most animated in practice is the assignment of movables to secure an obligation without transfer of the actual possession. This is facilitated through an agreement of the parties that the assignor shall continue to actually possess and enjoy use of the movable, while it is deemed to have been delivered to the assignee via constructive possession.[28] The Supreme Court of Korea considers such assignment for security to be a fiduciary transfer of title in that the assignor retains title only as against the assignee, whereas the assignee is the owner as against third parties and thus may seek delivery of the encumbered movable from any third party.[29]

The approach with respect to creation is not different from that for a pledge. In the case of movable property, both security agreement and publicity, albeit via the fictitious transfer of possession, are required. This generally poses concerns about the so-called 'hidden encumbrances,' as a third party would likely not be aware of the agreement between the assignor and assignee or otherwise be able to find out who has the title to the movable. In the case of receivables, while a security agreement is sufficient, likewise, the assignor has to notify the debtor of the receivable or the debtor of the receivable has to consent to the assignment in order for the assignment to be effective as against the debtor of the receivable and third parties.[30] This in practice often renders the use of a pool of receivables cumbersome and costly, since each would require notification, possibly to different debtors, while such pool fluctuates.[31]

The parties may agree on the enforcement method, and the assignor would generally not need to apply to a court as it could acquire the movable or dispose of it in satisfaction of the secured obligation.[32]

2-4. The Act on Security over Movables

The Act on Security over Movables addresses security rights over movable property, receivables, and intellectual property rights, and establishes registries for the purposes of registering such security rights.[33] Movable property that is subject to a mortgage as mentioned in Section 2-2 above is excluded from the scope of application as well as movable property represented by consignment notes, bills of lading and warehouse receipts, and certain types of securities.[34]

The approach with respect to creation follows that in the Civil Act. A security right over movable property under the Act on Security over Movables is created by the agreement of the parties to secure payment or other obligation (regardless of the denomination by the parties, and this covers an agreement on the assignment for security purposes mentioned in Section 2-3 above), and the registration in the registry.[35] Transfer of possession is not required. In the case of a security right over receivable, while it is created by a security agreement, registration is required for it to be effective against third parties. Moreover, the certificate of such registration needs to be delivered to the debtor of the receivable for the security right to be effective against such person.[36] While such differential treatment of security rights may be inevitable, it is clearly undesirable.[37]

A security right in a pool of movables, whether present or future, may be registered, as long as the movables can be identified by their kind, location, quantum, or another similar method.[38] In the case of a security right in a pool of receivables, whether present or future, the identification may be by the kind, cause or date of accrual, or the like.[39]

The priority among security rights in the same asset is determined by the order of registration in the registry.[40] However, if there is a delivery of possession of the movable property, including via constructive possession for the purposes of assignment for security, the rule in Article 7(3) of the Act on Security over Movables is that priority is determined by the order of the event, i.e., the registration or possession, whichever occurs first. This poses a problem as it is rather difficult to determine the point in time of the delivery of possession, particularly if there is an agreement on constructive possession between the parties. It is thus for the courts, which have not upheld the later-in-time assignment where there have been double assignments of the movable for security purposes, let alone the second security agreement itself, to rule on priority where registration of a security right under the Act on Security over Movables follows an assignment for security purposes.[41]

With regard to receivables, the priority may become complex as it is possible not only to create a security right over receivables under the Act, but also to create a pledge (Section 2-1) and to assign for security purposes (Section 2-3). In such case, priority is determined by the order of registration or notification to or acknowledgement of the debtor of the receivable, whichever occurs first.[42] Therefore, it would be prudent for a potential creditor to inquire from the debtor of the receivable and further search the registry for existence of any competing claimants.[43]

The principal enforcement process of a security right over movable property is an auction, and it is only where a justifiable ground exists that the secured creditor may take possession of collateral in satisfaction or appropriate the proceeds of sale.[44] While such non-parallel approach derives, again, from the Civil Act,[45] it is hardly desirable.[46] However, Article 31(1) allows the parties to otherwise agree on the enforcement. In the case of security rights over receivables, the secured creditor may directly seek payment.[47]

2-5. Summary: A Melange of Security Rights

As illustrated above, the legal framework for using movable assets as security in Korea is fragmented, depending on the type of asset. There are multiple devices that a creditor could use for purposes of security, yet with different requirements. In a nutshell, a variegated legal regime for a patchwork of security rights in movable property and receivables has been developed short of a comprehensive framework to cover all types of movable assets, tangible or intangible, present or future.

In terms of movable property, the dispossession required for pledge has led to the development of assignment for security purposes. However, the downside of such fiduciary transfer of title is that potential creditors would find it difficult to tell whether the grantor has rights in the asset to be encumbered or if there is any competing security right in the same asset. While the security right over movable property under the Act on Security over Movables is non-possessory, it coexists with the pre-existing pledge and assignment for security.

Although the Act on Security over Movables is indeed a legal paradigm shift,[48] it remains to been seen if it indeed vitalises the secured credit market.

3. THE UNCITRAL MODEL LAW ON SECURED TRANSACTIONS

To assist States in developing a modern secured transactions law dealing with security rights in movable assets,[49] UNCITRAL adopted in 2016 the UNCITRAL Model Law on Secured Transactions.

For many businesses, movable assets are the main type they can offer as collateral. Legislative reform based on the Model Law would thus make it easier for businesses, particularly small and medium-sized enterprises, to access credit using the types of assets that they are likely to have. Such reform can also reduce the cost of credit and make it possible for businesses to obtain credit for longer periods. Readily available credit at a reasonable cost helps businesses grow and prosper. This would likely have a positive impact on the economic prosperity of a State as a whole, which is the rationale underlying the Model Law and its preparation.[50]

Prepared by the core legal body of the United Nations system with the aim of providing a benchmark secured transactions law for States with different legal traditions and with active Korean participation in the sessions, the fundamental principles and corresponding provisions of the Model Law could shed light on possible reform of Korea's legal framework for secured transactions.

3-1. Functional, Integrated, and Comprehensive Approach

The Model Law suggests a functional, integrated, and comprehensive approach to secured transactions. The functional approach is reflected in the definition of 'security right' in Article 2 (kk) so that the Model Law applies to all transactions under which a property right in a movable asset is created by agreement of parties to secure payment or other performance of an obligation, regardless of the form of transaction, the terms used by the parties to describe the transaction, or whether the assets are owned by the grantor or the secured creditor. This means that the Model Law applies not only to transactions in which the grantor grants a security right in an asset that it already owns, but also to transactions that take the form of the creditor retaining or being transferred title to an asset to secure performance of an obligation, for example, retention-of-title arrangements and financial leases.[51] This may be a major distinction from the traditional position in Korea where such transactions are treated differently, as its legislation has denominated such rights in movables in different ways. In particular, as assignments for security purposes depend on court precedents and the rules on such rights remain unclear.

The comprehensive approach of the Model Law is reflected in its article 1, which provides that a single law should apply to security rights in all types of movable assets unless specifically excluded.[52] Considering that the legal framework in Korea has developed on asset-by-asset and as-needed bases with distinct rules on movable property and receivables, whereas receivables are considered to be one type of movable assets under the Model Law, taking this approach may be another challenge for Korea.

The integrated approach of the Model Law ensures that a common set of rules govern creation, third-party effectiveness, priority, and enforcement of a security right in movable assets. This allows a secured creditor to be certain of the ways it could obtain a security right and furthermore, of the rights that it will have upon default of the debtor. The situation in Korea is somewhat far from integration, in the sense that a creditor has various security devices to choose from, yet with different requirements to meet, and that it may be difficult at times to determine the priority among competing claimants that have utilised different security devices in the same asset. For example, a piece of equipment that a manufacturer owns may be an object of a pledge under the Civil Act, of a mortgage under the Act on Mortgage on Motor Vehicles and Other Specific Movables or the Factory and Mining Assets Mortgage Act, or if unregistered, of a security right under the Act on Security over Movables. Further, it could be assigned to a creditor for security purposes.

The integrated approach is reinforced in the Model Law as it suggests that apart from the enforcement provisions, the same rules should apply to outright transfers of receivables.[53] Therefore, the term 'security right' in the Model Law includes the right of the transferee under an outright transfer of a receivable by agreement,[54] and the term 'secured creditor' includes such a transferee,[55] since it is often difficult to tell whether a person is transferring receivables outright or granting a security right in them. While applying the provisions of the Model Law to both types of transactions reduces the need to make this distinction, another benefit is that it allows the provisions of the Model Law to determine priority among all competing security rights in the same receivable, including the rights of an outright transferee.[56] In the Korean context, transactions involving receivables are again subject to the variegated regime. While efforts have been made in the Act on Security over Movables to address the requirements of the Civil Act with respect to assignment of receivables and potentially various priority conflicts,[57] it may be necessary to further address certain contractual limitations on the creation of security rights in receivables and the rights and obligations of the debtor of the receivable.[58]

3-2. Creation and Third-Party Effectiveness

The Model Law makes it easy to create a security right. The parties only need to enter into a security agreement that satisfies some simple requirements.[59] To create a security right in a movable asset that is effective against the grantor, the grantor must have rights in the asset to be encumbered or the power to encumber it.[60] Unlike in Korea, registration is not a requirement for the creation of a security right under the Model Law.[61]

Similar to the Act on Security over Movables, the Model Law allows for the creation of a security right not only in assets that the grantor already has, but also in assets which do not yet exist or in which the grantor does not yet have rights at the time the security agreement is entered into, i.e., future assets.[62] To allow for this, the Model Law requires that the assets in the security agreement be described in a manner that reasonably allows their identification,[63] as it might not be possible to include a specific description of future assets, and such a requirement may pose a question whether the future asset is the object of the security right. In this regard, it remains to be seen how the courts would interpret the identification requirements in Articles 3(2) and 34(2) of the Act on Security over Movables.

A secured creditor will want to ensure that its security right is also effective against third parties, as the security right will otherwise not be of much benefit particularly when the grantor becomes insolvent.[64] The primary way of making a security right effective against third parties under the Model Law is to register a notice in the general security rights registry (the "Registry") established under Article 28.[65] This is different from the registration foreseen in the Act on Security over Movables, which is rather akin to a document registration,[66] as the registrant under the Model Law is required to submit a simple notice containing only the basic information about the security right.[67] While authorisation of the grantor is required for the registration, the security agreement need not be submitted with the notice, which further facilitates advance registration.[68] In contrast, the Act on Security over Movables requires that the parties apply jointly for registration.[69] The records in the Registry are indexed by reference to the name of the grantor and not by the asset,[70] which is the same as the approach taken in the Act on Security over Movables.[71]

While the Registry allows a secured creditor to publicise the existence of a security right over assets of the grantor, registration of a notice is not a requirement for creation under the Model Law. However, a reasonable secured creditor would register a notice in the Registry as soon as possible, to achieve third-party effectiveness, as the priority among the secured creditors would be determined by the order of registration. Furthermore, by subjecting all security devices as well as outright transfers of receivables to registration under the Registry, it can function as the key reference for all financing purposes to determine whether there is an existing or potential security right over the assets of a borrower. This addresses concerns with regard to hidden encumbrances and security rights unknown to other secured creditors.

This aspect of registration is particularly relevant with regard to the assignment for security purposes, which may be registered under the Act on Security over Movables, but not so required. Unless the requirement of registration applies equally to assignments for security purposes or a mechanism is introduced to encourage their registration, from the perspective of a potential creditor, the risk arising from hidden encumbrances might be too high for it to engage in any financial transaction. Outright transfers of receivables, which are not subject to any registration requirements, could have benefitted from the use of the registry in place under the Act on Security over Movables.[72] Korea could further consider the benefits of notice filing.[73]

3-3. Priority

It goes without saying that a secured creditor should have priority over an unsecured creditor, including in insolvency proceedings. An event of default is a defining moment in a secured transaction as the priority of a security right becomes the key issue. Thus, obtaining priority is crucial to creditors when they plan to lend. If a creditor does not have priority against competing claimants, the encumbered assets might be of no value as a higher-ranking creditor would be entitled to first take most, if not all, of the value of the collateral.

A secured creditor may find that its security right in an encumbered asset is in competition with the rights of competing claimants in the same asset, and such rights may have been in existence before the secured creditor entered into the secured transaction or may have arisen afterwards. Further, the priority of a security right may change over the life of the transaction. Ultimately, its rank will be determined at the time it enforces against the encumbered asset.[74]

This calls for establishment of clear and predicable priority rules that allow prospective creditors to determine the priority of their security rights from the very outset of the secured transaction in a reliable, timely, and cost-efficient manner. The Model Law provides for such rules in its chapter V. The Model Law addresses not only priority competitions between secured creditors, which is determined generally by the order of registration,[75] but also competitions arising from the sale, lease, or licence of the asset, and the grantor's insolvency.[76] The Model Law further suggests the need to clearly set forth in the law any preferential claim (for example, claims of employees for unpaid wages and of the State for unpaid taxes) that would have priority over a security right.[77] It also sets forth rules to provide super-priority to creditors that have extended credit to enable the grantor to acquire rights in the asset, referred to in the Model Law as an "acquisition secured creditor," over other secured creditors.[78]

Such provisions may shed light on how to treat retention of title, financial lease, and other similar devices in Korea.

As noted above, the Act on Security over Movables includes rules for determining priority where there is, on the one hand, a registration of a security right and on the other, transfer of possession in the case of movable property, or a notice to or the consent of the debtor of the receivable in the case of receivables.[79] However, as mentioned above in Section 2-4, the co-existence of assignment for security purposes and security right over movable property poses some interesting questions and challenges. Under the former, the assignee need not register its right and is considered to have title as against third parties. Under the latter, the secured creditor needs to register in order to establish such security right.

Suppose Company X transfers title of a piece of equipment by way of security to Bank Y. While Bank Y would have ownership as against third parties, as Company X retains possession, it is difficult for Bank Z to tell whether the asset is encumbered. Bank Z would have to inquire from Company X about the equipment. The problem is that it may not be possible for Company X, the assignor, to subsequently grant a security right in the same asset, since court precedents deem assignment for security to be a so-called fiduciary transfer of title and do not find the later-in-time assignments valid, where there have been multiple assignments of the movable for security purposes. In any case, Bank Y's right in the equipment would have priority over Bank Z's security right regardless of whether it was registered.[80]

3-4. Enforcement of a Security Right

As noted above in Section 3-3, the occurrence of an event of default is when the secured creditor will rely most on the effectiveness of its security right.[81] A security right makes it possible for the secured creditor to recover what it is owed from the value of the encumbered asset, and the Model Law provides a number of ways to do this.[82] The security agreement can provide the secured creditor with additional enforcement options, as long as they are not in conflict with the Model Law.[83]

Under the Model Law, while a secured creditor can exercise its post-default rights by applying to the court,[84] a secured creditor need not go to court and can instead enforce the security right itself.[85] This may mean a significant change in many jurisdictions,[86] including Korea. Although out-of-court enforcement can make it possible for a secured creditor to recover what it is owed more quickly and efficiently, the Model Law imposes conditions on how a secured creditor can undertake such measures to minimise the risk of misuse.[87] Moreover, enforcement is also subject to the general standard of conduct in article 4 that one "must exercise its rights and perform its obligations under this Law in good faith and in a commercially reasonable manner."

The Model Law proffers a secured creditor with a number of ways to enforce its security right. A secured creditor can sell the encumbered asset and recover what it is owed from the proceeds, lease or license the encumbered asset and recover what it is owed from the rent or royalty payments, or acquire the encumbered asset in total or partial satisfaction of the amount due.[88] A secured creditor's choice of how to enforce will depend on a number of factors, including the type of asset and commercial circumstances.[89] With regard to receivables, Article 82(2) of the Model Law provides for collection of payment even before default, if the grantor consents.

While the Act on Security over Movables may permit enforcement methods similar to the Model Law, the primary and default method for enforcement remains to be 'public' auction, which might take longer for the secured creditor to recover what it is owed. The secured creditor might not be able to recover as much from a public auction than through a private sale. Another issue relates to equitable treatment with an assignor in an assignment for security who would not be subject to the same rules under the Act on Security over Movables. Considering this imbalance and as creditors would likely prefer the methods available in an assignment for security, the utility of the security right under the Act may be questioned.

4. CONCLUDING REMARKS

As noted in the introduction (Section 1), access to credit is crucial to business growth and economic prosperity of a State. It is no wonder that increasing access to credit at affordable rates has been the focus of the work of the World Bank Group and other development banks. UNCITRAL is on the point of embarking on work on access to credit for micro, small, and medium-sized enterprises,[90] which highlights the prominence the topic has gained.

Reform of secured transactions regimes is not just about the legal framework. It entails broader discussion about the social and economic policies of a State. For example, governments sometimes unlock finance for certain businesses. It also involves regulatory aspects. For instance, national prudential regulation may, or may not, consider movables in mitigating the credit exposures of financial institutions. Furthermore, infrastructure improvements may be required to support the lending practice. As witnessed in the plan the Financial Services Commission outlined in 2018, collateral valuation mechanisms, information sharing by financial institutions, and secondary markets need to be developed. In short, legislative reform is only one part of the entire reform process that needs to involve all relevant stakeholders and considerations.

One must also not forget that getting credit is only one side of the story. One can get credit only when another is willing to provide it. While secured transaction laws may furnish the structure to enable businesses to utilise the value inherent in their movable assets to obtain credit, such structure must also incline financial institutions to extend loans secured by those movable assets and prompt competition in the market. Otherwise, secured credit will unlikely be readily available to businesses at affordable cost. This is why any legislative framework for secured transactions must take into account not only the credit needs of business, but also willingness of banks and other financial institutions to extend credit. Further, as secured transactions often involve third parties, legitimate interests of all parties affected by a secured transaction should be balanced.

In this context, the bill the Ministry of Justice has been preparing to introduce appears to be a step forward. If the Act on Security over Movables were to be amended accordingly, it would establish another security device that may be created to encumber different types of assets, movable property and receivables. However, this does not equate to an 'all-asset security right,' which the Model Law facilitates, and it is hoped that in any event, fragmentation does not become a trend.

As highlighted above, due diligence that potential creditors would have to conduct on the assets to be encumbered to ensure that they obtain priority over other creditors and the requirements that they would need to meet for creation or third-party effectiveness would depend on the type of asset and vary significantly. This translates into 'costs' to the lenders, which further result in higher interest rate and even cause reluctance to lend based on movable assets.

While the legal tradition that underpins the Korean law should be respected, a number of economies with different legal traditions have already considered and implemented secured transaction law reform based on the Model Law. It may indeed be difficult and not practical to amend the Civil Act,[91] but the Model Law may be adapted to the legal system. Patching up the legislation cannot be a long-term plan. In this regard, Korea should take a more holistic approach to secured transactions law reform, and may wish ultimately to implement the functional, integrated, and comprehensive approach of the Model Law, as a way to facilitate lending to businesses.

REFERENCES

Somin Chung, "Proposal for the Reform of the Secured Transactions," Kyungpook National University Law Journal 67 (2019) [in Korean], pp. 169-193.

Suhn-Kyoung Hong and Jang-Ho Kim, "Chapter 32: South Korea," in JOHNSTON William (ed.), Security over Receivables: An International Handbook, (2008), pp. 481-495.

Woo-jung Jon, Cross-border Transfer and Collateralisation of Receivables: A Comparative Analysis of Multiple Legal Systems, (2018).

Hyoung-Seok Kim, "New Security Rights on Movables and Claims: An Overview," Seoul Law Journal 52(3) (2011) [in Korean], pp. 191-243.

Hyunjin Kim, "Modernization of security transaction by UNCITRAL and a proposal for reform of Security over Movable Property and Receivables," The Journal of Comparative Private Law 25(4) (2018) [in Korean], pp. 1145-1188.

Jae-Hyung Kim, "Development of Security Rights Law since the Codification of the Civil Code of Korea," Journal of Korean Law 13(2) (2014), pp. 271-299.

Jae-Hyung Kim, "The Main Issues in the Act on Security of Movable Property, Receivables, etc. – A Discussion on the Legislative Process –," The Korean Journal of Civil Law 61 (2012) [in Korean], pp. 3-35.

Youngjoon Kwon, "An Overview on the UNCITRAL Model Law on Secured Transactions and its Implication," The Journal of Comparative Private Law 24(2) (2017) [in Korean], pp. 599-638.

Jae Sung Lee, UNCITRAL Legislative Guide on Secured Transactions and its Implications on the Korean Legal Regime, (2008).

Kwang-Hyun Suk, "UNCITRAL Legislative Guide on Secured Transactions and the Security Right Regime on Movables and Receivables under Korean Law," International Trade Law 88 (2009) [in Korean], pp. 173-217.

Kwang-Hyun Suk and Woo-Jung Jon, "South Korea," in CAMPBELL Dennis (ed.), International Secured Transactions, Binder 2, (2010).

Notes

1. World Bank, Doing Business 2020: Comparing Business Regulation in 190 Economies, (2020), available at https://openknowledge.worldbank.org/handle/109 86/32436.
2. Act No 10366.
3. Financial Services Commission, "Plan to Facilitate the Use of Movable Assets as Collateral," Press Release 23 May 2018, http://fsc.go.kr/downManager?bbsid =BBS0048&no=126471.
4. Ministry of Economy and Finance, "2020 Economic Policies," Press Release 19 December 2019, http://english.moef.go.kr/pc/selectTbPressCenterDtl.do?boardCd= N0001&seq=4805.
5. Approximately USD 2.5 billion.
6. Financial Services Commission, "Key Tasks in Financial Policy for 2020," Press Release 23 December 2019, http://fsc.go.kr/downManager?bbsid=BBS0048&no= 147739.
7. Ministry of Justice Announcement No 2019-359. *See also*, Somin Chung, "Proposal for the Reform of the Secured Transactions," Kyungpook National University Law Journal 67 (2019) [in Korean], pp. 184~185.
8. The text of the Model Law is available at https://uncitral.un.org/sites/uncitral.un. org/files/media-documents/uncitral/en/19-08779_e_ebook.pdf.
9. UNCITRAL Model Law on Secured Transactions: Guide to enactment, (2017) (the "Guide to Enactment"), paras. 5-6. The text of Guide to Enactment is available at https://uncitral.un.org/sites/uncitral.un.org/files/media-documents/uncitral/ en/mlst_guide_to_enactment_e.pdf.
10. Kwang-Hyun Suk and Woo-Jung Jon, "South Korea," in CAMPBELL Dennis (ed.), International Secured Transactions, Binder 2, (2010) ("Suk and Jon"), p. KOR-1.
11. Article 329 of the Civil Act provides that "[a] pledgee of movables is entitled to hold possession of the movables which he has received from the debtor or a third person as security for his claim, and to obtain satisfaction of his claim out of the movables in preference to other creditors."
12. Civil Act, art. 330.
13. Civil Act, art. 345.
14. Civil Act, art. 346.
15. Civil Act, art. 349.
16. Civil Act, art. 338.
17. Civil Act, art. 339. Article 59 of the Commercial Act states that this "shall not apply to pledges established for the purpose of securing claims arising out of commercial activities," permitting consent to extrajudicial enforcement before the secured obligation falls due. *See also*, Supreme Court Judgment of 18 July

2017, Docket No 2017Da207499, unofficial English translation available at http://library.scourt.go.kr/SCLIB_data/decision/18_2017Da207499.htm.

18. Civil Act, art. 353.

19. Civil Act, art. 356.

20. Civil Act, art. 186.

21. Civil Act, art. 358.

22. Civil Act, art. 372.

23. Article 787(1) of the Commercial Act provides that "[a] registered ship may be used for purposes of a mortgage" and article 790 provides for mutatis mutandis application to "ships under construction."

24. Act on Mortgage on Motor Vehicles and Other Specific Movables, art. 3. The Act prohibits the creation of a pledge over these specific movables (Article 9) and requires registration to make effective any acquisition, loss, or change of such mortgage (Article 5).

25. Factory and Mining Assets Mortgage Act, arts. 13 and 53. This variant is favoured by creditors in Korea that seek to establish a blanket security right in a factory, (Suk and Jon, *supra* note 10, p. KOR-15).

26. Civil Act, art. 363.

27. Jae-Hyung Kim, "Development of Security Rights Law since the Codification of the Civil Code of Korea," Journal of Korean Law 13(2) (2014) ("KIM JH"), pp. 287~288; Woo-Jung Jon, Cross-border Transfer and Collateralisation of Receivables: A Comparative Analysis of Multiple Legal Systems, (2018) ("Jon"), pp. 23~24.

28. Civil Act, art. 189.

29. *See e.g.*, Supreme Court Judgment of 28 October 2004, Docket No 2003Da 30463.

30. Civil Act, art. 450.

31. Jae-Hyung Kim, *supra* note 27, p. 290; Hyoung-Seok Kim, "New Security Rights on Movables and Claims: An Overview," Seoul Law Journal 52(3) (2011) [in Korean] ("KIM HS"), pp. 193. *See also*, Suhn-Kyoung Hong and Jang-Ho Kim, "Chapter 32: South Korea," in JOHNSTON William (ed.), Security over Receivables: An International Handbook, (2008), para. 32.07.

32. *See also*, Supreme Court Judgment of 7 September 1999, Docket No 98Da47283.

33. Act on Security over Movables, art. 2.

34. Act on Security over Movables, art. 3(3).

35. Act on Security over Movables, arts. 2 and 7.

36. Act on Security over Movables, art. 35.

37. Kwang-Hyun Suk, "UNCITRAL Legislative Guide on Secured Transactions and the Security Right Regime on Movables and Receivables under Korean Law," International Trade Law 88 (2009) [in Korean] ("SUK"), p. 186.

38. Act on Security over Movables, arts. 2.2 and 3(2).

39. Act on Security over Movables, arts. 2.3 and 34(2).

40. Act on Security over Movables, art. 7(2).

41. In the case of receivable, see Supreme Court Judgment of 14 July 2016, Docket No 2015Da71856, 71863.

42. Act on Security over Movables, art. 35(3).

43. Hyoung Seok Kim, *supra* note 31, p. 233.

44. Act on Security over Movables, art. 21(2). Further notification requirements are provided for in Article 23.

45. Article 338 of the Civil Act is as follows: "(1) A pledgee may sell the pledged article by auction to obtain satisfaction of his claim. (2) A pledgee may apply to the court to have the pledged article appropriated to the satisfaction of the debt to the extent of its value appraised by an expert, provided there is a justifiable reason for doing so. In such case, the pledgee must give the debtor and pledger notice of the application in advance."

46. Suk, *supra* note 37, p. 197. *See also,* Hyunjin Kim, "Modernization of security transaction by UNCITRAL and a proposal for reform of Security over Movable Property and Receivables," The Journal of Comparative Private Law 25(4) (2018) [in Korean], pp. 1176 and 1181.

47. Act on Security over Movables, art. 36; Civil Act, art. 353.

48. Jae-Hyung Kim, *supra* note 27, p. 297.

49. Guide to Enactment, para. 5.

50. UNCITRAL Practice Guide to the Model Law on Secured Transactions, (2019) (the "Practice Guide"), para. 4. The text of the Practice Guide is available at https://uncitral.un.org/sites/uncitral.un.org/files/media-documents/uncitral/en/19-10 910_e.pdf.

51. Practice Guide, para. 10.

52. Model Law, art. 1(1) and (3). This is also one of the aspects included in the strength of legal rights index of the Doing Business report.

53. Model Law, art. 1(2).

54. Model Law, art. 2(kk)(ii).

55. Model Law, art. 2(ff).

56. Practice Guide, para. 81.

57. Act on Security over Movables, art. 35.

58. Model Law, arts. 13 and 61-67.

59. Model Law, art. 6; Practice Guide, para. 11.

60. Model Law, art. 6(1).

61. In Korea, with respect to security rights in movable property, such as pledge, assignment for security, and security right over movable property, an additional act to publicise is treated as a prerequisite not only to achieving third-party effectiveness, but also to the creation (Civil Act, art. 330; Act on Security over Movables, art. 7(1)).

62. Model Law, arts. 2(n) and 6(2); Practice Guide, para. 49.

63. Model Law, art. 9(1).

64. Practice Guide, para. 13.

65. Model Law, art. 18. Another method for achieving the third-party effectiveness of a security right is physical possession of a tangible encumbered asset by the secured creditor, as intangible assets are not capable of physical possession (Guide to Enactment, para. 123). The Model Law also provides other methods for achieve third-party effectiveness for bank accounts, negotiable documents, and uncertificated non-intermediated securities (Articles 25-27).

66. Act on Security over Movables, art. 43(1).

67. Model Law, Model Registry Provisions, art. 8.

68. Model Law, Model Registry Provisions, arts. 4 and 8.

69. Act on Security over Movables, art. 41(1).

70. Model Law, Model Registry Provisions, art. 22(a); Guide to Enactment, paras. 228-229.

71. Movable Security Act, art. 2.8.

72. Suk, *supra* note 37, pp. 180 and 207; Jon, *supra* note 27, p. 34.

73. Youngjoon Kwon, "An Overview on the UNCITRAL Model Law on Secured Transactions and its Implication," The Journal of Comparative Private Law, 24 (2) (2017) [in Korean], pp. 630~631.

74. Practice Guide, para. 272.

75. Model Law, art. 29.

76. Model Law, arts. 34-35.

77. Model Law, art. 36.

78. Model Law, arts. 2(a) and 38-39.

79. Act on Security over Movables, arts. 7(3) and 35(3).

80. Jae-Hyung Kim, "The Main Issues in the Act on Security of Movable Property, Receivables, etc. – A Discussion on the Legislative Process –," The Korean Journal of Civil Law 61 (2012) [in Korean], pp. 23~25.

81. Practice Guide, para. 299.

82. Practice Guide, para. 302.

83. Model Law, art. 72(1)(b). Cf. Civil Act, art. 339 ("No pledger shall, by a contract effected before the debt becomes due, agree that the pledgee shall, by way of satisfaction of his/her claim, acquire the ownership of the pledged article or dispose of it otherwise than in the manner provided for by Acts.").

84. The enacting State may specify another authority.

85. Model Law, art. 73(1).

86. Practice Guide, para. 304.

87. Model Law, arts. 77-80.

88. Practice Guide, para. 305.

89. Practice Guide, para. 306.

90. A/74/17, para. 192(a); A/CN.9/WG.I/WP.119.

91. Jae Sung Lee, UNCITRAL Legislative Guide on Secured Transactions and its Implications on the Korean Legal Regime, (2008), p. 74.

RECENT DEVELOPMENTS

Law and Practices of the ADIZs over the East China Sea

KIM Han-Taek
Professor
Kangwon National University, Chuncheon, Korea

Key Words

ADIZ, CADIZ, KADIZ, JADIZ, UNCLOS, EEZ, FIR, ICAO, Chicago Convention, East China Sea

1. INTRODUCTION

Russian and Chinese bombers and reconnaissance planes have occasionally entered the South Korea's Air Defense Identification Zone (hereinafter KADIZ) in recent years. On October 22, 2019 six Russian military aircraft entered KADIZ, prompting the Republic of Korea Air Force (hereinafter ROKAF) to scramble fighter jets to turn them back.[1] On November 29, 2019 a Chinese military plane violated KADIZ, prompting ROKAF to deploy its fighters to drive it out. The plane, presumed to be its Y-9 surveillance aircraft, first entered KADIZ and exited the zone. It later reentered the zone two more times before its last exit in a day.[2] Actually Russia and China did not recognize KADIZ and the Japan's Air Defense Identification Zone (hereinafter JADIZ) declared by Japan. And Republic of Korea (hereinafter, "Korea") and Japan did not recognize the China's Air

Defense Identification Zone (hereinafter CADIZ) over the East China Sea which was declared by the Chinese Government on November 23, 2013.[3]

2. ADIZs OVER THE EAST CHINA AND INTERNATIONAL LAW

CADIZ caused a significant repercussion effect to Korea, Japan and the United States. Especially, CADIZ covers the Senkaku Islands (Chinese name 釣魚島; Diaoyu Islands) of Japan, made up of five islets and three barren rocks covering an area of 7 square kilometers which is the island chain, claimed by China, Taiwan and Japan and the Ieodo base of Korea. The Ieodo (Socotra Rock, Chinese name 蘇岩礁), which is a submerged rock on which South Korea has constructed a scientific research station, is within the South Korea's Exclusive Economic Zone (hereinafter EEZ) and also is within the China's EEZ. The Ieodo base is 170km away from the Jeju Island in South Korea. While neither country claims the rock as territory, China has objected to Korean activities there as a breach of its EEZ rights. CADIZ established until approximately 300 miles from the Chinese coast is the zone established for detecting, identifying a flying object approaching to the mainland China and taking proper measures. CADIZ overlaps with JADIZ by more than a half and it also overlaps partially with KADIZ and Taiwan's ADIZ. Actually the military activities of other countries in EEZ are not prohibited under the UN Convention on the Law of the Sea (hereinafter UNCLOS) in 1982, but China is one of a few countries that are very sensitive to the security of its EEZ.

Although over 20 countries maintain ADIZs, CADIZ is problematic because the Chinese Government expects all aircraft traversing the heavily trafficked airspace of the East China Sea to submit flight plans and obey air traffic controllers, even if the aircraft have no intention of approaching China. According to the announcement, aircraft that fail to follow instructions are subject to unspecified "defensive emergency measures." The implied threat, of course, is that if aircraft do not comply, China might shoot them down.

Korea also declared the expansion of KADIZ on December 8, 2013 in response to the CADIZ. KADIZ includes the southern airspace of Marado Island and Hongdo Island as well as the airspace of Ieodo base to the south by matching the southern boundary line with the Incheon Flight Information Region (hereinafter FIR) allocated to Korea by the International Civil Aviation Organization (hereinafter ICAO).[4] Therefore, the range of KADIZ has increased to two thirds of the total area of South Korea. As far as KADIZ over the East Sea (also called the Sea of Japan by Japanese Government) is concerned old KADIZ established first by the United States Air Force in 1950 during the Korean War is valid. Especially KADIZ on the airspace of the East Sea almost adjoins JADIZ which was originally established by the United States and inherited by Japan in 1969. Since FIR does not overlap between countries, the FIR is relatively persuasive as the standard for establishing ADIZs over the East China Sea especially in the coastal countries of Northeast Asia such as China, Japan, Taiwan and South Korea.

Since there are some news that China is establishing a plan to establish CADIZ in the South China Sea, it might create tension to ASEAN countries.[5] As far as the islands, reefs, banks, and other features of the region are concerned, the possible disputes among states in the South China Sea include the Spratly Islands, Paracel Islands, Scarborough Shoal, Pratas Islands and various boundaries in the Gulf of Tonkin. The Situation in the South China Sea is much more politically complex than in the East China Sea, largely because of competing territorial claims by numerous claimants such as China, the Philippines, Brunei, Vietnam, Taiwan and Malaysia etc.

ADIZs are the air sectors that countries establish on EEZ or sky of high seas in order to defend their territorial airspace and ADIZs are declared unilaterally based on the right of self defense under the international law.[6] So there is no standard to establish or prohibit the establishment of ADIZs and there is no international regulatory organization that could control ADIZs. Since the Chicago Convention of 1944 (The Convention on International Civil Aviation) that established the ICAO only deals with civil aircraft, ADIZs are not explicitly mentioned in the convention and the organization. In fact there is no provision in the international law that specifies the legal authority for the relevant country to declare ADIZ unilaterally. Although the ADIZ is not part of a country's air space, the role of ADIZs is to provide a means of anticipatory self-defense from incoming and immediate threats emanating above the high seas. ADIZs can only be legally applied in relation to preventing the unauthorized entry of aircraft into the national airspace. ADIZs cannot be used to control foreign aircraft not intending to enter the national airspace. States only enjoy exclusive sovereignty over the airspace above their territory, a right which ends at the 12 nautical mile border of the territorial sea. Beyond this territorial belt, all states enjoy the high seas freedoms, including freedom of overflight, a customary principle memorialized in UNCLOS of 1982. In the absence of a treaty or convention concerning ADIZs, state practice and government statements set the norms of conduct relating to the declaration and maintenance of ADIZs.

3. CONCLUSION

In conclusion as far as ADIZs over the East China Sea is concerned, the best way to solve these problems, is the urgent need of consultation among Korea, China, Japan and Russia. There is a model such as "The Letter Regarding the Prevention of Accidental Contingencies between Korean Military Aircraft and Japanese Self-Defense Force Aircraft" concluded in 1999. In this letter a Korean military aircraft should give a notice to the air control unit of Japan at least 30 minutes in advance when it flies to JADIZ and a Japanese military aircraft flying to KADIZ applies in the same way.

Notes

1. (3rd LD) 6 Russian military aircraft intrude into S. Korea's air defense zone, Yonhap News Agency, October 22, 2019.

2. Chinese warplane violates Korea's air defense zone again, The Korea Herald, November 29, 2019.

3. China creates new air defense zone in East China Sea amid dispute with Japan, The Washington Post, November 23, 2013.

4. South Korea Announces Expansion of Its Air Defense Zone, The New York Times, December 8, 2013.

5. Jae Woon Lee, "Tension on the Air: The Air Defense Identification Zones on the East China Sea," 7 Journal of East Asia and International Law, 2014, pp. 280~281.

6. Nicholas Grief, "Public International Law in the Airspace of the High Seas," Martinus Nijhoff Publishers, 1994, p. 153; Dais A. Welch, "What's an ADIZ?, Why the United States, Japan, and China Get It Wrong," Foreign Affairs, December 9, 2011.

KYIL

The U.S. Nuclear Regulatory Commission's (NRC) Standard Design Certification Approval of Korean Nuclear Advanced Power Reactor (APR1400)

WON Jae-Chun
Professor
Handong International Law School, Pohang, Korea

1. INTRODUCTION

On September 2019, Korea Hydro & Nuclear Power Co., Ltd. (KHNP) and Korea Electric Power Corporation (KEPCO) of the Republic of Korea (hereinafter, "Korea") received a design certificate for its APR1400 reactor from the U.S. Nuclear Regulatory Commission (hereinafter, "NRC"). The Korean companies submitted the design to NRC in September 2013 and then submitted a revised version of the application in December 2014; in September 2018, the APR1400 obtained the Standard Design Approval (hereinafter, "SDA"), and in September 2019 it received a design certificate valid for 15 years from the NRC.[1] The APR1400 is the first non-U.S. nuclear reactor certified by the NRC.

It should be noted that prior to the U.S. NRC certification, in October 2018, the APR1400 was also granted European design certification from the European Utility Requirements (hereinafter, "EUR"). The APR 1400 is the only non-U.S. reactor which has both European and U.S. certification, meeting the highest possible industry

257

standards for its safety, reliability, and functional efficiency. In the absence of an international nuclear reactor design regulatory mechanism, European Certification and the U.S. Certification serves as the international industry standard in nuclear reactor design.

2. APR1400 CERTIFICATION PROCESS: US TITLE 10 CFR PROCEDURE

In the USA, the whole nuclear reactor design approval and certification procedure is applied as a U.S. legal and regulatory proceeding. Regarding the SDA and Design Certification[2] Activities (hereinafter, "DCA"), the NRC must review the nuclear reactor by following the thorough process, which is specifically stipulated in Title 10 of the Code of Federal Register[3] (CFR), from Parts 1 to 199. For example, in Part 52 CFR (*Licenses, Certifications, and Approvals for Nuclear Power Plants*), exhaustive sets of legal procedures follow, such as *General Provisions*, eight different *Subparts* with explicit texts on each subpart's scope of applicability, interpretation, and all procedures that must be meticulously followed through. The certification procedure is a rigorous and time-consuming process; however, such law on approval and certification procedure firmly establishes a set standard to secure the safety and protection of the people and the environment.

Based on the ratification of 1953's Korea-U.S. nuclear energy cooperation treaty,[4] from the very beginning, nuclear energy development in Korea primarily applied and improved the U.S. standard of safety in Korean nuclear reactors thus, Korea has become familiar with the technical protocol of U.S. nuclear regulations and procedures. Accordingly, unnecessary burdens in the certification process were curtailed as APR1400 has achieved technological compatibility with U.S. nuclear safety standards and design protocol in accordance with the U.S. law and regulation process.

3. TREATY BASED KOREA-U.S. NUCLEAR ENERGY COOPERATION

In order to promote the peaceful civilian use of nuclear energy,[5] the U.S. intentionally supported the spread of nuclear reactors, as they shared many design ideas and patents through international cooperation agreements.[6] In the case of Korea, the U.S. signed three agreements on cooperation regarding the production of nuclear energy. On February 3, 1953, Korea and the U.S. signed the *Agreement for Cooperation Between the Government on the Republic of Korea Concerning Civil Use of Atomic Energy* and continued with the signing of the *Agreement for Cooperation Between the Government of the Republic of Korea and the Government of the United States concerning Civil Use of Atomic Energy* on November 24, 1972. Most recently, on April 22, 2015, the two nations updated the agreement, allowing vibrant nuclear energy research and industry operation with the *Agreement for Cooperation Between the Government of the Republic of Korea and the Government of the United States of America Concerning Peaceful Uses of Nuclear Energy.*

According to the *Power Magazine*, numerous U.S. engineering, licensing, consulting, and supply chain partners, including AECOM, Jensen and Hughes, MPR Associates, Structural Integrity, and Westinghouse were involved in working together to bring innovation and design licensing process of APR1400.[7] Therefore, the constructive cooperation between and among participatory companies of Korea and the U.S. would enhance APR1400's standing in international nuclear energy market, and invigorate further nuclear safety research.

Furthermore, as a source of clean energy, above mentioned nuclear energy cooperation of the peaceful use of nuclear energy would contribute to the reduction of Carbon dioxide emissions in compliance with the Paris Agreement on Climate Change, and it would meet the energy needs for the IT-based the Fourth Industrial

Revolution.

4. NATIONAL CERTIFICATION PROCESS AS A MEANS OF INTERNATIONAL REGULATORY STANDARD

Since the Second World War, the U.S. implemented a policy to internationalize the peaceful use of nuclear energy. Using bilateral treaties, the U.S. shared nuclear reactor technology with countries such as Korea and Japan. Accordingly, APR1400 validates the original intent and purpose of the U.S. nuclear policy, and it is one of the best-practiced case examples of how the U.S. standard can be applied to a non-U.S. nuclear reactor design for global use. The certified design, construction, and operation of APR1400 would further test and validate the credibility and reliability of the U.S. approval and certification process.

Safety is one of the most fundamental concerns regarding the approval and certification of nuclear reactors. In contemporary times, the six countries, U.S., Korea, Japan, China, France, and Russia, are known to possess sufficient nuclear reactor design capacity, as they have the capacity to export their nuclear reactor. In the absence of an international certification regime, the nuclear reactor design safety regulation is a primarily localized and national process, which brings a dangling uncertainty in the safety of the nuclear reactors and the standard for such operation.

The NRC's approval and certification of APR1400 is a noticeable case on how a national regulatory process could set the international regulatory standard, equivalent to the international customary law standard in the area of nuclear energy and safety.

5. CONCLUSION

The APR1400 received design approval and certification from both the U.S. and the EUR; since the U.S. and EUR set the highest industry standard, APR1400 is expected to qualify for design approval and certification from multiple other national regulatory jurisdictions

Whether the U.S. NRC approval and certification should be the formal international standard is the question of its own. Nevertheless, the U.S. has the longest scientific and peaceful industrial use of nuclear energy, and the approval and certification procedure is transparent and strictly scrutinized, compared to other national processes. In the absence of an international certification process, for all intents and purposes, the U.S. Nuclear Related Laws and Regulations have become an international certification process equivalent.

Notes

1. Nuclear Engineering International Magazine, *Korea's APR-1400 certified by US NRC*, September 2, 2019.

2. The *Standard Design Approval or Design Approval* means an NRC staff approval, issued under subpart E of Part 52 CFR, of a final standard design for a nuclear power reactor of the type described in 10 CFR 50.22. The approval may be for either the final design for the entire reactor facility or the final design of major portions thereof.

3. Following Title 10 of the Code of Federal Regulations (CFR), the principal set of rules and regulations regarding nuclear energy in the U.S. is issued by the federal agencies.

4. *Agreement for Cooperation Between the Government on the Republic of Korea Concerning Civil Use of Atomic Energy*, 1953.

5. The U.S. Congress created the *Atomic Energy Commission* in 1946 to promote the development of nuclear energy for peaceful civilian purposes.

6. World Nuclear Organization Report, *International Standardization of Nuclear Reactor Designs*, January 2010.

7. Sweeney, et al., Power, *Bringing the APR1400 Reactor to Market*, July 2019.

Deportation of North Korean Fishermen by the Republic of Korea

PARK Eon-Kyung
Visiting Professor
Kyung Hee University, Office of Career Development, Seoul, Korea

1. BRIEF OVERVIEW OF THE CASE

The Republic of Korea (hereinafter, "Korea") deported two fishermen from the Democratic of People's Republic of Korea (DPRK) who were found on a fishing vessel captured in the waters near the Northern Limit Line (NLL) in the West (Yellow) Sea. According to the Korea's joint investigation, the two killed 16 other fishermen on the ship and were apprehended by the Korea Navy during their attempt to flee to the DPRK from the NLL showing no desire to defect. The Korea judged that they had no sincere desire to defect in consideration of their crime, the actions they took within the DPRK after having committed the crime and during the arrest of the ship. The Korea then decided to deport them although they provided their written request to defect during the investigation. The Ministry of Unification notified the DPRK of its decision to deport the two and transfer the ship on November 5, 2019. The sailors were repatriated on November 7, 2019 and the vessel was transferred on November 8, 2019. This is the first case where the Korea deported DPRK nationals who were escaping from the DPRK. A Unification Ministry spokesman stated that the Korea decided to expel the fishermen based on the result of inter-departmental discussions because they were "non-political, serious criminals who did not receive protection and could pose a threat to the lives and safety of our people if accepted into our society, and brutal criminals could not be recognized as refugees under international laws."[1]

2. LEGAL AND POLITICAL GROUNDS FOR THE DEPORTATION OF THE DPRK FISHERMEN

The Ministry of Unification reported the deportation case of the fishermen and the National Assembly conducted questioning at the 7th meeting of the Foreign Affairs and Unification Committee of the National Assembly held on November 15, 2019. The major legal issues discussed during the meeting were as follows:

2-1. Constitution of the ROK

Article 3 of the Constitution stipulates that the territory of the Korea shall consist of the Korean peninsula and its adjacent islands. The Supreme Court[2] has held that the residents of the DPRK also fall under the category of citizens of the Korea based on Article 3, and lower courts[3] have maintained the same position.[4] Under international law, residents escaping from the DPRK are dual citizens of the DPRK and the Korea, but according to local law, the residents of the DPRK are also nationals of the Korea. In this regard, the Korea stated that the duality of inter-Korean relations is considered when applying the act in practice, and defectors from the DPRK are accepted as North Korean refugees only after determining the sincerity of their desire to defect.[5]

2-2. North Korean Refugee Protection and Settlement Support Act

The North Korean Refugee Protection and Settlement Support Act (hereinafter referred to as the North Korean Refugee Act) enacted in January 1997 aims to provide residents escaping from the DPRK with protection and support necessary for settlement in the Korea (Article 1). This Act applies to residents escaping from the DPRK who have expressed their intention to be protected by the Korea (Article 3) and any person escaping from the DPRK who intends to be protected under this Act should apply for protection in person with the head of any administrative agency. However, in making a decision on whether to provide protection, offenders of nonpolitical and serious crimes, such as murder, may not be designated as persons eligible for protection (Subparagraph 1 of Paragraph 1 of Article 9).

The Korea judged that the two fishermen were vicious criminals who could pose a threat to the lives and safety of Korea nationals and that they lacked sincerity in their desire to defect and thus, decided on their deportation.[6] The government said the fishermen lacked sincerity despite their expressed desire to defect because their motive, purpose, and preparations were not to defect but to avoid punishment for their murderous acts and their attempt to escape. Some claimed that the two should be punished in the Korea, but the government judged that it would be difficult to proceed with a criminal investigation and prosecution in the Korea as it would not be easy to collect relevant evidence.[7]

3. INTERNATIONAL LEGAL ISSUES

One of the other issues raised and considered was whether the fishermen possessed refugee status. Should the DPRK fishermen be determined to be refugees, the Korea's action to repatriate them would be illegal. Regarding this issue, the government judged that the Refugee Act did not apply to the fishermen since they were DPRK residents and they were not considered to be refugees as they committed a non-political criminal act.[8]

There were also claims at the meeting of Foreign Affairs and Unification Committee of the National Assembly that the extradition of criminals to the DPRK which the Korea has not signed an extradition treaty with was without legal basis and that the repatriation violated the UN Convention against Torture.

4. REVIEW

The Supreme Court of the Korea has recognized that the residents of the DPRK are citizens of the Korea based on Article 3 of the Constitution. However, due to practical limitations, it is not possible to exercise jurisdiction over the residents of the DPRK, and they are subject to protection in accordance with the North Korean Refugee Act after having defected to the Korea.

The Korea did not accept their refugee status and subsequently deported the fishermen in accordance with the North Korean Refugee Act which does not accept offenders of nonpolitical and serious crimes, such as murder committed by persons escaping from the DPRK. The government reconfirmed the principle that a resident escaping from the DPRK becomes a national of the Korea after a determination of their sincere desire to defect.

The incident sparked controversy, and it revealed that there was a gap in judging the legal status of the residents of the DPRK and implementing policies. It is a case that raised the need to prevent recurrence of similar incidents by supplementing related laws.

Notes

1. Refer to National Assembly Secretariat, 371st National Assembly (regular meeting) Foreign Affairs and Unification Committee Meeting No. 7, November 15, 2019.
2. Supreme Court Decision 89Nu6396 decided September 28, 1990.
3. Seoul High Court 99La130, October 12, 1999; Seoul Central District Court 2002Na60862, June 27, 2003.
4. Hyo-Won Lee, "Analysis on the Judicial Precedents about the Relationship between the South and North Korea," *Seoul Law Journal* Vol. 52 No. 3, September 2011, p. 6.
5. National Assembly Secretariat, *supra* note 1, p. 9.
6. *See ibid.*, pp. 4, 11-12.
7. *Ibid.*, p. 6.
8. *Ibid.*, p. 36.

A Summary of Recent WTO Cases involving the Republic of Korea

OH Sun-Young
Associate Professor
Soongsil University, Seoul, Korea

1. INTRODUCTION

Republic of Korea (hereinafter, "Korea") has actively participated in virtually all aspects of World Trade Organization ("WTO") work, and it is one of the major users of dispute settlement procedures under the WTO jurisprudence. Korea initiated three WTO dispute complaints against other member states in 2019. In the same period four cases were brought against Korea; the Appellate Body issued its reports in two cases brought by Japan against Korea, which reports were adopted in 2019.

2. BRIEF SUMMARY OF CASES ADOPTED BY DSB

2-1. Korea — Import Bans & Testing & Certification Requirements for Radionuclides (DS 495)[1]

After the Fukushima Dai-ichi Nuclear Power Plant ("FDNPP") accident on Japan's northeastern coast on 11 March 2011, Korea imposed import bans and additional testing and certification requirements in relation to a broad range of fish and non-fishery products from Japan to ensure food safety in the face of the possible presence of radionuclides in the food imports. Japan challenged Korea's requirement to test for additional radionuclides if caesium or iodine is detected, as applied to both non-fishery and fishery products, and it challenged Korea's product-specific import bans on two fishery products, as well as the blanket import ban dated 2013 on all fishery products from 8 prefectures for 28 fishery products.

Before the Panel, Japan raised claims against the Korean measures under SPS Agreement Articles 2.3, 5.6, 7, and 8 and Annexes B and C. The Panel found violations of Articles 2.3, 5.6, 5.7, 7 by ruling that Korea caused "arbitrarily and unjustifiably" discrimination against Japan and they were "more trade restrictive than required" to achieve Korea's appropriate level of protection ("ALOP"). The Appellate Body concluded that the Panel erred by not accounting for all of these elements of Korea's ALOP in its assessment under Article 5.6. The Appellate Body thus reversed the Panel's finding that Korea's measures were inconsistent with Article 5.6. The Appellate Body also found that the Panel erred in its interpretation of Article 2.3 by considering that relevant "conditions" under this provision may be exclusively limited to "the risk present in products," to the exclusion of other conditions, including territorial conditions, which have the potential to affect the products at issue.

2-2. Korea — Anti-dumping Duties on Pneumatic Valves from Japan (DS 504)[2]

Korea imposed definitive anti-dumping duties of 11.7-22.8 percent on Japanese pneumatic valves over five years in 2015. Pneumatic valves are vital cogs in cars, electronics and other machines, and Japanese valves for pneumatic transmission previously accounted for more than 70 percent of the Korean market. In 2016,

Japan challenged the measure before the WTO dispute settlement body by arguing that Korea's imposition of anti-dumping duties is inconsistent with the Anti-Dumping Agreement due to defects in the determination of injury and a causal relationship as well as the lack of transparency in the investigation procedure conducted by the Korea Trade Commission ("KTC") and the KTC's Office of Trade Investigation.

Before the Panel, Japan raised claims against the Korean measures under Anti-Dumping Agreement Articles 1, 3.1, 3.2, 3.4, 3.5, 6.5, 6.5.1, 6.9.1, 12.2, 12.2.2, and Article VI of the GATT 1994. The Panel found that Korea had acted inconsistently with some provisions of the Anti-Dumping Agreement; in particular, Korean Investigating Authorities acted inconsistently with Articles 3.1 and 3.5 of the Anti-Dumping Agreement in their causation analysis as a result of flaws in their analysis of the effect of the dumped imports on prices in the domestic market, and Article 6.5 with respect to their treatment of information provided by the applicants as confidential without requiring that good cause be shown. The Appellate Body found that the Panel did not err in finding that Japan's claims concerning causation, as well as its claims concerning the confidential treatment of information were within its terms of reference. The Appellate Body, however, found that the Panel erred in finding that Japan's claims concerning the definition of domestic industry, the volume of the dumped imports, the price effects of the dumped imports, the disclosure of essential facts and part of Japan's claim concerning the impact of the dumped imports on the domestic industry were outside its terms of reference. Interestingly, South Korea and Japan have issued differing interpretations of the Appellate Body's holdings, both insisting that they have won the case.

3. AFTERWORD

Five out of seven pending cases involving Korea at the WTO will be left in limbo due to the suspended operation of its dispute settlement body. The panel reports for these five cases are scheduled to be delivered in 2020. The five cases are as follows: (1) Korea — Measures Affecting Trade in Commercial Vessels (DS 571, complainant is Japan, and the Panel was composed on 6 November 2018); (2) United States — Anti-Dumping and Countervailing Duties on Certain Products and the Use of Facts Available (DS 539, the Panel was composed on 5 December 2018); (3) Korea — Sunset Review of Anti-Dumping Duties on Stainless Steel Bars (DS 553, complaint is Japan, and the Panel was composed on 21 January 2019); (4) United States — Safeguard measure on imports of large residential washers (DS 546, Panel was composed on 1 July 2019); and (5) Japan — Measures Related to the Exportation of Products and Technology to Korea (DS 590, consultations were requested on 11 September 2019).

Notes

1. Report of the Appellate Body, KOREA - IMPORT BANS, AND TESTING AND CERTIFICATION REQUIREMENTS FOR RADIONUCLIDES, April 11, 2019, WT/DS495/AB/R.
2. Report of the Appellate Body, KOREA - ANTI-DUMPING DUTIES ON PNEUMATIC VALVES FROM JAPAN, September 10, 2019, WT/DS504/AB/R.

An Overview of the United Nations Convention on International Settlement Agreements Resulting from Mediation

LEE Gyooho
Professor of Law
Chung–Ang University School of Law, Seoul, Korea

1. INTRODUCTION

Cross-border alternative dispute resolution mechanisms such as mediation and arbitration are widely used. To promote arbitration as an effective method of resolving international commercial disputes, the Convention on the Recognition and Enforcement of Foreign Arbitral Awards (New York, 1958) (hereinafter "New York Convention") entered into force on June 7, 1959. Korea became a contracting state on February 8, 1973. New York Convention aims in providing that foreign and non-domestic arbitral awards will not discriminated against and it forces contracting states to ensure such awards are generally recognized and enforced in their jurisdiction in the same way as domestic arbitral awards.[1] However, in spite of increasing importance of mediation in transnational disputes, a harmonized international instrument has lacked until the adoption of the United Nations Convention on International Settlement Agreements Resulting from Mediation (hereinafter the "Singapore Convention on Mediation").

The Singapore Convention on Mediation was adopted on December 20, 2018 by resolution 73/198 during the seventy-third session of the General Assembly of the United Nations. It was open for signature on August 7, 2019 in Singapore and, thereafter, at the United Nations headquarters in New York. The Republic of Korea (hereinafter "Korea") became a signatory of Singapore Convention on Mediation on August 7, 2019. As of January 29, 2020, 52 countries including China, India, Singapore and United States of America are signatories of Singapore Convention on Mediation. In accordance with Article 14(1) of the Singapore Convention on Mediation, it shall enter into force six months after deposit of the third instrument of ratification, acceptance, approval or accession. As of January 29, 2020, the Singapore Convention on Mediation is not yet in force.[2] The Singapore Convention on Mediation is consistent with the UNCITRAL Model Law on International Commercial Mediation and International Settlement Agreements resulting from Mediation (2018). Each country is free to adopt either the Singapore Convention on Mediation, the Model Laws or both.[3]

2. OBJECTIVES

The Singapore Convention on Mediation purports to establish an effective and uniform legal framework for the right to invoke settlement agreements, and for their enforcement as well. It is expected to promote legal certainty and stability to international mechanism on mediation.

3. KEY PROVISIONS

The Singapore Convention on Mediation consists of preamble and 16 provisions. The term, "Mediation," under the Singapore Convention on Mediation refers to "a process, irrespective of the expression used or the basis upon which the process is carried out, whereby parties attempt to reach an amicable settlement of their dispute with the assistance of a third person or persons ("the mediator") lacking the authority to impose a solution upon the parties to the dispute." (Article 2, paragraph 3).

3-1. Scope of Application

The Singapore Convention on Mediation applies to international settlement agreements resulting from mediation and concluded in writing by parties to resolve an international commercial dispute (Article 1, paragraph 1). A settlement agreement is "in writing" if its content is recorded in any form including an electronic one (Article 2, paragraph 2). The nature of a commercial dispute is international in a case where at least two parties to the settlement agreement have their places of business in different nations, or in a case where the nation in which the parties to the settlement agreement have their places of business is different from either the nation which a substantial part of the obligations under the settlement agreement is performed or the nation with which the subject matter of the settlement agreement is most closely connected (Article 1, paragraph 1).

The application of the Singapore Convention on Mediation is excluded from settlement agreements concluded by a consumer for personal, family or household purposes, or relating to family, inheritance or employment law (Article 1, paragraph 2). Also, the Singapore Convention on Mediation does not apply to a settlement agreement that has been approved by a court or concluded before a court and is enforceable as a judgment in the nation of that court and to a settlement agreements that has been recorded and is enforceable as an arbitral award (Article 1, paragraph 3). It is intended to avoid potential overlapping application with existing and future international instruments such as New York Convention, the Convention on Choice of Court Agreements (2005) and the Convention on the Recognition and Enforcement of Foreign Judgments in Civil or Commercial Matters (2019).[4]

3-2. General Principles: Obligations of Contracting Parties to the Singapore Convention on Mediation

The signatories to the Singapore Convention on Mediation are obliged to enforce a settlement agreement based on the Convention (Article 3, paragraph 1). Also, a Party to the Convention shall permit a disputing party to invoke a settlement agreement under the Singapore Convention on Mediation in a case where a dispute occurs in terms of a matter that was claimed to be already resolved by the settlement agreement, so as to show that the matter has already been resolved by the settlement agreement (Article 3, paragraph 2).

3-3. Formality requirements for reliance on settlement agreements

Article 4 of the Singapore Convention on Mediation provides the formalities for relying on a settlement agreement. When it comes to the formalities for reliance on settlement agreements, a party relying on a settlement agreement shall supply to the competent authority of the Party to the Singapore Convention on Mediation the settlement agreement signed by them and evidence that settlement resulted from mediation (Article 4, paragraph 1). Furthermore, Article 4 (2) provides the formality requirement in terms of an electronic communication. The competent authority may compel the disputing party to submit any necessary document so as to verify that the formalities for relying on the settlement agreement are abided by under the Singapore Convention (Article 4, paragraph 4).

3-4. Grounds for Refusing to Grant Relief

When certain requirements are met, the competent authority may refuse to grant relief at the request of the party against whom the relief is sought or on its own initiative. The competent authority may refuse to grant relief at the request of the party against whom the relief is sought only if that party furnished to the competent authority proof that, for example, a party to the settlement agreement was under some incapacity (Article 5, paragraph 1 (a)). Furthermore, the competent authority of the Party to the Singapore Convention on Mediation may, *sua sponte*, refuse to grant relief if granting relief is contrary to the public policy of that Party or the subject matter of the dispute is not capable of settlement by mediation under the law of that Party (Article 5, paragraph 2).

3-5. Parallel Applications or Claims

If an application or a claim relating to settlement agreement has been made to a court, an arbitral tribunal or any other competent authority which may affect the relief sought, the competent authority of the Party to the Singapore Convention on Mediation may, if it considers it proper, adjourn the decision and may also, on the request of a party, order the other party to give suitable security (Article 6).

3-6. Relationship to Other Laws or Treaties

The Singapore Convention on Mediation provides for the application of most favorable framework for settlement agreements. Hence, the Singapore Convention on Mediation is not allowed to deprive an interested party of any right may have to avail itself of a settlement agreement in the manner and to the extent allowed by the other laws or the treaties of the Party to the Singapore Convention on Mediation (Article 7).

3-7. Reservations

Only two reservations are permitted under the Singapore Convention on Mediation (Article 8, paragraphs 1 and 2). A Party to the Singapore Convention on Mediation may declare that it shall not apply the Convention to settlement agreements to which it is a party, or to which any governmental agencies or any person acting on behalf of a governmental agency is a party, to the extent specified in the declaration (Article 8, paragraph 1 (a)). Also, a Party to the Singapore Convention on Mediation may declare that it shall apply the Convention only to the extent that the parties to the settlement agreement have agreed to the application of the Convention (Article 8, paragraph (b)).

Any reservation of the Singapore Convention on Mediation shall apply only to settlement agreements prospectively. In other words, it shall apply only to settlement agreements which have been concluded after the entry into force of the Singapore Convention on Mediation for the Party to the Convention concerned (Article 9).

Notes

1. United Nations Commission on International Trade Law, Convention on the Recognition and Enforcement of Foreign Arbitral Awards (New York, 1958), p. 1 (2015), available at https://treaties.un.org/pages/ViewDetails.aspx?src=TREATY &mtdsg_no=XXII-4&chapter=22&clang=_en (last visit on January 29, 2020).

2. *Id.*

3. United Nations Commission on International Trade Law, United Nations Convention on International Settlement Agreements Resulting from Mediation (New York, 2018) (the "Singapore Convention on Mediation"), available at https://uncitral.un.org/en/texts/mediation/conventions/international_settlement_agree ments (last visit on January 28, 2020).

4. *Id.*

Resolutions related to International Law Adopted in the 2nd Half of the 20th National Assembly

CHUNG Min-Jung
Legislative Research Officer
National Assembly Research Service, Seoul, Korea

As of December 16, 2019, there was a total of two resolutions under the National Assembly Foreign Affairs and Unification Committee adopted at the plenary session during the 2nd half of the 20th National Assembly (May 30, 2016 to May 29, 2020). (Refer to Table 1)[1]

Table 1. Resolutions Related to International Law Adopted in the 2nd Half of the 20th National Assembly

(As of Dec. 16, 2019)

Bill Number	Bill Name	Date of Adoption at the Plenary Session
2021817	Resolution calling for the end of the activity that threatens regional security of Northeast Asia	August 2, 2019
2021601	Resolution calling for the repeal of retaliatory export restrictions by the Japanese government	August 2, 2019

※ Source: National Assembly Bill Information System (Last search date: Dec. 16, 2019), <http://likms.assembly.go.kr/bill/BillSearchResult.do>.

1. RESOLUTION CALLING FOR THE END OF THE ACTIVITY THAT THREATENS THE REGIONAL SECURITY OF NORTHEAST ASIA

The main contents of the "Resolution calling for the end of the activity that threatens the regional security of Northeast Asia" adopted at the plenary session of the National Assembly on August 2, 2019 are as follows:

On July 23, 2019, four Chinese and Russian military aircrafts entered into the Korean Air Defense Identification Zone (KADIZ) without permission for a joint military training. One Russian early warning and control aircraft trespassed into Dokdo airspace twice. The Korean National Assembly strongly condemns such actions as they increase the likelihood of military crises.

The Korean National Assembly strongly demands that its surrounding countries including China and Russia do not use the Korean Peninsula and its surroundings as a stage for an arms race. The military measures of using warning shots to resolutely respond to the first invasion of our airspace since the Korean War are considered justified and appropriate. We also call on our government to prepare firm and effective countermeasures to prevent a repeat of the unauthorized entry into the Air Defense Identification Zone and our airspace.

Meanwhile, we strongly condemn the Japanese government for criticizing the response of our military during the invasion of our airspace by the Russian warships.

The Korean National Assembly has the following positions in order to protect the sovereignty of Korea and secure the peace and stability of Northeast Asia:

"1. The Korean National Assembly points out that the actions of Russian warships invading into Dokdo airspace are an infringement of our sovereignty and a threat to the stability of Northeast Asia. As to the Russian government, who is denying the invasion of our airspace, we strongly demand that they confirm the facts according to the evidence presented by our government, immediately apologize, and promise that such actions will not be repeated.

2. The Korean National Assembly strongly condemns the invasion into our Air Defense Identification Zone of the Chinese and Russian warships, and sternly demands that both countries respect our Air Defense Identification Zone and not enter without permission.

3. The Korean National Assembly once again reaffirms that Dokdo clearly belongs to South Korea historically, geographically, and legally. We demand that the unlawful claims of sovereignty by Japan regarding Dokdo be immediately stopped and rescinded.

4. The Korean National Assembly demands that our government immediately prepare firm and effective countermeasures to ensure that the political and military landscapes of the Korean peninsula and Northeast Asia remain peaceful and stable.

5. The Korean National Assembly confirms that the US-Korea alliance is at the core of peace and stability in the Korean peninsula, and demands that our government maintains and strengthens strong combined defense readiness based on the spirit of such alliance."

2. RESOLUTION CALLING FOR THE REPEAL OF RETALIATORY EXPORT RESTRICTIONS BY THE JAPANESE GOVERNMENT

The main contents of the "Resolution calling for the repeal of retaliatory export restrictions by the Japanese government" adopted at the plenary session of the National Assembly on August 2, 2019 are as follows:

"The Korean National Assembly strongly denounces the anti-Korean export restriction measures by the Japanese government as a retaliatory measure against our judiciary's ruling on the issue of forced labor during Japanese occupation.

1. The Korean National Assembly is greatly concerned that the series of actions by the Japanese government against Korea including restrictions on the export of three semiconductor materials on July 4th and the exclusion from the whitelist that provides priority for export processes of strategic materials on August 2nd, not only damage the foundations of the friendly relationship between Korea and Japan, but also make the people of both countries suffer, and harm global free trade. We demand that the Japanese government immediately rescind its series of retaliatory export restrictions.

2. The Korean National Assembly is concerned that the friendly relationship between Korea and Japan will deteriorate due to the prolonging of conflicts between the two countries and the expansion of economic damage. Therefore, we urge the Korean and Japanese government to actively take action for a diplomatic solution to reestablish a forward-looking relationship.

3. The Korean National Assembly expresses great disappointment on the unfounded criticism of the Japanese government and some political figures, including suspicions on South Korean violations of North Korean sanctions restrictions, and demands that such criticism be immediately rescinded.

4. The Korean National Assembly calls on the government to protect the industry and economy from the export restrictions by Japan, and to actively respond to such unjustified measures."

Notes

1. National Assembly Bill Information System (last visited: December 16, 2019), <http://likms.assembly.go.kr/bill/BillSearchResult.do>.

CONTEMPORARY PRACTICE AND
JUDICIAL DECISIONS

Judicial Decisions in Public International Law (2019)

Edited by
LEE Seryon
Professor, Jeonbuk National University, Jeonju, Korea

Constitutional Court Case No. 2019Hun-Ma419
Decided on May 8, 2019

Main Issue

Unconstitutionality of Article 30 (1) of the Act on National Human Rights Commission

Disposition

The request for adjudication at issue is dismissed as a whole.

Reasoning

1. Case Overview

(1) The complainant was sentenced to ten years' imprisonment on charges of rape and bodily injury through intrusion upon another's residence under the Act on Special Cases concerning the Punishment of Sexual Crimes and rape under the Criminal Act and to the order

to attach an electronic tracking device for ten years under Articles 5 (1) 3 and 9 (1) 1 of the Act on Probation and Electronic Monitoring of Specific Criminal Offenders in the Seongnam Branch of Suwon District Court (2015Go-hap145) on November 26, 2015. Upon this, he appealed to the high court (Seoul High Court Decision 2015No3536) and then to the Supreme Court [Supreme Court Decision 2016Do8689 and Supreme Court Decision 2016Jun-do102 (Consolidated); hereinafter referred to as "judgment at issue"], but the appeals were all rejected and the original judgment became final and conclusive. Thus, he became subject to registration of personal information under Article 42 (1) of the Act on Special Cases concerning the Punishment of Sexual Crimes.

(2) The complainant filed the constitutional complaints several times, claiming that the Supreme Court decision at issue infringes upon his fundamental rights, including the right to equality, but the Constitutional Court rejected all such complaints on grounds that they do not qualify as an exceptional case where a constitutional complaint can be filed against a court judgment (Constitutional Court Decision 2016Hun-ma940 decided November 15, 2016; Constitutional Court Decision 2016Hun-ma1023 decided December 13, 2016; Constitutional Court Decision 2017Hun-ma1275 decided December 5, 2017). The complainant also filed a petition with the National Human Rights Commission of Korea, alleging that the Supreme Court decision at issue infringes upon his personal rights, including the right to equality, but the National Human Rights Commission of Korea refused to accept the petition on grounds that the National Human Rights Commission of Korea Act excludes court judgments from the objects of investigation by the National Human Rights Commission of Korea.

(3) Thus, the complainant filed the constitutional complaint at

issue on April 22, 2019, claiming that his fundamental rights, including the right to a fair trial, are infringed upon as Article 30 (1) of the National Human Rights Commission of Korea Act and Article 68 (1) of the Constitutional Court Act do not include any provision concerning communication of the remedy procedure pursuant to international law available for violation of the complainant's human rights, based on the individual communication system under the 'International Covenant on Civil and Political Rights.'

2. Subject Matter of Review

The subject matter of review in this case is whether "Article 30 (1) of the National Human Rights Commission of Korea Act not including communication pursuant to the individual communication system under the 'International Covenant on Civil and Political Rights'" and "Article 68 (1) of the Constitutional Court Act not including communication pursuant to the individual communication system under the 'International Covenant on Civil and Political Rights'" (hereinafter collectively referred to as "legislative omission in this case") infringe upon the fundamental rights of the complainant. The provisions at issue are as follows.

Provisions at Issue

National Human Rights Commission of Korea Act (amended by Act No. 11413 on March 21, 2012) Article 30 (Matters Subject to Investigation by Commission)

(1) In any of the following cases, a person who has suffered a violation of human rights or been discriminated against (hereinafter referred to as "victim"), or any other person or organization that is aware of such violation or discrimination, may file a petition with the Commission:

1. Where any of the human rights guaranteed in Articles 10 through 22 of the Constitution of the Republic of Korea has been violated or a discriminatory act has been committed in connection with the performance of duties (excluding legislation by the National Assembly and trials by a court or the Constitutional Court) by a State agency, a local government, a school established by Article 2 of the Elementary and Secondary Education Act, Article 2 of the Higher Education Act, and other Acts, a public service-related organization pursuant to Article 3-2 (1) of the Public Service Ethics Act, or a confinement or caring facility;

2. Where a discriminatory act has been committed by a legal entity, an organization or a private individual.
Constitutional Court Act (amended by Act No. 10546 on April 5, 2011)

Article 68 (Grounds for Request)

(1) Any person whose fundamental right guaranteed by the Constitution is infringed due to exercise or non-exercise of the governmental power, excluding judgment of the courts, may request adjudication on a constitutional complaint with the Constitutional Court: Provided, That if any remedial process is provided by other statutes, no one may request adjudication on a constitutional complaint without having exhausted all such processes.

Judgment

(1) The individual communication system under the 'International Covenant on Civil and Political Rights' (hereinafter referred to as the "ICCPR"), which is provided in the Optional Protocol to the International Covenant on Civil and Political Rights ratified by the Republic of Korea, means a system under which, if an individual claiming that any of his/her rights under the ICCPR is infringed fails

to receive relief in spite of exhaustion of all available domestic remedies, he/she submits his/her communication to the ICCPR Committee, which, in turn, forwards the State Party concerned and the individual its views about whether the State Party concerned has violated any provision of the Covenant after considering the communication received (see Articles 1, 2, 4 (1), and 5 of the Optional Protocol to the ICCPR) (see Constitutional Court Decision 2011Hun-ma306 decided July 26, 2018, etc.).

(2) The complainant is contesting legislative lack of Article 30 (1) of the National Human Rights Commission of Korea Act and Article 68 (1) of the Constitutional Court Act that do not adopt the individual communication system under the ICCPR. However, Article 30 (1) of the National Human Rights Commission of Korea Act provides that a victim any of whose human rights guaranteed in Articles 10 through 22 of the Constitution has been violated or against whom a discriminatory act has been committed by a State agency, etc., or against whom a discriminatory act has been committed by a legal entity, a private individual, etc., may file a petition with the National Human Rights Commission of Korea, and Article 68 (1) of the Constitutional Court Act provides that a person any of whose fundamental rights guaranteed by the Constitution is infringed due to exercise or non-exercise of the governmental power may request adjudication on a constitutional complaint with the Constitutional Court. Even though the fundamental rights, etc. described in the Constitution partially overlap with the rights recognized under the ICCPR, the system for petitions and investigations under the National Human Rights Commission of Korea Act or the system for adjudication on constitutional complaints under the Constitutional Court Act and the individual communication system under the ICCPR are completely separate ones in that the former is a domestic remedial process for individuals whose

fundamental rights, etc. guaranteed by the Constitution are infringed, while the latter is an international remedial process for individuals whose rights recognized under the ICCPR are infringed. These systems serve as part of various remedies for individuals whose human rights are infringed, but do not constitute a uniform or phased unity as remedies for infringement of human rights. Thus, according to the purposes, system, and objects of the relevant statutes, regulations and treaties, this case falls under a case where legislation concerning the individual communication system under the ICCPR is not made incompletely or insufficiently, but not made at all, which constitutes genuine legislative omission.

(3) A request for adjudication on constitutionality of genuine legislative omission is only allowed when the legislature has neglected legislation expressly delegated by the Constitution to guarantee fundamental rights or when, though it is clear in terms of constitutional interpretation that the State's legislative obligation to protect the fundamental rights of a specific person has arisen, the legislature has not taken any legislative action (see Constitutional Court Decision 2012Hun-ma840 decided August 29, 2013). However, legislative obligation under which the legislature shall specify in the National Human Rights Commission of Korea Act or the Constitutional Court Act the fact that there is a remedial process available for infringement of human rights based on the individual communication system under the ICCPR is neither expressly described in the Constitution, nor recognized in terms of constitutional interpretation. Therefore, the request for adjudication at issue, which is filed for genuine legislative omission that does not qualify as the object of a constitutional complaint, shall not be accepted because there is not any explicit legislative delegation against such legislative omission in the Constitution and the aforementioned legislative obligation is not recognized in terms of constitutional interpretation.

Conclusion

Based on this reasoning, the request for adjudication at issue is unlawful as a whole, and dismissed in accordance with Article 72 (3) 4 of the Constitutional Court Act. Decision is rendered as set forth in the above Disposition by the unanimous consent of all the participating Justices.

Presiding Justice Lee Jong-seok, Justice Lee Seon-ae, Justice Moon Hyung-bae

Seoul High Court's Sixth Administration Division Case
No. 2018Nu68676 Decided on April 3, 2019

Main Issue

Revocation of denial of refugee status
Judgment of the First Instance: Seoul Administrative Court Decision
2017Gu-dan76503 decided September 12, 2018

Disposition

1. The judgment of the first instance is revoked.
2. The disposition of denial of refugee status rendered against the plaintiff on March 30, 2016 by the defendant is revoked.
3. The total court costs shall be borne by the defendant.

Reasoning

1. Detailed process of disposition

The plaintiff (born on October 2, 1988), a citizen of the Federal Democratic Republic of Ethiopia (hereinafter referred to as "Ethiopia"), entered the Republic of Korea with a short-term visit (C-3) visa on October 28, 2014, and applied to the defendant for recognition of refugee status on November 11, 2014 on the grounds that 'the plaintiff has been arrested several times by the police for supporting the opposition UDJ Party in Ethiopia and has the fear of being persecuted by the Ethiopian government for participating in protests against the Ethiopian government while staying in the Republic of Korea.' However, the defendant rendered a decision not to grant the plaintiff refugee status (hereinafter referred to as "disposition at issue") on March 30, 2016 on the below grounds.

[Documentary evidence] Entries in Gap Evidence Nos. 1 and 3, and the whole purport of pleadings

2. Whether the disposition at issue is legitimate

(1) The summary of the plaintiff's claims

The plaintiff had much interest in politics under the influence of TL, his childhood play-mate, from a very young age. In early 2008 A.D. (around Ethiopian calendar 2001; the Ethiopian calendar is the unique calendar only used in Ethiopia. A gap of seven to eight years exists between the Ethiopian and Gregorian calendars, but not exactly. Hereinafter the West's ordinary calendar applies, except as otherwise specified), the plaintiff joined the opposition Unity for Democracy and Justice Party (hereinafter referred to as the "UDJ Party") on TL's recommendation, and was arrested and detained by the police while acting as its member. In addition, the plaintiff was arrested and detained, along with TL, by the police for participating in a demonstration condemning the Ethiopian government for indifference toward the treatment of Ethiopian workers residing overseas. After that, the plaintiff and TL decided to leave Ethiopia to escape persecution by the Ethiopian government. TL first left Ethiopia and was granted refugee status in the United States. The plaintiff entered Korea and has been engaging in activities against the Ethiopia's ruling party. Thus, if the plaintiff returns to Ethiopia, he has a well-founded fear of being persecuted by the Ethiopian government. Therefore, the court of original judgment erred in making the disposition at issue.

(2) Relevant legal principles

According to subparagraph 1 of Article 2 and Article 18 of the Refugee Act, Article 1 of the Refugee Convention and Article 1 of the Refugee Protocol, a foreigner who is unable or unwilling to avail himself of the protection of the country of his nationality in well-founded fear that he is likely to be persecuted for reasons of race, religion, nationality, membership of a specific social group, or political opinion, or a stateless foreigner who is unable or does not desire to return to the country in which he/she resided before entering the Republic of Korea in such fear, must be recognized as a refugee; and 'persecution,' which is required for recognition of refugee status, means 'a threat against life, body or freedom as well as an act causing serious injury upon essential human dignity or discrimination.' A foreigner seeking refugee status bears the burden of proving the "well-founded fear" of being persecuted. However, it is difficult to impose upon the foreigner the burden of proving the entirety of the alleged facts by objective evidence, considering the foreigner's special circumstances. Thus, the alleged facts shall be deemed as proven if it is reasonable to recognize them based upon the consistency and persuasiveness in his allegations and the credibility of his entire statement in light of the following: the route of entry into the country, the period between the entry into the country and the filing of the application for recognition of refugee status, the circumstances surrounding the application for recognition of refugee status, the circumstances in the country of nationality, the degree of fear to which the foreigner is feeling subjectively, the political, social, cultural environment of the region where the applicant had been residing, and the degree of fear felt by an ordinary person residing in the relevant region under similar situations (see Supreme Court Decision 2007Du3930 decided July 24, 2008). Therefore, well-founded fear as basis for refugee status should be considered to be established when the facts of alleged persecutions are rationally acceptable in accordance with the aforementioned evaluation, unless under unique circumstances where domestic situation in the country of nationality has changed so drastically that the possibility of persecution has been completely eliminated (see

Supreme Court Decision 2010Du27448 decided April 26, 2012).

(3) Established facts

1) Political unrest in Ethiopia

Ethiopia is a federal republic consisting of nine states. It adopts the parliamentary government system under which the Prime Minister is in charge of state affairs as head of the Executive Branch though the President plays a symbolic and ceremonial role as Head of State. It has two chambers, which consist of the House of People's Representatives (lower chamber with total 547 members serving five-year terms) and the House of the Federation (upper chamber with total 153 members serving five-year terms); and the supreme power is vested in the House of People's Representatives. The EPRDF (Ethiopian People's Revolutionary Democratic Front), the ruling party that holds the real power in the House of People's Representatives, was a political party established in 1989 by a group of organizations to overthrow Derg regime, which is a socialist military junta. There has been virtually no opposition since 1991, so the EPRDF maintains one-party rule by winning 493 of the total 547 seats of the House of People's Representatives in the first general election held on May 7, 1995, 481 of the total 547 seats of the House of People's Representatives in the second general election held in May 2000, and 327 of the total 547 seats of the House of People's Representatives in the third general election held in May 2005. However, the political situation in Ethiopia was unstable as student protests, which had begun in April 2001, demanding democratization in school, developed into large-scale anti-government protests, resulting in the resignation of the President in June 2001 and the exile of the Speaker of the House of the Federation to the United States in August 2001. In December 2003, hundreds of people were killed in tribal conflicts over land and the right of residence in western Gambela, and large-scale student demonstrations erupted around the Ethiopia's capital Addis Ababa and Oromo in January 2004. Like this, intertribal clashes and demands for democratization persisted in Ethiopia. In the third general election of May 2005, the opposition alleged that voting fraud was committed, which led to protests by opposition parties and university students. 40 protesters were killed and about 100 wounded in Addis Ababa when the riot police fired on June 8, 2005. In 2008, the UDJ Party was formed around party members who withdrew from the former CUD (Coalition for Unity and Democracy). The UDJ Party largely opposes the racial federal system, and demands respect for workers' rights and interests, guarantee of farmers' land ownership, release of opposition activists, and abolition of anti-terrorism laws. The UDJ Party's leadership is composed mainly of highly educated and professionally trained members, and it has members from almost every region and tribe in Ethiopia. In July 2009, an anti-terrorism bill passed the Parliament. Thereupon, the international community raised concerns that it would limit freedom of expression and fair trial. Around May 2010, major opposition candidates were killed and terror bombings occurred during and after the election campaigns for the fourth general election. In the fourth general election, the ruling EPRDF and its allies won 545 of the total 547 seats in the House of People's Representatives, while Medrek and an independent candidate each captured 1 seat. Medrek is a party coalition founded in 2008, joined by the UDJ Party in 2009. Medrek criticizes the EPRDF for its policies deepening economic inequality. The fifth general election was held in May 2015. The ruling EPRDF had a huge victory in the election by winning 500 seats in the House of People's Representatives, with its allies taking the remaining 47 seats.

2) Ethiopian nationals under the ruling party's surveillance

According to the Human Rights Watch World Report 2006 - Ethiopia, the Ethiopian ruling party used various forms of human rights abuse to deter and punish criticism of the government, exaggerating concerns about armed insurgency and terrorism to justify the torture and imprisonment of its critics and even ordinary citizens. Hundreds of students were actually arrested in 2004 in student protests at Addis Ababa University and secondary schools. After 2005 demonstrations, coercive measures were used to control the free speech rights of students and teachers alike.

According to the Human Rights Watch - Ethiopian National Surveillance Data March 2010, Ethiopia had been watching its own citizens through the '5:1 system' since early 2009 with the aim of deterring opposition parties from participating in elections. Where a member of an opposition party engages in political activities, such as attending a meeting, it has a system to report such fact to the superior authority. According to the Human Rights Watch - Ethiopian National Surveillance Data March 2014, as the Internet and mobile communication technology developed, the Ethiopian ruling party has monopolized the telecommunications industry through the state-owned enterprise, Ethio Telecom, since 2010. It suppressed freedom of expression by frequently blocking oppositional websites, independent media sites, blogs, and other international media, as well as radio and TLV broadcasts, and recruited informants through Ethiopian embassies abroad to collect intelligence on Ethiopians residing both in Ethiopia and abroad.

3) Plaintiff's personal history in Ethiopia

The plaintiff grew up in a neighborhood with his close friend, TL, since elementary school (1992 to 2003). He entered a high school (there is no middle school) in 2004 and graduated in 2007. After joining the UDJ Party with two friends on TL's recommendation in 2008 (Ethiopian calendar 2001), he formed a group with three friends, including TL, which mainly engaged in UDJ Party member-ship recruitment, booklet publication, placard designs, etc. Its work was carried out by TL with the plaintiff, etc. under the direction of the UDJ Party leadership. The plaintiff was arrested by the police who broke in through the door while legally recruiting and educating UDJ Party members in the Ponghe region of southern Ethiopia in 2008 (Ethiopian calendar 2001), and was released in three days after suffering beatings and insults. Later, the plaintiff entered Alpha University College in Addis Ababa, capital of Ethiopia, in 2010 to major in business administration, but gave up the College course halfway in 2013. In November 2013, he participated in a peaceful demonstration with TL in front of the Saudi Embassy in Ethiopia, calling for improved treatment of Ethiopian workers in Saudi Arabia. However, Ethiopian police arrested about 100 protesters for participation in the demonstration. The plaintiff and TL were also arrested by the police, detained, beaten, and insulted in the central investigation center (known as Maekelawi), and released in three days after contacting a police officer they had known. About two weeks after release, TL departed Ethiopia for the United States, where he was granted refugee status on June 13, 2014. TL paid an agent for issuance of a visa, and went to the United States with the visa. Just before the departure, the plaintiff told TL about threats to his life due to his political activities.

4) Plaintiff's activity after entering the Republic of Korea

The plaintiff was issued a passport on February 28, 2014, entered the Republic of Korea with a short-term visit (C-3) visa on October 28, 2014, and applied for recognition of refugee status to the defendant on November 11, 2014. Since 2015, he has kept company with SB in charge of members of the Korea branch of Ginbot 7. Ginbot 7 was designated as a terrorist group by the Ethiopian government. The plaintiff participated in a gathering hosted by the Korea branch of Ginbot 7 on December 27, 2015 to protest against the unfair demarcation of a borderline between the Ethiopian government and the Sudanese government in front of the Embassy of the Republic of Sudan in the Republic of Korea. The borderline demarcation brought political benefit to the Ethiopian ruling EPRDF, but caused serious harm to the Ethiopians living along the border. The plaintiff had an interview for recognition of refugee status on March 15, 2016, attended the Ginbot 7's fundraising event in April 2016, and participated in a gathering in October 2016 to protest against the massacre of Oromo, one of the Ethiopian peoples.

5) Plaintiff's family and political companions under the Ethiopian government's surveillance

The plaintiff's brother AA (born in 1984) entered Italy on August 27, 2016 with a passport issued on February 4, 2014, where he was issued a visa with the validity of September 9, 2016 to September 23, 2017. On March 15, 2018, the plaintiff made a statement to the effect that 'he was under threat to his life from the Ethiopian ruling party EPRDF for joining the UDJ Party, and the plaintiff and his entire family were blacklisted and placed under constant surveillance by the government; intelligence agents came to his house to arrest him; after he departed from the country, they continuously attempted to find out his whereabouts, and investigated his family at a police station, concluding that his departure was evidence that he was involved in terrorism; and to escape such surveillance, he fled to Italy around July 2016, with his wife and newborn baby left in Ethiopia.'

Judgment

Summing up the documentary evidence, entries in Gap Evidence Nos. 29 and 31 and Eul Evidence Nos. 8, 9, 14 and 15, appellant's interrogatory answer, and the whole purport of pleadings, the following facts, besides the foregoing, can be recognized. Considering such facts in light of the aforementioned legal principles, the plaintiff is in 'well-founded fear that he is likely to be persecuted by the government of Ethiopia, the country of his nationality, for reasons of political opinions,' so if he returns to Ethiopia, it is very unlikely that he would be protected by the country of his nationality. Therefore, the plaintiff's complaint is well-grounded.

① Plaintiff's affiliation with UDJ Party and party activity

The plaintiff's statement concerning the process of joining the UDJ Party, the recruitment of party members after joining, and arrest and detention by the police is made in detail, quite vividly, and consistently in the entire process of refugee interview to hearing of appeal (though the plaintiff's statement is somewhat inconsistent in the dates of occurrence of events, it is acceptable in light of the plaintiff's use of the Ethiopian calendar and the lapse of about ten years since the occurrence of events, not decisively undermining the consistency of the statement). Comparing and contrasting the plaintiff's UDJ Party membership card with the UDJ Party membership card-related materials prepared by the Immigration and Refugee Board of Canada, we don't find that circumstances exist to suspect that the appearance or form of or the entry in the plaintiff's membership card is forged or altered. The fact is that the plaintiff joined the UDJ Party around 2008 when the UDJ Party was established, though the process of his membership acquisition did not exactly meet the UDJ Party membership procedure including a three-month probationary period and the branch's recommendation. It seems virtually impossible to expect that the process of membership acquisition would strictly follow the UDJ Party's rules.

② Level of plaintiff's understanding of Ethiopian political situations

The plaintiff's statement about the fourth general election held in May 2010, which was given at the time of being interviewed for refugee status, does not exactly coincide with the details of the Ethiopian overview report prepared by the Ministry of Foreign Affairs as of 2015. However, quite unlike the details of the above Ethiopian overview report prepared by the Ministry of Foreign Affairs, there are foreign news reported on June 21, 2010 in relation to the fourth general election of Ethiopia, which says that 'the UDJ Party joined Medrek in December 2009 in preparation for the 2010 fourth general election, and in the fourth general election, the Medrek joined by the UDJ Party won one seat in the House of People's Representatives,' along with materials relating to the UDJ Party and Medrek. Thus, it is not reasonable to conclude from the statement made by the plaintiff at the time of being interviewed for refugee status that the plaintiff was ignorant of the political situation in Ethiopia.

③ The level of the plaintiff's experience of persecution and fear in Ethiopia

The plaintiff appears to have been blacklisted by the Ethiopian government after being arrested and detained in 2008 (Ethiopian calendar 2001). In November 2013, he participated in a demonstration with TL, etc. to protest against the unfair treatment of Ethiopian workers in Saudi Arabia in front of the Saudi Embassy in Ethiopia, and was arrested, detained, beaten, and insulted by the police and released in three days. The Ethiopian government issued a press release to the effect that protesters were arrested on charges of 'unauthorized assembly.' However, since, in those days, the press was controlled and freedom of expression was extremely limited in Ethiopia, we cannot conclude from the Ethiopian government's release that the demonstration had nothing to do with anti-government activities. Moreover, 'unfair treatment of Ethiopian workers,' which was the main issue of the demonstration, is a matter in line with the political stance mostly taken by the UDJ Party, such as the guarantee of workers' rights and interests. Thus, it may be said that the plaintiff was persecuted for his political activity criticizing the Ethiopian government's policy on Ethiopian workers residing overseas. It does not matter whether the plaintiff participated in the demonstration in the capacity of UDJ Party member. If the plaintiff did not escape from Ethiopia, it is very likely that he could feel the fear that his political view or activity would endanger his life or physical safety.

④ TL granted refugee status

The plaintiff joined the UDJ Party on the TL's recommendation, and engaged in party activity that recruits new members and manufactures placards under the direction of the UDJ Party leadership through TL. TL was in the middle management position of the UDJ Party as its early member, and arrested and detained for participating in a demonstration in front of the Saudi Embassy in Ethiopia in November 2013. Under such circumstances, he felt that he would no longer be safe in Ethiopia. So he left Ethiopia without delay and entered the United States, where he was granted refugee recognition several months later. Like this, the plaintiff, along with TL, one of the Ethiopian ruling party's main targets, has been engaging in political activity against the ruling party EPRDF in Ethiopia for a considerable period of time and has been interacting with TL through e-mail, etc. until now. TL also clarified in his statement the surveillance and personal danger the plaintiff had suffered in Ethiopia due to his political views and activities against the EPRDF, largely in accord with the plaintiff's statement.

⑤ Plaintiff and his family under the Ethiopian government's surveillance

According to annual Human Rights Watch World Reports on Ethiopia, the Ethiopian ruling party has controlled government critics by exaggerating the threat of terrorism, and was criticized by the international community for severely restricting the freedom of expression through the anti-terrorism bill passed in July 2009. The Ethiopian ruling party has been operating the system to surveil Ethiopian citizens, while controlling mass media and Internet media and monitoring Ethiopian citizens outside the country through its embassies in foreign countries. In this context, the plaintiff's statement is credible that the plaintiff's family, as well as the plaintiff, were put under surveillance by the Ethiopian government due to his anti-government activities in Ethiopia. In this regard, the plaintiff's brother made a statement to the effect that he had fled to Italy around July 2016 to avoid the ongoing surveillance and investigation by the Ethiopian government. The details of the statement are supported by objective data, such as the visa the plaintiff's brother was issued in Italy.

⑥ Detailed process through which the plaintiff was issued a passport

The plaintiff was issued a passport in Ethiopia on February 4, 2014. Just a few months earlier, TL, who had been arrested and released during protests along with the plaintiff, left Ethiopia and entered the United States in November 2013, though he was on a list of surveillance by the Ethiopian ruling party. There are no grounds to suspect that TL forged his passport or smuggled himself into the United States in the process of exit and entry. According to the UK Home Office's country of origin information, Ethiopia's border security was somewhat unstable. The plaintiff's interrogatory answer regarding the issuance or renewal of the passport and the detailed process of passport examination at the Ethiopian airport is quite convincing.

⑦ Political activity and application for recognition of refugee status after entering the Republic of Korea

The Ethiopian government designated Ginbot 7 as a 'terrorist group,' but the plaintiff participated in Ginbot 7's activities after entering the Republic of Korea. This showed that the plaintiff was against the Ethiopian ruling party as ever. Even though the plaintiff did not engage in certain political activities for about one year after applying for recognition of refugee status and was not a UDJ Party member as at the time of being interviewed for refugee status, it is just a short-term gap in his political career following change of his party affiliation after entering another country to escape persecution from the Ethiopian ruling party, and there are no exceptional circumstances to have doubt about the detailed process of his application for recognition of refugee status. The Ethiopian government is now adopting an appeasement policy about Ginbot 7, but it is just a temporary and transitional measure taken after the disposition at issue, which is under way after the election of the new Prime Minister. Thus, such fact is not sufficient evidence that the plaintiff will be safe from being persecuted for his political opinions.

(4) Subconclusion
    The disposition at issue is illegal and must be revoked.

Conclusion

The reasons for the plaintiff's claim are with merit, so it must be admitted. The judgment of the court of first instance is not justified in reaching its conclusion. The reasons for the plaintiff's appeal are with merit. Therefore, the judgment of the court of first instance is cancelled and the disposition at issue is revoked.

Presiding Judge Park Hyung-nam, Judge Jung Jae-oh, Judge Lee Sook-yeon

Supreme Court Decision 2018Du60847
Decided March 14, 2019

Main Issues and Holdings

[1] Meaning of each of the requirements to be deemed to have a domicile in the Republic of Korea, as prescribed in Article 2 (1) of the former Enforcement Decree of the Income Tax Act, which are "existence of a family member who makes a living together in the Republic of Korea" and "being deemed to continually reside in the Republic of Korea for at least one year in view of occupation or property status";

[2] Where an individual qualifies as both a domestic resident and an overseas resident under the Income Tax Act, so is deemed a person liable for tax, such as income tax, under foreign law, the method of determining the place of residence of that individual;

[3] Meaning of "permanent home" as prescribed in Article 4 (2) (a) of the "Convention between the Republic of Korea and Japan for the Avoidance of Double Taxation and the Prevention of Fiscal Evasion with respect to Taxes on Income," and where such permanent home exists in both Contracting States, meaning of "centre of vital interests," which is the secondary standard for determining the country of residence of a dual resident under the said Convention;

[4] Where Party A, a professional football player playing in a football club owned by Company B, a Japanese stock corporation, filed a final return on global income tax on his annual income, and made payment accordingly, and the tax authority increased the amount of the assessed global income tax and notified Party A of the revised tax assessment, the case holding that, even though Party A was deemed to have a permanent home in both the Republic of

Korea and Japan in light of all circumstances, the Contracting State more closely related to Party A in terms of personal and economic relations was Japan, not the Republic of Korea, and accordingly, Party A was a resident of Japan under the "Convention between the Republic of Korea and Japan for the Avoidance of Double Taxation and the Prevention of Fiscal Evasion with respect to Taxes on Income."

Summary of Decision

[1] In Article 2 (1) of the former Enforcement Decree (amended by Presidential Decree No. 26067, Feb. 3, 2015) of the Income Tax Act, which prescribes the requirements to be deemed to have a domicile in the Republic of Korea, "family member who makes a living together in the Republic of Korea" refers to a close relative sharing living expenses or a place of residence in the Republic of Korea, and "being deemed to continually reside in the Republic of Korea for at least one year in view of occupation or property status" refers to, in light of the purport of deeming a resident a person liable for income tax, being closely connected to the Republic of Korea in terms of the person's location, such as where it seems that residing in the Republic of Korea for at least one year is necessary for him/her to maintain his/her employment or work relationship or that the management, disposition, etc. of his/her property take at least one year of residence in the Republic of Korea;

[2] Where an individual qualifies as both a domestic resident and a foreign resident under the Income Tax Act, so is deemed a person liable for tax, such as income tax, under foreign law, that individual is at risk of double taxation. To avoid such an event, tax treaties have been signed among countries to provide for separate provisions. If a person subject to taxation is recognized as qualifying as a dual resident, that individual's country of residence must be determined

pursuant to relevant tax treaties concluded with the pertinent Contracting State;

[3] The main sentence of Article 4 (1) of the "Convention between the Republic of Korea and Japan for the Avoidance of Double Taxation and the Prevention of Fiscal Evasion with respect to Taxes on Income" (hereinafter referred to as the "Korea-Japan Tax Convention") provides that "For the purposes of this Convention, the term 'resident of a Contracting State' means any person who, under the laws of that Contracting State, is liable to tax therein by reason of his domicile, residence, place of head or main office or any other criterion of a similar nature." In addition, providing that "Where by reason of the provisions of paragraph (1) an individual is a resident of both Contracting States, then his status shall be determined as follows": Article 4 (2) specifies in subparagraph (a) that "he shall be deemed to be a resident only of the Contracting State in which he has a permanent home available to him; if he has a permanent home available to him in both Contracting States, he shall be deemed to be a resident of the Contracting State with which his personal and economic relations are closer (centre of vital interests)." Furthermore, subparagraphs (b) through (d) provide for a series of standards for determining the status of a resident under the Korea-Japan Tax Convention in a case where the pertinent matter cannot be determined by subparagraph (a).

In this context, a permanent home refers to all types of continuous residence for purposes other than short-term stay, such as travel or a business trip, available for use at any time. Thus, whether an individual owns or rents the residence is a circumstance that need not be considered in determining that individual's permanent home. When such permanent home exists in both Contracting States, the secondary standard for determining the country of residence of a dual resident under the Korea-Japan Tax Convention, which is where the centre of vital interests lies, that is, a Contracting State with which the individual's personal and economic interests are closer, must be examined. The centre of vital interests means a Contracting State with which the degree of relationship the individual has is deeper, in overall consideration of the individual's family relationship, social relationship, occupation, political and cultural activities, place of business, and place of property management;

[4] Where Party A, a professional football player playing in a football club owned by Company B, a Japanese stock corporation, filed a final return on global income tax on his annual income, and made payment accordingly, and the tax authority increased the amount of the assessed global income tax and notified Party A of the revised tax assessment, in light of the fact that (a) Party A had been playing in the Japanese professional football league since graduating from high school and signed a three-year contract with Company B, based on which he played as a professional football player in the Japanese football club, (b) Party A's residence in Japan, which was offered by Company B during the contract term, was not intended for Party A's short-term stay, but rather, a place of continuous residence during the contract term, and it was actually inhabited by Party A and his family continuously over a long period, and (c) the period of stay in the Republic of Korea was simply a temporary visit following Party A's appointment as a member of the national football team, and there exists no evidence of Party A's engagement in social or business activities in the Republic of Korea, the case held as follows: deeming Party A, who had a permanent home in both the Republic of Korea and Japan, to be a resident of Japan under the "Convention between the Republic of Korea and Japan for the Avoidance of Double Taxation and the Prevention of Fiscal Evasion with respect to Taxes on Income" is justifiable, for his personal and economic relations were closer with Japan, not the Republic of Korea; yet, the lower judgment determined the pertinent tax disposition valid by deeming Party A to be a domestic resident

under the above Convention, and in so determining, the lower court erred by misapprehending the relevant legal principle.

Provisions at Issue

[1] Articles 1-2 (1) and 2 (1) 1 of the former Income Tax Act (amended by Act No. 12852, Dec. 23, 2014); Article 2 (1) and (3) 2 of the former Enforcement Decree (amended by Presidential Decree No. 26067, Feb. 3, 2015) of the Income Tax Act. [2] Article 1-2 (1) 1 of the former Income Tax Act (amended by Act No. 12852, Dec. 23, 2014); Article 2 (1) and (3) of the former Enforcement Decree (amended by Presidential Decree No. 26067, Feb. 3, 2015) of the Income Tax Act. [3] Article 4 (1) and (2) of the Convention between the Republic of Korea and Japan for the Avoidance of Double Taxation and the Prevention of Fiscal Evasion with respect to Taxes on Income. [4] Article 4 (1) and (2) of the Convention between the Republic of Korea and Japan for the Avoidance of Double Taxation and the Prevention of Fiscal Evasion with respect to Taxes on Income; Article 1-2 (1) 1 of the former Income Tax Act (amended by Act No. 12852, Dec. 23, 2014); Article 2 (1) and (3) of the former Enforcement Decree (amended by Presidential Decree No. 26067, Feb. 3, 2015) of the Income Tax Act.

Reference Cases

[1] Supreme Court Decision 2013Du16876 decided Nov. 27, 2014 (Gong2015Sang, 77).

[2] Supreme Court Decision 2006Du3964 decided Dec. 11, 2008 (Gong2009Sang, 38); Supreme Court Decision 2014Du13959 decided Feb. 26, 2015.

Judicial Decisions in Private International Law (2019)

JANG Jiyong
Presiding Judge
Tongyeong branch of Changwon district court, Gyeongsangnam–do, Korea

1. JURISDICTION

Standard of determining international jurisdiction
Supreme Court Decision 2016Da33752
Decided on June 13, 2019 [Loan]

Facts

Party A, a Chinese national, who used to run a money lending business, entered the Republic of Korea to run a business of the same nature. Party B, etc., a couple with Chinese nationality, who used to operate real estate development business in China, took up residence in the Republic of Korea.

Party A brought a suit in the Republic of Korea court against Party B, etc. for the return of the loan which was lent in China.

Main Issues

[1] Meaning and standard of determining "substantive relations" in Article 2(1) of the Act on Private International Law

[2] Whether the jurisdictional provision in the Civil Procedure Act becomes the most important criteria for determining international jurisdiction (affirmative)

Whether the defendant's place of residence as the center of his/her interest lies becomes an important matter of consideration (affirmative)

[3] Reason for considering special jurisdiction in international jurisdiction, and, in a case where the defendant's assets are located within the Republic of Korea at the time of the Plaintiff's filing of lawsuit but without direct relevance to the Plaintiff's claim, method of determining international jurisdiction

[4] Standard of determining predictability in international jurisdiction, and in a case where the defendant has a foundation of livelihood or conducts economic activities by acquiring assets in the Republic of Korea, whether the predictability of a lawsuit against the defendant on his/her assets in the court of the Republic of Korea is recognized (affirmative)

[5] Whether international jurisdiction can concurrently exist (affirmative), and whether the Korean court's jurisdiction can readily be denied on the sole ground that the courts in other countries provide better convenience in terms of geography, language, and communications compared to the court in the Republic of Korea (negative)

Summary of Decision

[1] Article 2(1) of the Act on Private International Law states that "In case a party or a case in dispute is substantively related to the Republic of Korea, a court shall have the international jurisdiction. In this case, the court shall obey reasonable principles, compatible to the ideology of the allocation of international jurisdiction, in judging the existence of the substantive relations."

Here, the term "substantive relations" refers to having relevance with the concerned parties or the disputed matter to the extent that justifies the Korean court's exercise of jurisdiction. Determination of "substantive relations" must be rooted upon reasonable principles compatible to the idea of the allocation of international jurisdiction, including impartiality among interested parties, reasonableness of a trial, and promptness and the judicial economy. More specifically, such determination ought to take account of not only personal interests such as fairness as well as convenience and predictability of interested parties, but also the interests of the court and the state, including the reasonableness, promptness, efficiency of a trial, as well as the validity of a judgment. As such, there exist various interests of international jurisdiction. Determination on which interests deserve protection ought to be made on the basis of reasonable examination of the existence of "substantive relations" in individual cases.

[2] Article 2(2) of the Act on Private International Law states, "A court shall judge whether or not it has the international jurisdiction in the light of jurisdictional provisions of domestic laws and shall take a full consideration of the unique nature of international jurisdiction in the light of the purport of the provision of paragraph (1)," providing jurisdictional provisions of domestic laws as the specific criteria or method of determining "substantive relations" as prescribed in paragraph (1). As such, jurisdictional provisions in the Civil Procedure Act functions as the most important standard of determining international jurisdiction. However, considering that such jurisdictional provisions pertain to the provisions regarding venue on the domestic front, in some cases involving determination of international jurisdiction, these jurisdictional provisions must be modified and applied to the extent that they align with the idea of the allocation of international jurisdiction by considering the unique nature thereof.

The main text of Article 3 of the Civil Procedure Act stipulates, "General forum of a person shall be determined by his/her domicile," meaning that a place where an interested party keeps a living relation, i.e., the center on which that living relation is based, is the most general and universal source of land jurisdiction. Article 2 of the Civil Procedure Act states, "A lawsuit is subject to the jurisdiction of a court at the place where a defendant's general forum is located." This is because it is compatible to the impartiality of the interested parties in the allocation of jurisdiction to allow the plaintiff to bring a suit at the court within the jurisdiction where the defendant's domicile is located. A defendant's domicile is the center of living relation and is an important matter to be taken into consideration in the matter of international jurisdiction.

[3] Taking into account special jurisdiction in the matter of international jurisdiction is to recognize the jurisdiction of the state that has "substantive relations" to the disputed issue. Article 11 of the Civil Procedure Act stipulates, "A lawsuit concerning a property right against a person who has no domicile in the Republic of Korea or against a person whose domicile is unknown, may be brought to the court located in the place of the objects of a claim or those of the security, or any seizable property of a defendant." If the defendant's assets remain in the Republic of Korea at the time of the plaintiff's filing of a lawsuit, the plaintiff may bring a suit against the defendant at the Korean court. Upon the ruling in favor of the plaintiff, the court may immediately enforce the judgment to bring the actual result of the trial. As above, if the defendant's assets lie in the Republic of Korea, the Korean court's international jurisdiction may be recognized so as to protect the rights of the interested parties or to ensure the enforceability of the judgment. Nevertheless, indiscriminately recognizing international jurisdiction even in a case where the defendant's assets are accidentally placed in the Republic of Korea may put the defendant at a considerable disadvantage.

Therefore, where the plaintiff's claim has no direct relevance to the defendant's assets, the determination of international jurisdiction shall be made by considering the background leading up to the defendant's assets ending up in the Republic of Korea, the value of the pertinent assets, the need to protect the rights of the plaintiff, and the effectiveness of a judgment.

[4] Furthermore, Determination of predictability ought to be made on the basis of whether the defendant could have reasonably predicted the filing of a suit at the court in the relevant jurisdiction because of "substantive relations" between the defendant and the jurisdiction. A defendant, who has an established livelihood in the Republic of Korea or acquires assets and conducts economic activities, can easily foresee the filing of a suit against him/her relating to the assets at the Korean court.

[5] International jurisdiction is not exclusive jurisdiction, but it can exist concurrently with national jurisdiction. The jurisdiction of the Republic of Korea court shall not be readily denied on the sole basis of the fact that courts of other countries provide more convenience than the Republic of Korea court in terms of geography, language, and communications.

[6] The Court held as follows: (a) comprehensively considering the fact that (i) Party B, etc. purchased a real estate property and a car in the Republic of Korea, and possessed and used them; (ii) at the time of the instant lawsuit, Party B, etc. had an established livelihood in the Republic of Korea, raised children, and inhabited the acquired real estate property; (iii) at the time of the filing of the instant lawsuit, Party A entered the Republic of Korea, had been residing in the Republic of Korea for a considerable period of time, and planned to carry out business activities in the Republic of Korea going forward, it can be considered that both Party A and Party B, etc. laid substantial groundwork for livelihood activities in the Republic of Korea at the time of the filing of the instant lawsuit; (b)

after leaving China, Party B, etc. established livelihood in the Republic of Korea and acquired assets, making it difficult to assume that Party B, etc. did not possibly foresee the filing of the instant lawsuit against themselves at the Republic of Korea court; (c) since Party B, etc. possessed assets including a real estate property and a car in the Republic of Korea, which Party A held under provisional seizure, Party A had a practical interest in filing a suit at the Republic of Korea court to seek valid enforcement of the claim; (d) considering the fact that (i) Party A, a Chinese national, sought a trial by showing an explicit intent to be tried at the Republic of Korea court against Party B, etc., who are also Chinese nationals; (ii) Party B, etc. filed a countersuit by appointing a legal representative in the Republic of Korea; (iii) practical proceedings and deliberation took place with regard to the merits of the case for a considerable period of time; (iv) the facts that require attestation in the instant case can be proven through the evidentiary document, such as a contract or the history of account transfer records, and do not necessarily require an investigation in China; (v) whereas pursuing a litigation in the Republic of Korea may not be deemed considerably disadvantageous to Party B, etc., denying international jurisdiction of the Republic of Korea court and bringing the case back to the Chinese court for deliberation would seriously undermine judicial economy; (e) the concepts of international jurisdiction and applicable law are governed by different ideologies, and thus, the substantive relations between the foregoing lawsuit and the Republic of Korea court may not be readily denied on the sole basis of the fact that the law applicable to the legal relationship of the foregoing case is the Chinese law; (f) taking these matters into account, the lower court was justifiable to have determined that the foregoing lawsuit was substantively related to the Republic of Korea, and therefore, the Republic of Korea court had international jurisdiction.

2. GOVERNING LAW

2-1. Law applicable to torts

Supreme Court Decision 2015Da60689
Decided on April 23, 2019 [Indemnification]

Facts

The cargo ship entered Busan port, however it was found that the seal was dropped during the unloading process and the cargo was incinerated after being rejected for quarantine. Insurance Company A (the Plaintiff) filed a claim seeking indemnification against the consignor, Company B (the Defendant) after paying insurance money to the consignee.

Main Issues and Holdings

Whether 'the place where a tort occurred' in Article 32(1) of the Act on Private International Law includes the place of the legal interest at the violation of the legal interest as the place where damage (consequence) of the tort occurred (affirmative)

Summary of Decision

Courts *ex officio* examine applicable laws to the case and if there is a foreign element courts will apply laws according to the private international law. Article 32(1) of the Act on Private International Law stipulates that a tort shall be governed by the law of the place where it occurred, and the place where a tort occurred includes the place where damage from the tort occurred (see Supreme Court

Decision 93Da18167 on January 28, 1994, Supreme Court Decision 2005Da75071 on April 24, 2008).

As the loss of the sealing number was confirmed in Korea and the violated legal interest of the consignee was located in Korea, the right to claim damages subrogated by the Plaintiff is governed by the Korean law.

2-2. Insurable interest of the U.K. Life Assurance Act 1774

Supreme Court Decision 2017Da254600
Decided on May 30, 2019　〔Unjust Enrichment〕

Facts

Company A (the Defendant) and Insurance Company B (the Plaintiff) concluded an insurance contract, governed by U.K. law. According to the insurance contract, the regional coverage scope was limited to Antarctica and the insured parties were flight attendants and passengers who would be boarding the helicopter flown and managed by Company A, and Company B should pay a defined death or injury benefit to Company A in the event flight attendants or passengers either died or sustained injuries while boarding or flying during the insurance policy period. As the operator and manager of the instant helicopter, Company A is in a position to assume liability, i.e., providing compensation for damages in cases where flight attendants and passengers either die or sustain injuries caused by an accident that occurred while boarding or flying.

A passenger was injured due to an accident during the insurance policy period in which Company A's helicopter toppled over while landing in the South Pole. Upon having paid the entire insurance money to Company A and having received a written payment confirmation, Company B filed a claim against Company A seeking restitution of unjust enrichment equivalent to the foregoing insurance payout by asserting that the pertinent insurance contract was invalid as Company A, the assured had no insurable interest.

Main Issues and Holdings

Regarding an insurance contract according to which the assured is guaranteed a fixed payout upon the death or injury of an unspecified number of individuals that occurred over an extended period of time, in the event that the insured is in a position to assume pecuniary liability regarding the death or injury of such unspecified number of individuals and concluded said insurance contract for coverage of such legal liability, whether insurable interest is recognizable pursuant to the U.K. Life Assurance Act 1774 (affirmative)

Summary of Decision

[1] Governing Law: U.K. law

Given that the instant insurance contract has a foreign element limiting the regional coverage scope to the South Pole, the governing law ought to be set according to the Act on Private International Law. Article 25(1) main text of the Act on Private International Law provides that "A contract shall be governed by the law which the parties choose explicitly or implicitly." Inasmuch as the pertinent insurance contract is governed by U.K. law, any and all issues relating to the interpretation of the insurance contract and its validity shall be governed by the U.K. law.

[2] Insurable interest of the U.K. Life Assurance Act 1774

The section 1 of the U.K. Life Assurance Act 1774 requires insurable interest for the legality of the insurance, therefore every insurance on lives, or on any event, in which the assured has not an interest, shall be void. As the Life Assurance Act 1774 does not define 'insurable interest,' the courts in the U.K. recognize insurable interest on a case-by-case basis.

Whether the insurable interest exist on the part of an insured party in the type relevant to this case ought to be determined through interpretation of the insurance policy. Just because insured benefit falls under the purview of damages liability does not necessarily mean that an insurance contract should be concluded in the form of a liability insurance.

With regard to an insurance contract according to which the assured is guaranteed a fixed benefit payment upon the death or injury of an unspecified number of individuals that occurred over an extended period of time, insurable interest may be recognized pursuant to Section 1 of the Life Assurance Act 1774 in the event that the assured is in a position to assume pecuniary liability and concluded the insurance contract for coverage of such legal liability (see Feasey v. Sun Life Assurance Co. of Canada [2003] EWCA Civ 885).

The lower court recognized insurable interest of the pertinent insurance contract that was concluded between the Plaintiff and the Defendant, and subsequently determined that the instant insurance contract was valid under the U.K. law.

Persistent Pollutants Control Act

The Editorial Board
ILA Korean Branch

Act No. 8292, Jan. 26, 2007
Amended by Act No. 8371, Apr. 11, 2007
Act No. 8404, Apr. 27, 2007
Act No. 9433, Feb. 6, 2009
Act No. 10032, Feb. 4, 2010
Act No. 10034, Feb. 4, 2010
Act No. 10893, Jul. 21, 2011
Act No. 11263, Feb. 1, 2012
Act No. 11862, Jun. 4, 2013
Act No. 12464, Mar. 18, 2014
Act No. 13886, Jan. 27, 2016
Act No. 14532, Jan. 17, 2017
Act No. 15656, Jun. 12, 2018
Act No. 15841, Oct. 16, 2018

CHAPTER I GENERAL PROVISIONS

Article 1 (Purpose)

The purpose of this Act is to protect citizens' health and the environment from hazards posed by persistent pollutants and to promote international cooperation by prescribing matters necessary for the control of persistent pollutants, such as dioxins, mercury and mercury compounds, which are prescribed by both the Stockholm Convention on Persistent Organic Pollutants and the Minamata Convention on Mercury for the implementation thereof. *<Amended by Act No. 13886, Jan. 27, 2016>*

Article 2 (Definitions)

The terms used in this Act shall be defined as follows: *<Amended by Act No. 13886, Jan. 27, 2016>*

1. The term "persistent pollutants" means chemical substances that pose hazards to people and ecosystems, having the characteristics of toxicity, persistence, bioaccumulation, long-range transportability, etc., which are prescribed by the Stockholm Convention on Persistent Organic Pollutants (hereinafter referred to as the "Stockholm Convention") and the Minamata Convention on Mercury (hereinafter referred to as the "Minamata Convention"), and the details of which shall be prescribed by Presidential Decree;

2. The term "discharge facilities" means facilities, machines, implements, or other objects prescribed by Ordinance of the Ministry of Environment that discharge persistent pollutants;

3. The term "wastes containing persistent pollutants" means trash, burnt ashes, sludge, waste oil, waste acid, waste alkali, etc. contaminated with persistent pollutants exceeding the standards for persistent pollutants content prescribed by Ordinance of the Ministry of Environment among the commercial wastes as defined in subparagraph 3 of Article 2 of the Wastes Control Act, which are wastes prescribed by Presidential Decree among substances that become unnecessary for citizens' lives or their business activities.

Article 3 (Scope of Application)

This Act shall not apply to the control of persistent pollutants at sea (referring to the sea defined in Article 3 of the Framework Act on Marine Fishery Development). *<Amended by Act No. 13886,*

Jan. 27, 2016>

Article 4 (Relationship with other Acts)

(1) This Act shall apply to the control of persistent pollutants unless otherwise prescribed by the Toxic Chemicals Control Act, the Agrochemicals Control Act and other Acts. *<Amended by Act No. 13886, Jan. 27, 2016>*

(2) The Wastes Control Act shall apply to matters concerning the control of wastes containing persistent pollutants, not prescribed by this Act. *<Amended by Act No. 13886, Jan. 27, 2016>*

Article 5 (Master Plan for Control of Persistent Pollutants)

(1) The Minister of Environment shall establish a master plan for the control of persistent pollutants (hereinafter referred to as "Master Plan") every five years after consultation with the head of a related central administrative agency and the Special Metropolitan City Mayor, Metropolitan City Mayors, the Special Self-Governing City Mayor, Provincial Governors or the Special Self-Governing Province Governor (hereinafter referred to as "Mayor/Provincial Governor") and then deliberation of the Central Environmental Preservation Advisory Committee under Article 58 (1) of the Framework Act on Environmental Policy. The same shall apply to any planned modification to the matters herein prescribed by Presidential Decree. *<Amended by Act No. 10032, Feb 4, 2010; Act No. 13886, Jan. 27, 2016; Act No. 15841, Oct. 16, 2018>*

(2) The Master Plan shall contain the following matters: *<Amended by Act No. 13886, Jan. 27, 2016>*

1. General objectives of and direction-setting for advancement of the control of persistent pollutants;

2. Major plans for promoting the control of persistent pollutants;

3. Control conditions of persistent pollutants and prospect thereof;

4. Plans to raise funds for various projects concerning the control of persistent pollutants;

5. Plans for cooperation with international organizations and with foreign and domestic agencies concerning the control of persistent pollutants;

6. Matters necessary for the control of persistent pollutants.

(3) Other matters necessary for the establishment of the Master Plan shall be prescribed by Presidential Decree.

Article 6 (Implementation Plans for Persistent Pollutants)

(1) The Minister of Environment and the head of a related central administrative agency shall establish and implement a detailed plan for the implementation of the Master Plan (hereinafter referred to as "implementation plan") every year. In such cases, the head of the related central administrative agency shall submit the implementation plan and the results of advancement to the Minister of Environment.

(2) Matters necessary for the establishment and implementation of an implementation plan, submission of the results of advancement, etc. shall be prescribed by Presidential Decree.

Articles 7 and 8 Deleted. *<by Act No. 10034, Feb. 4, 2010>*

Article 9 (Establishment of Maximum Permissible Daily Exposure)

(1) The Government may establish a maximum permissible daily exposure as a standard at which a body may be continuously exposed to persistent pollutants through respiration, skin contact, ingestion, etc. during a whole lifetime without any apprehension of influence on health. *<Amended by Act No. 13886, Jan. 27, 2016>*

(2) The maximum permissible daily exposure by kind of persistent pollutant under paragraph (1) shall be prescribed by Presidential Decree. *<Amended by Act No. 13886, Jan. 27, 2016>*

Article 10 (Establishment of Environmental Standards)

(1) The Government shall establish environmental standards for

persistent pollutants in order to protect the health of people and to create a comfortable environment, and shall strive to have the appropriateness thereof maintained as the environmental conditions change. *<Amended by Act No. 13886, Jan. 27, 2016>*

(2) The environmental standards under paragraph (1) shall be prescribed by Presidential Decree.

Article 11 (Installation and Operation of Measurement Network)

(1) The Minister of Environment shall install a persistent pollutant measurement network (hereinafter referred to as "measurement network") to ascertain the situation of pollution by persistent pollutants of air, water, soil, river, sediment, living organisms nationwide, and measure pollution levels. *<Amended by Act No. 13886, Jan. 27, 2016>*

(2) The Mayor/Provincial Governor and the head of a City/Country/District (referring to the head of an autonomous District; hereinafter the same shall apply) may install a measurement network to ascertain the situation of pollution by persistent pollutants in his/her jurisdiction, and measure the pollution level. *<Amended by Act No. 13886, Jan. 27, 2016>*

(3) The Minister of Environment shall establish a plan for the installation of a measurement network, which clearly states the location, district, items to be measured, measurement period, measuring frequency, etc. under paragraph (1).

(4) Paragraph (3) shall apply mutatis mutandis to cases where a Mayor/Do Governor or the head of a Si/Gun/Gu installs a measurement network pursuant to paragraph (2).

(5) Where a Mayor/Do Governor or the head of a Si/Gun/Gu installs and operates a measurement network, the Minister of Environment may provide financial and technological support within budgetary limits.

Article 12 (Use of Land, etc.)

(1) The Minister of Environment, a Mayor/Do Governor or the

head of a Si/Gun/Gu may use land, or building or fixtures on the land in the district necessary for the installation of a measurement network or for the investigation into the conditions of pollution.

(2) The Act on Acquisition of and Compensation for Land, etc. for Public Works shall apply mutatis mutandis to the procedures of use under paragraph (1) or to the compensation for loss, etc.

CHAPTER II PROHIBITION OF OR RESTRICTION ON MANUFACTURE, EXPORTATION, IMPORTATION OR USE OF PERSISTENT POLLUTANTS

Article 13 (Prohibition of, or Restriction on, Manufacture, Exportation, Importation, or Use of Persistent Pollutants)

(1) No person shall manufacture, export, import, or use banned persistent pollutants (referring to the persistent organic pollutants prescribed in Annex A to the Stockholm Convention, however, excluding restricted substances and prohibited substances under Article 32 of the Toxic Chemicals Control Act and pesticides under the Pesticide Control Act; hereinafter referred to as "banned persistent pollutants"): Provided, That the same shall not apply to cases falling under any of the following: *<Amended by Act No. 11263, Feb. 1, 2012; Act No. 13886, Jan. 27, 2016>*

1. Where banned persistent pollutants, the production or use of which is permitted for specific purposes under Annex A to the Stockholm Convention are manufactured, imported, exported, or used for such specific purposes;

2. Where banned persistent pollutants are manufactured, imported, exported, or used for purposes of testing, research or examination.

(2) Those who intend to manufacture, export, import, or use banned

persistent pollutants pursuant to the proviso to paragraph (1) shall comply with the standards for control prescribed by Presidential Decree, such as labeling on their containers or packages for safety control. *<Newly Inserted by Act No. 11263, Feb. 1, 2012; Act No. 13886, Jan. 27, 2016>*

(3) Restricted persistent pollutants (referring to persistent organic pollutants prescribed in Annex B to the Stockholm Convention and mercury and mercury compounds prescribed in the Minamata Convention, however, excluding restricted chemicals and prohibited chemicals under subparagraphs 4 and 5 of Article 2 of the Chemical Substances Control Act and pesticides under the Pesticide Control Act; hereinafter referred to as "restricted persistent pollutants") may be manufactured, exported, imported, or used only in any of the following cases: Provided, That no mercury emissions from chlor-alkali plants shall be manufactured, exported, imported, or used: *<Newly Inserted by Act No. 13886, Jan. 27, 2016>*

1. Where restricted persistent pollutants are manufactured, imported, exported, or used for purposes under Annex B to the Stockholm Convention;

2. Where restricted persistent pollutants are manufactured, imported, or exported for a purpose other than those for which the manufacture, import, or export is prohibited according to the phase-out date specified in Article 6 of the Minamata Convention and Part 1 of Annex A thereto;

3. Where restricted persistent pollutants are used for a purpose other than those for which the use is prohibited according to the phase-out date specified in Annex B to the Minamata Convention;

4. Where restricted persistent pollutants are manufactured, imported, exported, or used for purposes prescribed by Presidential Decree, such as testing, research or examination.

(4) Those who intend to manufacture, export, import, or use restricted persistent pollutants shall comply with the standards for control prescribed by Presidential Decree, such as labeling on the containers or packages of restricted persistent pollutants for safety control. *<Amended by Act No. 11263, Feb. 1, 2012; Act No. 13886, Jan. 27, 2016>*

(5) A person falling under any of the following subparagraphs shall each time submit an application for export approval, specifying the main use, the country of import, the export volume, etc., and obtain approval from the Minister of Environment as prescribed by Ordinance of the Ministry of Environment. The same shall also apply to any modification to important matters prescribed by Ordinance of the Ministry of Environment among those so approved: *<Amended by Act No. 15841, Oct. 16, 2018>*

1. A person who seeks to export banned persistent pollutants, falling under paragraph (1) 1;

2. A person who seeks to export restricted persistent pollutants, falling under paragraph (3) 1;

3. A person who seeks to export mercury among restricted persistent pollutants, falling under paragraph (3) 2 or 3.

CHAPTER III REGULATION ON DISCHARGE OF PERSISTENT POLLUTANTS

Article 14 (Permissible Discharge Standards)

(1) Permissible discharge standards for persistent pollutants to be discharged from discharge facilities in the form of exhaust gas, waste water, etc. shall be prescribed by Ordinance of the Ministry of Environment. *<Amended by Act No. 11263, Feb. 1, 2012; Act No. 13886, Jan. 27, 2016>*

(2) When the Minister of Environment intends to legislate or

amend the Ordinance of the Ministry of Environment under paragraph (1), he/she shall consult with the head of a related central administrative agency in advance.

(3) A person who operates discharge facilities (hereinafter referred to as "discharge business operator") shall comply with the permissible discharge standards under paragraph (1) (excluding the permissible discharge standards for persistent pollutants in the form of waste water, in cases of persons who operate a zero wastewater discharge facility established under the proviso to Article 33 (1) and (2) of the Water Environment Conservation Act, among the discharge facilities established under subparagraph 2 of Article 15). <Amended by Act No. 11263, Feb. 1, 2012; Act No. 14532, Jan. 17, 2017>

(4) When the Minister of Environment prescribes permissible discharge standards under paragraph (1), he/she shall consider whether the environmental standards under Article 10 can be maintained or achieved, whether the technology of reducing persistent pollutants is economical, applicable, etc. <Amended by Act No. 13886, Jan. 27, 2016>

Article 15 (Standards for Installation of Discharge Facilities)

Any person who intends to obtain or file any of the following permits, approval, or reports shall be equipped with the facilities that can meet the permissible discharge standards under Article 14 (hereinafter referred to in "permissible discharge standards"), in addition to the standards for facilities prescribed by the relevant Acts: <Amended by Act No. 8371, Apr. 11, 2007; Act. No. 8404, Apr. 27, 2007; Act No. 11263, Feb. 1, 2012; Act No. 14532, Jan. 17, 2017>

1. A permit, report, modification permit, or modification report under Article 23 (1) through (3) of the Clean Air Conservation Act;

2. A permit, report, modification permit, or modification report under Article 33 (1) through (3) of the Water Environment

Conservation Act;

3. A permit, modification permit, or modification report for the waste control business under Article 25 (3) or (11) of the Wastes Control Act;

4. Approval, report, modification approval or modification report under Article 29 (2) or (3) of the Wastes Control Act.

Article 16 (Orders of Improvement, Orders of Suspension of Use and Orders of Closure)

(1) Where the level of persistent pollutants discharged from the discharge facilities exceeds the permissible discharge standards, the Minister of Environment may order the use of all or some of the discharge facilities suspended for a period of up to six months, as prescribed by Ordinance of the Ministry of Environment: Provided, That with respect to discharge facilities prescribed by Ordinance of the Ministry of Environment, such as the discharge facilities in which the degree of violation of the permissible discharge standards is minor, the Minister of Environment may order the relevant discharge business operator to take measures necessary to lower the discharge density of the persistent pollutants below the permissible discharge standards (hereinafter referred to as "improvement order"), in consideration of the measures necessary for improvement, the period for installation of facilities, etc. *<Amended by Act No. 13886, Jan. 27, 2016; Act No. 15656, Jun. 12, 2018>*

(2) Where a person ordered to suspend use under paragraph (1) fails to comply with such order, or where compliance with the permissible discharge standards is deemed impossible due to the structure of the relevant discharge facilities, deterioration of prevention facilities, etc., the Minister of Environment may order the closure of such discharge facilities. *<Amended by Act No. 15656, Jun. 12, 2018>*

(3) Where an administrative disposition taken to order a discharge

business operator the suspension of use under paragraph (1) or the closure under paragraph (2) becomes final and conclusive, the Minister of Environment may announce the name of the relevant discharge facility and the details of the offense and disposition, as prescribed by Ordinance of the Ministry of Environment. *<Newly Inserted by Act No. 15841, Oct. 16, 2018>*

Article 17 (Disposition of Penalty Surcharges)

(1) Where the Minister of Environment has to order suspension of use under Article 16 (1) to a discharge business operator and where such suspension of use of facilities is deemed likely to substantially hinder the national economy and other public interests, such as the livelihood of residents, external credibility, employment, commodity prices, etc., he/she may impose a penalty surcharge not exceeding 300 million won in place of an order of suspension of use. *<Amended by Act No. 15656, Jun. 12, 2018>*

(2) The criterion for penalty surcharges according to the kind, scale, etc. of discharge facilities and other necessary matters shall be prescribed by Presidential Decree.

(3) Where a discharge business operator fails to pay the penalty surcharge under paragraph (1) within the deadline, the Minister of Environment shall collect it in the same manner as delinquent national taxes are collected: Provided, That the authority of the Minister of Environment to impose and collect a penalty surcharge has been delegated to a Mayor/Do Governor, it may be collected in the same manner as delinquent local taxes are collected.

(4) Penalty surcharges collected under paragraph (1) shall be the revenue of the special accounts for environmental improvement under the Framework Act on Environmental Policy. *<Amended by Act No. 10893, Jul. 21, 2011>*

(5) Where the Minister of Environment delegates his/her authority

to impose and collect a penalty surcharge to a Mayor/Do Governor, he/she may appropriate part of the penalty surcharge collected as expenses of collection, as prescribed by Presidential Decree.

Article 18 (Investigations of Sources of Discharge and Quantity of Discharge)

(1) The Minister of Environment may investigate the discharge sources of persistent pollutants and the discharged quantity thereof nationwide in order to establish and implement the master plan rationally. *<Amended by Act No. 13886, Jan. 27, 2016>*

(2) The Minister of Environment may request the head of a related agency to submit necessary data or to provide assistance for the investigation of the discharge sources of persistent pollutants and the discharged quantity thereof under paragraph (1). In such cases, the head of the related agency in receipt of such request shall comply therewith except in extenuating circumstances. *<Amended by Act No. 13886, Jan. 27, 2016>*

(3) Matters concerning the methods and procedures for investigating the discharge sources of persistent pollutants and the discharged amount thereof, methods for calculating the quantity, etc. under paragraph (1) shall be prescribed by Ordinance of the Ministry of Environment. *<Newly Inserted by Act No. 11263, Feb. 1, 2012; Act No. 13886, Jan. 27, 2016>*

Article 19 (Measurement of Persistent Pollutants, Impact Assessment on Surrounding Areas, etc.)

(1) Each discharge business operator shall directly measure persistent pollutants discharged from the relevant discharge facility according to the fair examination standards of environmental pollution under Article 6 (1) 10 of the Environmental Examination and Inspection Act, or request a measuring organization prescribed by Ordinance of the

Ministry of Environment to measure them, and record the result of measurement and preserve it during the period prescribed by Ordinance of the Ministry of Environment. In such cases, the extent of persistent pollutants, methods for, and frequency of, measurement, and other necessary matters shall be prescribed by Ordinance of the Ministry of Environment. *<Amended by Act No. 11263, Feb. 1, 2012; Act No. 13886, Jan. 27, 2016>*

(2) A discharge business operator who operates a discharge facility of at least a scale prescribed by Presidential Decree, which is likely to cause serious pollution to the environment of surrounding areas shall investigate the impacts of the operation of the discharge facility on the surrounding areas every three years, independently or jointly, or request a measuring organization prescribed by Ordinance of the Ministry of Environment to investigate such impacts, and submit the result thereof to the Minister of Environment. In such cases, matters necessary for the method for and extent of investigations, report of the result of investigations, etc. shall be prescribed by Ordinance of the Ministry of Environment. *<Amended by Act No. 11263, Feb. 1, 2012>*

(3) Where any discharge business operator fails to perform the duty to measure under paragraph (1) or fails to investigate the impacts under paragraph (2), the Minister of Environment may order the measurement of persistent pollutants or impact assessments upon specifying a period, as prescribed by Ordinance of the Ministry of Environment. *<Amended by Act No. 13886, Jan. 27, 2016>*

(4) The Minister of Environment may order discharge business operators who fail to comply with an order issued under paragraph (3) to suspend the use of such discharge facilities or to close them.

(5) The result of measurement under paragraph (1) may be kept and preserved in electronic form pursuant to subparagraph 1 of Article 2 of the Framework Act on Electronic Documents and Transactions. *<Newly Inserted by Act No. 11263, Feb. 1, 2012; Act No. 15841, Oct. 16, 2018>*

Article 20 (Emergency Measures and Reporting in Time of Accident, Measures, etc. to Prevent Recurrence)

(1) Where persistent pollutants have been discharged into the air or public waters defined in subparagraph 9 of Article 2 of the Water Environment Conservation Act due to any breakdown or damage of a discharge facility or other accidents, the relevant discharge business operator shall, without delay, take necessary emergency measures according to the guidelines for handling accidents prescribed by Ordinance of the Ministry of Environment, and remove or dispose of the discharged persistent pollutants promptly and safely. *<Amended by Act No. 11263, Feb. 1, 2012; Act No. 14532, Jan. 17, 2017; Act No. 13886, Jan. 27, 2016>*

(2) Where an accident referred to in paragraph (1) has occurred, the relevant discharge business operator shall report the status of the accident to the Minister of Environment without delay.

(3) The Minister of Environment may order the discharge business operator of the discharge facility in which an accident has occurred to take measures necessary to prevent the spread of the accident or recurrence thereof.

CHAPTER IV DISPOSAL OF WASTES CONTAINING PERSISTENT POLLUTANTS

Article 21 (Classification, Control, etc. of Wastes Containing Persistent Pollutants)

Wastes containing persistent pollutants shall be deemed controlled wastes as defined in subparagraph 4 of Article 2 of the Wastes Control Act. *<Amended by Act No. 13886, Jan. 27, 2016>*

Article 22 (Standards for Disposal, etc. of Wastes Containing Persistent Pollutants)

Those who intend to collect, transport, keep or dispose of wastes containing persistent pollutants shall comply with the standards and methods prescribed by Ordinance of the Ministry of Environment. *<Amended by Act No. 13886, Jan. 27, 2016>*

Article 23 (Restriction on Recycling)

(1) Any person who intends to recycle wastes containing persistent pollutants shall recycle such wastes only for the kinds and uses prescribed by Ordinance of the Ministry of Environment for eco-friendly recycling. *<Amended by Act No. 13886, Jan. 27, 2016>*

(2) Deleted. *<By Act No. 13886, Jan. 27, 2016>*

(3) The Minister of Environment may order a person who recycles wastes containing persistent pollutants, for the kinds and uses, other than those prescribed in paragraph (1), to suspend the use thereof, or to close the relevant facility. *<Amended by Act No. 11263, Feb. 1, 2012; Act No. 13886, Jan. 27, 2016>*

CHAPTER V CONTROL OF INSTRUMENTS, ETC. CONTAINING PERSISTENT POLLUTANTS

Article 24 (Making List of Contaminated Implements, etc.)

The Minister of Environment may make a list of instruments, facilities, and products containing persistent pollutants exceeding a level set out in the standards prescribed by Presidential Decree (hereinafter referred to as "contaminated implements, etc.") in order to prevent hazards to the human body. *<Amended by Act No. 13886, Jan. 27, 2016>*

[This Article Wholly Amended by Act No. 11263, Feb. 1, 2012]

Article 24-2 (Reporting, etc. on Implements, etc. Subject to Control)

The owner of an instrument, facility, or product prescribed by Presidential Decree, such as a transformer (hereinafter referred to as "implements, etc. subject to control"), shall report the matters prescribed by Ordinance of the Ministry of Environment, such as the manufacturer, date of manufacture, and replacement of insulating oil, to the competent Mayor/Provincial Governor. The same shall also apply to any modification to important matters prescribed by Ordinance of the Ministry of Environment among the reported matters, such as replacement of insulating oil.

[This Article Newly Inserted by Act No. 11263, Feb. 1, 2012]

Article 24-3 (Restriction on Importation and Exportation of Implements, etc. Subject to Control)

No person shall import or export any implements, etc. subject to control containing insulating oil, the concentration of persistent pollutants of which exceeds a level set out in the standards prescribed by Presidential Decree. *<Amended by Act No. 13886, Jan. 27, 2016>*

[This Article Newly Inserted by Act No. 11263, Feb. 1, 2012]

Article 25 (Safety Control of Contaminated Implements, etc.)

(1) The owner of contaminated implements, etc. shall take the following safety control measures:

1. Indication of cautions for safety;

2. Attaching an identification device to verify whether they are contaminated.

(2) Detailed matters necessary for the safety control measures under paragraph (1) shall be prescribed by Ordinance of the Ministry of Environment.

(3) Where the owner of contaminated implements, etc. fails to take the safety control measures under paragraphs (1) and (2), the competent Mayor/Do Governor may order such

owner to take measures necessary for safety control by specifying a period, as prescribed by Ordinance of the Ministry of Environment. *<Amended by Act No. 11263, Feb. 1, 2012>*

Article 26 (Deadline for Disposal of Contaminated Implements, etc.)

The owner of contaminated implements, etc. who has finished using such implements shall properly dispose of them in accordance with the standards and methods provided in Article 22 within the deadline prescribed by Ordinance of the Ministry of Environment.

CHAPTER VI SUPPLEMENTARY PROVISIONS

Article 27 (Assistance in Installation, etc. of Facilities)

The Minister of Environment may install and operate any of the following facilities, or render assistance necessary for the development, dissemination, etc. of technology to reduce environmental pollution due to persistent pollutants for the proper management of the persistent pollutants: *<Amended by Act No. 13886, Jan. 27, 2016>*

1. A facility to eliminate or reduce persistent pollutants discharged from the discharge facility;
2. A facility to collect, transport, keep or dispose of wastes containing persistent pollutants.

Article 28 (International Cooperation)

The Government shall exchange information and technology relating to persistent pollutants and cooperate in the exchange of human resources, joint investigations, research and development, etc. through international cooperation with international organizations and countries relating to the Stockholm Convention and the Minamata Convention, and proactively participate in international endeavor to prevent and reduce hazards of persistent pollutants to health or the environment. *<Amended by Act No. 13886, Jan. 27, 2016>*

Article 29 (Reporting, Examination, etc.)

(1) The Minister of Environment or a Mayor/Provincial Governor may order each of the following persons to file a report or to submit data on the matters prescribed by Ordinance of the Ministry of Environment, and may authorize related public officials to access their facilities or places of business and to investigate the discharge sources of persistent pollutants and the discharged quantity thereof pursuant to Article 18 or collect samples or inspect relevant documents, facilities, equipment, etc. to verify whether they meet the prohibition of, or restriction on, manufacture, exportation, importation, or use of persistent pollutants under Article 13, the permissible discharge standards, the standards for disposal of wastes containing persistent pollutants under Article 22 or the deadline for disposal of contaminated implements, etc. under Article 26: *<Amended by Act No. 11263, Feb. 1, 2012; Act No. 13886, Jan. 27, 2016>*

1. Persons who manufacture, export, import, or use persistent pollutants under Article 13;

2. Discharge business operators;

3. Persons who collect, transport, keep or dispose of wastes containing persistent pollutants under Article 22;

4. Persons who recycle wastes containing persistent pollutants under Article 23;

5. Owners of contaminated implements, etc. under Article 24;

6. Owners of implements, etc. subject to control under Article 24-2.

(2) When issuing any order to file a report or to submit data, to collect samples or conduct an inspection (hereinafter referred to as "inspection, etc.") under paragraph (1), a plan regarding the date and time, reasons, details, etc. of inspection, etc. shall be notified to the person subject to such inspection, etc. by no later than seven days before the start of the inspection,

etc.: Provided, That in cases of emergency or where it is deemed that any prior notification might cause the destruction of evidence, etc. to defeat the purpose of such inspection, etc., this shall not apply.

(3) Any public official who gains access and conducts an inspection pursuant to paragraph (1) shall carry a certificate indicating his/her authority and produce it to persons involved.

Article 29-2 (Submission of Annual Reports)

(1) Each Mayor/Provincial Governor shall submit an annual report on the control of persistent pollutants to the Minister of Environment. <Amended by Act No. 13886, Jan. 27, 2016>

(2) Matters necessary for the methods of preparing annual reports under paragraph (1) and the timing of submission thereof shall be prescribed by Ordinance of the Ministry of Environment.

[This Article Newly Inserted by Act No. 11263, Feb. 1, 2012]

Article 30 (Hearings)

When the Minister of Environment or a Mayor/Provincial Governor intends to issue an order of closure pursuant to Article 16 (2), 19 (4) or 23 (3), he/she shall hold a hearing. <Amended by Act No. 11263, Feb. 1, 2012; Act No. 15656, Jun. 12, 2018>

Article 31 (Delegation and Entrustment of Authority)

(1) The Minister of Environment may partially delegate his/her authority under this Act to Mayors/Do Governors, the President of the National Institute of Environmental Research, or the director general of a regional environmental office, as prescribed by Presidential Decree.

(2) The Minister of Environment may entrust each of the following business affairs to the related specialized agencies, such as the Korea Environment Corporation established under the Korea Environment Corporation Act, as prescribed by Presidential Decree: <Amended by Act No. 9433, Feb. 6, 2009; Act No. 11263, Feb. 1, 2012; Act No. 13886, Jan. 27, 2016>

1. Business affairs regarding the establishment and operation of a measurement network under Article 11;
2. Business affairs regarding the investigations of the discharge sources and the discharged quantity of persistent pollutants under Article 18 (1);
3. Business affairs regarding the installation and operation of facilities for the collection, transport, storage, and disposal of wastes containing persistent pollutants under subparagraph 2 of Article 27;
4. Business affairs regarding the access, collection of samples, and inspections under Article 29 (1) (only for cases required for verifying compliance with the permissible discharge standards under Article 14 (3) or for investigating the discharge sources and discharged quantity of persistent pollutants under Article 18 (1)).

Article 31-2 (Statutory Treatment as Public Officials for Purposes of Penal Provisions)

For the purposes of penal provisions under Articles 129 through 132 of the Criminal Act, any executive or employee of the related specialized agencies who engages in business affairs entrusted pursuant to Article 31 (2) shall be deemed a public official.
[This Article Newly Inserted by Act No. 11263, Feb. 1, 2012]

CHAPTER VII PENAL PROVISIONS

Article 32 (Penal Provisions)

Any person who manufactures, exports, imports, or uses banned persistent pollutants for any purpose other than the permitted purpose, in violation of Article 13 (1), shall be punished by imprisonment for not more than five years or by a fine not exceeding 100 million won. *<Amended by Act No. 15656, Jun. 12, 2018>*
[This Article Newly Inserted by Act No. 13886, Jan. 27, 2016]

Article 32-2 (Penal Provisions)

Any person who fails to comply with an order of closure issued under Article 16 (2), 19 (4) or 23 (3) shall be punished by imprisonment for not more than five years, or by a fine not exceeding 50 million won. *<Amended by Act No. 12464, Mar. 18, 2014; Act No. 15656, Jun. 12, 2018>*

Article 33 (Penal Provisions)

Any person who manufactures, exports, imports, or uses restricted persistent pollutants for any purpose other than the permitted purpose, in violation of Article 13 (3), shall be punished by imprisonment for not more than three years or by a fine not exceeding 50 million won. *<Amended by Act No. 15656, Jun. 12, 2018>*
[This Article Newly Inserted by Act No. 13886, Jan. 27, 2016]

Article 33-2 (Penal Provisions)

Any of the following persons shall be punished by imprisonment for not more than three years, or by a fine not exceeding 30 million won: *<Amended by Act No. 11263, Feb. 1, 2012; Act No. 12464, Mar. 18, 2014; Act No. 15656, Jun. 12, 2018>*

1. Deleted; *<by Act No. 13886, Jan. 27, 2016>*
2. A person who fails to comply with an order of improvement or an order of suspension of use issued under Article 16 (1);
3. A person who fails to comply with an order of suspension of use issued under Article 19 (4);
4. A person who recycles wastes containing persistent pollutants for the kinds and uses other than those prescribed by Ordinance of the Ministry of Environment, in violation of Article 23 (1);
5. A person who fails to comply with an order of suspension of use issued under Article 23 (3);
5-2. A person who imports or exports implements, etc. subject to control, in violation of Article 24-3;
6. A person who fails to properly dispose of contaminated implements, etc. within the deadline, in violation of Article 26.

Article 34 (Penal Provisions)

Any of the following persons shall be punished by imprisonment for not more than two years, or by a fine not exceeding 20 million won: *<Amended by Act No. 11263, Feb. 1, 2012; Act No. 12464, Mar. 18, 2014; Act No. 13886, Jan. 27, 2016>*

1. A person who fails to meet the standards for control regarding the manufacture, export, import, or use of banned persistent pollutants, in violation of Article 13 (2);

1-2. A person who fails to comply with the standards for the manufacture, export, import, or use of restricted persistent pollutants, in violation of Article 13 (4);

2. A person who exports restricted persistent pollutants without obtaining approval or modification approval, or after obtaining approval or modification approval fraudulently, in violation of Article 13 (5);

3. A person who fails to comply with the permissible discharge standards, in violation of Article 14 (3);

4. A person who fails to comply with an order of measurement of persistent pollutants or an order of impact assessment on the surrounding area issued under Article 19 (3);

5. A person who fails to comply with an order to take measures issued under Article 20 (3);

6. A person who pollutes the surrounding environment by collecting, transporting, storing, or disposing of wastes containing persistent pollutants, in violation of Article 22.

Article 35 (Penal Provisions)

Any person who fails to comply with an order to take measures issued under Article 25 (3) shall be punished by a fine not exceeding one million won.

Article 36 (Joint Penal Provisions)

Where the representative of a corporation, or an agent, employee or other servant of the corporation or an individual commits an offence under Articles 32 through 35 in connection with the business of the corporation or individual, not only shall such offender be punished, but the corporation or individual be also punished by a fine as prescribed in the corresponding provisions: Provided, That this shall not apply where such corporation or individual has not been negligent in giving due attention and supervision concerning the relevant business to prevent such offence.

[This Article Wholly Amended by Act No. 11263, Feb. 1, 2012]

Article 37 (Administrative Fines)

(1) Any of the following persons shall be punished by an administrative fine not exceeding ten million won: *<Amended by Act No. 11263, Feb. 1, 2012; Act No. 13886, Jan. 27, 2016>*

   1. A person who fails to measure persistent pollutants or preserve the record thereof, makes or preserves a false record, or fails to investigate the impacts on the surrounding area or to submit the result thereof, in violation of Article 19 (1) or (2);

   2. A person who fails to take emergency measures, or to remove or dispose of discharged persistent pollutants promptly and safely, or to file an accident report, in violation of Article 20 (1) or (2);

   3. A person who collects, transports, stores, or disposes of wastes containing persistent pollutants (excluding any person falling under subparagraph 6 of Article 34), in violation of Article 22.

(2) Any of the following persons shall be punished by an administrative fine not exceeding three million won: *<Amended by Act No. 11263, Feb. 1, 2012>*

   1. Deleted; *<by Act No. 13886, Jan. 27, 2016>*

   2. A person who fails to file a report or modification report of instruments, etc. subject to control, in violation of Article 24-2, or files a false report or false modification report.

(3) A person who fails to submit a report or data under Article 29, or submits a false report or data, or refuses, interferes with or evades access, collection of samples or inspections by related public officials shall be punished by an administrative fine not exceeding one million won.

(4) Administrative fines under paragraphs (1) through (3) shall be imposed and collected by the Minister of Environment or the competent Mayor/Do Governor, as prescribed by Presidential Decree. *<Amended by Act No. 11263, Feb. 1, 2012>*

(5) through (7) Deleted. *<by Act No. 11263, Feb. 1, 2012>*

ADDENDA

Article 1 (Enforcement Date)

This Act shall enter into force one year after the date of its promulgation.

Article 2 (Transitional Measures concerning Standards for Installation of Discharge Facilities)

Any discharge business operator who has installed and is operating a discharge facility as at the time this Act enters into force shall meet the standards for the installation of discharge facilities under Article 15 (1) and (2) within one year from the date this Act enters into force.

Article 3 (Transitional Measures concerning Measurement, etc.)

(1) Where a measurement has been taken under Article 31 (2) of the Wastes Control Act before this Act enters into force, such measurement shall be deemed taken under Article 19 (1) of this Act. *<Amended by Act No. Act No. 8371, Apr. 11, 2007>*

(2) Where an investigation has been conducted under Article 31 (3) of the Wastes Control Act before this Act enters into force, such investigation shall be deemed conducted under Article 19 (2) of this Act. *<Amended by Act No. Act No. 8371, Apr. 11, 2007>*

Article 4 Omitted.

ADDENDA <Act No. 8371, Apr. 11, 2007>

Article 1 (Enforcement Date)

This Act shall enter into force on the date of its promulgation. (Proviso Omitted.)

Articles 2 through 10 Omitted.

ADDENDA <Act No. 8404, Apr. 27, 2007>

Article 1 (Enforcement Date)

This Act shall enter into force on the date of its promulgation. (Proviso Omitted.)

Articles 2 through 14 Omitted.

ADDENDA <Act No. 9433, Feb. 6, 2009>

Article 1 (Enforcement Date)

This Act shall enter into force on January 1, 2010.

Articles 2 through 11 Omitted.

ADDENDA <Act No. 10032, Feb. 4, 2010>

Article 1 (Enforcement Date)

This Act shall enter into force three months after the date of its promulgation.

Articles 2 and 3 Omitted.

ADDENDUM <Act No. 10034, Feb. 4, 2010>

This Act shall enter into force three months after the date of its promulgation.

ADDENDA <Act No. 10893, Jul. 21, 2011>

Article 1 (Enforcement Date)

This Act shall enter into force one year after the date of its promulgation.

Articles 2 through 6 Omitted.

ADDENDA *<Act No. 11263, Feb. 1, 2012>*

Article 1 (Enforcement Date)

This Act shall enter into force one year after the date of its promulgation: Provided, That the amended provisions of the proviso to Article 13 (1), Article 14, the part concerning the entrustment of investigation to a measuring organization in the amended provisions of Article 19 (2), Article 19 (5), subparagraph 1 of Article 33, Articles 36 and 37 (1) 3 shall enter into force on the date of its promulgation, and the amended provisions of Articles 13 (excluding the proviso to paragraph (1)) and 34 shall enter into force six months after the date of its promulgation.

Article 2 (Transitional Measures concerning Administrative Fines)

For the purposes of the provisions concerning administrative fines (limited to Article 37 (1) 3), any violation committed before this Act enters into force shall be governed by the former provisions.

ADDENDA *<Act No. 11862, Jun. 4, 2013>*

Article 1 (Enforcement Date)

This Act shall enter into force on January 1, 2015.

Articles 2 through 12 Omitted.

ADDENDUM *<Act No. 12464, Mar. 18, 2014>*

This Act shall enter into force on the date of its promulgation.

ADDENDA *<Act No. 13886, Jan. 27, 2016>*

Article 1 (Enforcement Date)

This Act shall enter into force on the date when the Minamata Convention becomes effective in the Republic of Korea.

Article 2 (Transitional Measures concerning Master Plan, etc.)

(1) A master plan for the control of persistent organic pollutants formulated under the previous provisions of Article 5 (1) before this Act enters into force shall be deemed a master

plan for the control of persistent pollutants formulated under the amended provisions of Article 5 (1).

(2) An implementation plan for persistent organic pollutants formulated under the previous provisions of Article 6 (1) before this Act enters into force shall be deemed an implementation plan for persistent pollutants formulated under the amended provisions of Article 6 (1).

Article 3 (Transitional Measures concerning Administrative Fines)

For the purposes of the provisions concerning administrative fines, any violation committed before this Act enters into force shall be governed by the previous provisions.

Article 4 Omitted.

Article 5 (Relationship to Other Statutes and Regulations)

At the time this Act enters into force, references in other statutes and regulations to the former Persistent Organic Pollutants Control Act or to the provisions thereof, if this Act includes any provisions corresponding thereto, shall be deemed references to this Act or the corresponding provisions thereof in lieu of the former Persistent Organic Pollutants Control Act or the provisions thereof.

ADDENDA *<Act No. 14532, Jan. 17, 2017>*

Article 1 (Enforcement Date)

This Act shall enter into force on the date of its promulgation: Provided, That the amended provisions of the Acts, which were promulgated before this Act enters into force, but the date on which they are to enter into force, has not arrived yet, among the Acts amended pursuant to Article 6 of the Addenda, shall enter into force on the enforcement dates of such Acts, respectively.

Articles 2 through 7 Omitted.

ADDENDA *<Act No. 15656, Jun. 12, 2018>*

Article 1 (Enforcement Date)

This Act shall enter into force six months after the date of its promulgation: Provided, That the amended provisions of Article 32-2 and subparagraph 2 of Article 33-2 of the Persistent Organic Pollutants Control Act, Act No. 13886, shall enter into force on the date when the Minamata Convention becomes effective in the Republic of Korea.

Article 2 (Applicability)

The amended provisions of Article 16 shall apply to violations of the permissible discharge standards that occur after this Act enters into force.

ADDENDA <Act No. 15841, Oct. 16, 2018>

Article 1 (Enforcement Date)

This Act shall enter into force on the date of its promulgation: Provided, That the amended provisions of Article 13 (5) of the Persistent Organic Pollutants Control Act, Act No. 13886, shall enter into force on the date when the Minamata Convention becomes effective in the Republic of Korea, and the amended provisions of Article 16 (3) of the Persistent Organic Pollutants Control Act, Act No. 15656, shall apply six months after the date of its promulgation.

Article 2 (Applicability concerning Announcement of Administrative Dispositions)

The amended provisions of Article 16 (3) of the Persistent Organic Pollutants Control Act, Act No. 15656, shall apply where the level of persistent organic pollutants discharged from discharge facilities exceeds the permissible discharge standards, so the order of suspension of use or the order of closure under Article 16 (1) or (2) of the Persistent Organic Pollutants Control Act, Act No. 15656, is given, after the enforcement date under the proviso to Article 1 of the Addenda.

Treaties/Agreements Concluded by the Republic of Korea

Treaties/Agreements
Concluded by the Republic of Korea[1]

The Editorial Board
ILA Korean Branch

1. BILATERAL AGREEMENTS

1-1. SOCIAL SECURITY

Administrative Arrangement for the Implementation of the Agreement on Social Security between the Republic of Korea and the Republic of Peru
[**Signed** November 22, 2018, **Entered into force** January 1, 2019][2]

Agreement on Social Security between the Republic of Korea and the Republic of Peru
[**Signed** March 2, 2017, **Entered into force** January 1, 2019]

Agreement on Social Security between the Government of the Republic of Korea and the Government of the Grand-Duchy of Luxembourg
[**Signed** March 1, 2018, **Entered into force** September 1, 2019]

---

1 Treaties are found at the homepage of Ministry of Foreign Affairs, Republic of Korea, http://www.mofa.go.kr/.

2 Entered into force for the Republic of Korea.

Agreement on Social Security Between the Republic of Korea and the Republic of Slovenia
[**Signed** February 20, 2018, **Entered into force** October 1, 2019]

Agreement between the Republic of Korea and the Republic of Croatia on Social Security
[**Signed** December 18, 2018, **Entered into force** November 1, 2019]

1-2. MILITARY/SECURITY

Exchange of Notes Amending the Agreement between the Government of the Republic of Korea and the Government of the United Kingdom of Great Britain and Northern Ireland on the Protection of Classified Military Information
[**Signed** January 21, 2019, **Entered into force** March 18, 2019]

Agreement between the Republic of Korea and the United States of America concerning Special Measures Relating to Article V of the Agreement under Article IV of the Mutual Defense Treaty between the Republic of Korea and the United States of America Regarding Facilities and Areas and the Status of United States Armed Forces in the Republic of Korea
[**Signed** March 8, 2019, **Entered into force** April 5, 2019]

Arrangement to Amend the Memorandum of Understanding on Logistics and Defense Industry Cooperation between the Government of the Republic of Korea and the Government of the Republic of the Philippines
[**Signed** June 10, 2019, **Entered into force** July 10, 2019]

Agreement between the Government of the Republic of Korea and the Government of the United States of America concerning

Mutual Airlift Support Utilizing Aircraft Operated by/for the Military Forces of the Parties in Case of Military Hostilities in the Republic of Korea
[**Signed** July 11, 2019, **Entered into force** July 11, 2019]

Agreement between the Government of the Republic of Korea and the Government of the Kingdom of Thailand on the Mutual Protection of Classified Military Information
[**Signed** September 2, 2019, **Entered into force** October 10, 2019]

1-3. COOPERATION FUND

Framework Arrangement between the Government of the Republic of Korea and the Government of the Kingdom of Cambodia concerning Loans from the Economic Development Cooperation Fund for the Years 2019 through 2023
[**Signed** March 15, 2019, **Entered into force** March 15, 2019]

Framework Arrangement between the Government of the Republic of Korea and the Government of the Federal Democratic Republic of Ethiopia concerning Loans from the Economic Development Cooperation Fund for the Years 2019 through 2020
[**Signed** April 16, 2019, **Entered into force** April 16, 2019]

Framework Arrangement between the Government of the Republic of Korea and the Government of the Islamic Republic of Pakistan concerning Loans from the Economic Development Cooperation fund for the Years 2018 through 2020
[**Signed** April 24, 2019, **Entered into force** April 24, 2019]

Agreement between the Government of the Republic of Korea and the Government of Georgia concerning Loans from the Economic

Development Cooperation Fund
[**Signed** January 31, 2019, **Entered into force** May 1, 2019]

Arrangement between the Government of the Republic of Korea and the government of the Republic of Senegal concerning a Loan from the Economic Development Cooperation Fund for the Establishment of the national Oncology Center Project
[**Signed** July 18, 2019, **Entered into force** July 18, 2019]

Framework arrangement between the Government of the Republic of Korea and the Government of the Republic of the Union of Myanmar concerning Loans from the Economic Development Cooperation Fund for the Years 2018 through 2022
[**Signed** September 3, 2019, **Entered into force** September 3, 2019]

Framework arrangement between the Government of the Republic of Korea and the Government of the Lao People's Democratic Republic concerning Loans from the Economic Development Cooperation Fund for the Years 2020 through 2023
[**Signed** September 5, 2019, **Entered into force** September 5, 2019]

Agreement between the Government of the Republic of Korea and the Government of Solomon Islands concerning Loans from the Economic Development Cooperation Fund
[**Signed** November 14, 2019, **Entered into force** November 14, 2019]

Arrangement between the Government of the Republic of Korea and the Government of Solomon Islands concerning a Loan from the Economic Development Cooperation Fund for the Tina River Hydropower Development Project
[**Signed** November 15, 2019, **Entered into force** November 15, 2019]

Arrangement between the Government of the Republic of Korea and the Government of the Republic of Senegal concerning a Loan from the Economic Development Cooperation Fund for the construction of Refrigerated Warehouse Project
[**Signed** December 30, 2019, **Entered into force** December 30, 2019]

Arrangement between the Government of the Republic of Korea and the Government of the Republic of Senegal concerning a Loan from the Economic Development Cooperation Fund for the Supply of Refrigerated Trucks Project
[**Signed** December 30, 2019, **Entered into force** December 30, 2019]

1-4. VISA

Memorandum of Understanding between the Government of the Republic of Korea and the Government of the Kingdom of Saudi Arabia on the Facilitation of the Issuance of Visit Visas for the Nationals of the two Countries
[**Signed** April 24, 2018, **Entered into force** February 1, 2019]

Agreement between the government of the Republic of Korea and the Government of Turkmenistan on Mutual Waiver of Visa Requirements for Holders of Diplomatic, Official and Service Passports
[**Signed** April 17, 2019, **Entered into force** May 17, 2019]

Agreement between the Government of the Republic of Korea and the Government of the Republic of Indonesia on Visa Exemptions for Holders of Diplomatic and Official or Service Passports
[**Signed** November 25, 2019, **Entered into force** February 12, 2020]

1-5. TAX

Convention between the Republic of Korea and the Czech Republic for the Avoidance of Double Taxation and the prevention of Fiscal Evasion with respect to Taxes on income
[**Signed** January 12, 2018, **Entered into force** December 20, 2019]

Agreement between the Government of the Republic of Korea and the Government of the Republic of Singapore for the Elimination of Double Taxation with respect to Taxes on Income and the Prevention of Tax Evasion and Avoidance
[**Signed** May 13, 2019, **Entered into force** December 31, 2019]

Protocol amending the Convention between the Government of the Republic of Korea and the Government of Turkmenistan for the Avoidance of Double Taxation and the Prevention of Fiscal Evasion with respect to Taxes on Income signed at Seoul on April 13, 2015
[**Signed** April 17, 2019, **Entered into force** February 6, 2020]

Convention between the Republic of Korea and the United Arab Emirates for the Elimination of Double Taxation with respect to Taxes on Income and the Prevention of Tax Evasion and Avoidance
[**Signed** February 27, 2019, **Entered into force** February 29, 2020]

1-6. PROMOTION AND PROTECTION OF INVESTMENTS

Agreement between the Government of the Republic of Korea and the Government of the Republic of Armenia for the Promotion and Reciprocal Protection of Investments
[**Signed** October 19, 2018, **Entered into force** October 3, 2019]

1-7. FREE TRADE AREA

Protocol between the Government of the Republic of Korea and the Government of the United States of America amending the February 10, 2011 Exchange of Letters
[**Signed** September 18, 2018, **Entered into force** January 1, 2019]

Protocol between the Government of the Republic of Korea and the Government of the United States of America amending the Free Trade Agreement between the Republic of Korea and the United States of America
[**Signed** September 24, 2018, **Entered into force** January 1, 2019]

1-8. CUSTOMS

Agreement between the Government of the Republic of Korea and the Government of the Republic of Azerbaijan on Mutual Assistance and Cooperation in Customs Matters
[**Signed** June 29, 2019, **Entered into force** August 22, 2019]

1-9. GRANTS AID

Framework Agreement for Grant Aid between the Government of the Republic of Korea and the Government of the Republic of Azerbaijan
[**Signed** January 11, 2019, **Entered into force** August 28, 2019]

Framework Arrangement on Grant Aid for the years 2018-2023 between the Government of the Republic of Korea and the Government of the Republic of Kenya
[**Signed** October 23, 2019, **Entered into force** October 23, 2019]

Framework Agreement for Grant Aid between the Government of the Republic of Korea and the Government of the Republic of Tajikistan
[**Signed** July 16, 2019, **Entered into force** January 13, 2020]

1-10. AIR

Air Services Agreement between the Government of the Republic of Korea and the Government of the Republic of Latvia
[**Signed** September 28, 2018, **Entered into force** February 27, 2019]

Exchange of Notes for the Amendment to the Agreement between the Government of the Republic of Korea and the Government of the Republic of Poland for Air Services
[**Signed** October 2, 2019, **Entered into force** October 29, 2019]

Agreement on Air Services between the Republic of Korea and the Portuguese Republic
[**Signed** May 25, 2018, **Entered into force** December 12, 2019]

1-11. INTERNATIONAL ORGANIZATION

Agreement between the Government of the Republic of Korea and the Food and Agriculture Organization of the United Nations on the Establishment of an FAO Partnership and Liaison Office in the Republic of Korea
[**Signed** March 18, 2019, **Entered into force** May 9, 2019]

Agreement between the Government of the Republic of Korea and the United Nations Educational Scientific and Cultural Organization regarding the Establishment of the International Centre for Documentary Heritage under the Auspices of UNESCO

[**Signed** July 12, 2019, **Entered into force** August 13, 2019]

Agreement between the Government of the Republic of Korea and the United Nations Educational Scientific and Cultural Organization on the Establishment of the Asia-Pacific Centre of Education for International Understanding
[**Signed** October 11, 2019, **Entered into force** November 29, 2019]

Agreement between the Government of the Republic of Korea and the United Nations Educational Scientific and Cultural Organization (UNESCO) regarding the International Information and Networking Centre for Intangible Cultural Heritage in the Asia-Pacific Region under the Auspices of UNESCO (Category 2)
[**Signed** October 11, 2019, **Entered into force** December 3, 2019]

Accession Protocol of the Republic of Korea to the Constitutive Agreement of The Central American Bank for Economic Integration
[**Signed** December 28, 2018, **Entered into force** December 31, 2019]

1-12. CULTURE

Agreement between the Government of the Republic of Korea and the Government of Turkministan on Cooperation in the Field of Culture and Humanities
[**Signed** April 17, 2019, **Entered into force** May 17, 2019]

Agreement on Cultural Cooperation between the Government of the Republic of Korea and the Government of the Italian Republic
[**Signed** October 21, 2005, **Entered into force** November 27, 2019]

1-13. SCIENCE/TECHNOLOGY

Agreement between the Government of the Republic of Korea and the Government of the Italian Republic on Cooperation in the Fields of Science and Technology
[**Signed** February 16, 2007, **Entered into force** November 27, 2019]

Exchange of Notes to Extend the Agreement relating to Scientific and Technical Cooperation between the Government of the Republic of Korea and the Government of the United States of America
[**Signed** December 5, 2019, **Entered into force** December 26, 2019]

1-14. ECONOMY/TRADE

Agreement between the Government of the Republic of Korea and the Government of Georgia on Economic Cooperation
[**Signed** March 11, 2019, **Entered into force** May 24, 2019]

1-15. EDUCATION/CULTURE

Agreement between the Government of the Republic of Korea and the Government of the Democratic Socialist Republic of Sri Lanka on Cooperation in the Fields of Culture, the Arts, Education, Youth and Sports
[**Signed** November 29, 2017, **Entered into force** June 15, 2019]

1-16. AGRICULTURE

Exchange of Notes between the Republic of Korea and the United States of America concerning the Tariff-Rate Quota for Rice
[**Signed** December 12, 2019, **Entered into force** January 1, 2020]

Exchange of Notes between the Republic of Korea and the Socialist Republic of Viet Nam concerning the Tariff-Rate Quota for Rice
[**Signed** December 12, 2019, **Entered into force** January 1, 2020]

1-17. HEALTH CARE

Agreement on Mutual Reliance on Inspection Results of Good Manufacturing Practice for Medicinal Products between the Government of the Republic of Korea and the Swiss Federal Council
[**Signed** December 18, 2019, **Entered into force** January 15, 2020]

1-18. OTHERS

Agreement between the Government of the Republic of Korea and the Government of Belize on the Korea Overseas Volunteers Program
[**Signed** December 6, 2018, **Entered into force** January 5, 2019]

Agreement between the Government of the Republic of Korea and the Government of the Argentine Republic on a Working Holiday Programme
[**Signed** November 27, 2018, **Entered into force** January 26, 2019]

Exchange of Notes between the Government of the Republic of Korea and the Royal Government of Bhutan on the Dispatch of Korea Overseas Volunteers
[**Signed** February 27, 2019, **Entered into force** May 1, 2019]

Exchange of Notes between the Government of the Republic of Korea and the World Health Organization concerning the Establishment in the Republic of Korea of the WHO Asia-Pacific Centre for

Environment and health in the Western Pacific Region
[**Signed** August 2, 2019, **Entered into force** August 2, 2019]

Agreement between the Government of the Republic of Korea and the Government of the Socialist Republic of Vietnam on the Co-Production of Television Programs
[**Signed** March 26, 2019, **Entered into force** August 5, 2019]

2. MULTILATERAL AGREEMENTS

2-1. TRADE/COMMERCE/INDUSTRY

Amendment of the Trade Policy Review Mechanism
[**Signed** July 26, 2017, **Entered into force** January 1, 2019]

Decision to Endorse the Transposed Product Specific Rules in Appendix 2 of ANNEX 3 (Rules of Origin) of the ASEAN-KOREA Agreement on Trade in Goods
[**Signed** February 14, 2019, **Entered into force** September 1, 2019]

Free Trade Agreement between the Republic of Korea and the Republic of Central America
[**Signed** November 16, 2016, **Entered into force** October 1, 2019]

2-2. POST

Universal Postal Convention and Final Protocol to the Universal Postal Convention
[**Signed** September 7, 2018, **Entered into force** July 1, 2019]

Tenth Additional Protocol to the Constitution of the Universal

Postal Union
[**Signed** September 7, 2018, **Entered into force** July 1, 2019]

Second Additional Protocol to the General Regulations of the Universal Postal Union
[**Signed** September 7, 2018, **Entered into force** July 1, 2019]

2-3. FINANCIAL AGENCY

Agreement for the Administration of the Multilateral Investment Fund III
[**Signed** April 2, 2017, **Entered into force** December 27, 2019]

Agreement Establishing the Multilateral Investment Fund III
[**Signed** April 2, 2017, **Entered into force** December 27, 2019]

INDEX

AUTHOR GUIDELINES AND STYLE SHEET

I. SUBMISSION

Manuscripts should be submitted in Microsoft Word and electronically sent to ilakoreanbranch@gmail.com

II. GENERAL TERMS AND PEER-REVIEW SYSTEM OF PUBLICATION

All manuscripts are subject to initial evaluation by the KYIL Editorial Board and subsequently sent out to independent reviewers for a peer review. The Editorial Board accepts manuscripts on a rolling basis and will consider requests for an expedited review in appropriate cases.

III. FORMATING

1. ABSTRACT

Please include an abstract (no more than 150 words) at the beginning of an article.

2. TEXT

Main Text: Times New Roman, font size 12, 1.5 spacing
Endnotes: Times New Roman, font size 12, single spacing

3. CITING REFERENCE

The KYIL requires endnotes with subsequent numbering; the initial endnote should be indicated with '*,' if it is necessary to provide explanatory information about the manuscript.

Please include a reference list for all works the are cited at the end of the manuscript.

IV. NOTES

1. BOOKS

P. Malanczuk, *Akehurst's Modern Introduction to International Law*, 7th ed. (New York: Eoutledge, 1997), p. 1.

2. ARTICLES

Chao Wang, *China's Preferential Trade Remedy Approaches: A New Haven School Perspective*, Vol.21 No.1, Asia Pacific Law Review, (2013), p. 103.

3. ARTICLES IN COLLECTIONS

J. Paulsson & Z. Douglas, *Indirect Expropriation in Investment Treaty Arbitrations, in* Arbitration Foreign Investment Disputes 148 (N. Horn & S. Kroll eds., Kluwer Law International, 2004).

4. ARTICLES IN NEWSPAPER

YI Whan-Woo, *Korea, New Zealand embrace free trade pact*, Korea Times, November 14, 2014.

5. UNPUBLISHED MATERIALS

PARK Jung-Won, *Minority Rights Constraints on a State's Power to Regulate Citizenship under International Law*, Ph.D thesis (2006), on file with author.

6. WORKING PAPERS AND REPORTS

OECD, *'Indirect Expropriation' and the 'Right to Regulate' in International Investment Law*, OECD Working Paper, 2014/09.

7. INTERNET SOURCES

C. Schreuer, The Concept of Expropriation under the ETC and Other Investment Protection Treaties (2005), http://www.univie,ac,at/intlaw/pdf/csunpuyblpaper_3pdf. [Accessed on September 22, 2015]

V. GUIDELINE FOR AUTHORS

1. ARTICLE

Manuscripts must be in the form of a regular paper including endnotes and references. The length for an articles should not exceed 10,000 words in English excluding notes and references.

2. SPECIAL REPORT

Manuscripts for Special Report must be in the form of a descriptive report which covers the international law issues related to Korea in the past 5 years. Special Report must include author's comments with less than 10 endnotes and 5 references. The length for a special report should be no more the 5,000 words.

3. RECENT DEVELOPMENT

Manuscripts must cover the trends in international law related to Korea in the preceding year. Recent Development must be in the form of a short report, including less than 5 endnotes. The length for Recent Development should be no more than 2,000 words.